D.B. Cooper

D.B. Cooper
The Real McCoy

By Bernie Rhodes

Research by Russell P. Calame

University of Utah Press
Salt Lake City

∞ The paper in this book meets the standards for permanence and
durability established by the Committee on Production Guidelines
for Book Longevity of the Council on Library Resources

Library of Congress Cataloging-in-Publication Data

Rhodes, Bernie A., 1932–
   D.B. Cooper, the real McCoy / by Bernie A. Rhodes ; research by
Russell P. Calame.
      p.   cm.
   Includes index.
   ISBN 0–87480–377–2 (cloth : alk. paper)
   1. Cooper, D. B.   2. McCoy, Richard Floyd, 1942–1974.
3. Criminals—United States—Biography.   4. Hijacking of aircraft—
United States—Case studies.   I. Calame, Russell P.   II. Title.
HV6248.C6617R49   1991
364.1'552'0973—dc20   91–50332
                                                            CIP

This book is dedicated to
sweet Anna Margaret
my mother and still best friend

Contents

D.B. Cooper

Introduction

On 24 November 1971, a lone male Caucasian, using the name of Dan (misidentified by the press as D. B.) Cooper, hijacked Northwest Orient Airlines Flight 305 between Portland and Seattle and parachuted from the rear stairs that cold, rainy Thanksgiving Eve with $200,000 of the airline's money. Cooper was never found. None of the ten thousand twenty-dollar bills extorted from the airline was ever found in circulation, although many years later $5,880 in damaged bills was dug up—literally excavated from a sandbar—along the Columbia River. The Cooper case still remains on the FBI books as the only unsolved airplane hijacking in American history.

Five months after the Cooper hijacking, Richard Floyd McCoy, Jr., a Mormon Sunday-school teacher and Vietnam vet from Provo, Utah, using the name James Johnson, hijacked United Airlines Flight 855 and also parachuted in the dark of night from its rear stairs with half a million dollars. McCoy was caught and convicted in federal court 29 June 1972 in Salt Lake City, Utah. After serving only two years of a forty-five-year sentence, he escaped from one of the U.S. government's maximum-security prisons. After several months as a fugitive, McCoy was killed in a shootout with the FBI in Virginia Beach, Virginia.

During the course of my investigations back in 1972, I became convinced that Cooper and McCoy were the same man. This, then, is the story of the life of the man who had the ingenuity and courage to execute both of these hijackings. This is also the story of the difficulties and confusion that envelop law enforcement when someone concocts a completely new type of crime—in this case, holding an airline at ransom, then jumping with the money at night from the back stairs of a commercial airliner in flight. Cooper was the first ever to do this, and, while initially caught off guard, law enforcement quickly adapted to counter this criminal innovation.

My name is Rhodes. I was the chief United States probation and parole officer for the District of Utah in 1972 when McCoy came to trial. My job as chief investigator for the federal courts was different from the FBI's. I wasn't so much interested in the crime itself as I was in the criminal and what provoked him to commit the crime. By the time a criminal case was referred to my office, the crime had been solved, an arrest had been made, and either a plea of guilty had been entered or a jury verdict had been rendered. Then it was my turn to look the offender over, determine why he did it, how he went about it, who got hurt, and, if given the chance, whether he would do it again.

By 1972, I had pulled a hitch in Korea, started a family, graduated with a B.S. in criminology from the University of Houston, and worked as a federal probation and parole officer for a little over ten years. Eleven years later, with twenty-eight years of marriage on the rocks, I'd had enough. I retired. After a couple of years in Pacific Beach, California, getting the cobwebs out of my head, I was invited by friends to use their summer home on Skopelos, an island on the Aegean side of mainland Greece. That was in 1985, the year this book was started. After a little less than a year in Europe, I returned to Salt Lake City. It was at a Christmas party in 1985 that I ran into Russell P. Calame, former special agent in charge of the Salt Lake City FBI office. That was a stroke of luck, because without him, the story would have died the following year. Calame agreed to do the research. He's done much more than that. In many ways, the story is more his than mine.

I knew Richard McCoy. In 1972, following his conviction, I interviewed him and most of his immediate family. However, I never felt comfortable sharing the contents of those interviews with the public. By 1986, I had decided it might not be ethical or in keeping with the integrity of the federal court to use interviews conducted while I was an officer of that court. I had also concluded it would be impossible to tell the story without the interviews. But what I'd overlooked in Russ Calame was that, although he had been retired from the Federal Bureau of Investigation since 1972, he could still pull rabbits out of his hat.

Not by accident, Calame found out that in 1972 the McCoy family had planned to publish a book and contracted with an attorney in Provo, Utah, Thomas S. Taylor, to act as their agent. The project eventually fell apart, but Taylor had kept the transcripts—almost two hundred pages of typed, yellow legal-sized sheets that had been gathering dust in his basement for almost fifteen years. Taylor graciously gave his entire file to us in late 1986. It was thirty hours or more of rambling, colorful interviews with Richard McCoy, his wife, Karen, his mother, Myrtle, his brother, Russell, and Karen's sister, Denise Burns.

From these transcripts, I have reconstructed, in the participants' own words, their roles in Richard McCoy's short and troubled life without feeling that I have broken a trust or misused my office. Because the information in those transcripts duplicates most of the information in my own shorter interviews, I have written the interviews as though I conducted all of them to give more immediacy to the dialogue. I have also omitted the usual apparatus of ellipses when necessary in putting the circumlocutions and repetitions of conversation into more readable form.

In 1986, I filed a lawsuit under the Freedom of Information Act, asking the federal court to require William Webster, director of the FBI, and Edwin Meese, the attorney general of the United States, to release connecting material from the Richard McCoy and D. B. Cooper files. Some things, after almost twenty years, had been destroyed by routine purgings of the file at the legal, ten-year mark. Other items had unaccountably been lost. Our search for these materials is part of this story. Among the many documents in our files are transcripts of FBI interviews; correspondence with the Department of Justice and with the FBI agencies in Utah, Washington, Oregon, California, Nevada, and Virginia; reports of FBI laboratory results; copies of telegrams and teletypes among FBI offices; Air National Guard duty rosters; and searches of newspaper files in six states. Transcripts of the trial, appeals, and private correspondence with agents who worked both cases are part of the documentation that buttresses our reconstruction. Nor is that all. Calame and I, over the past five years, have also conducted over 180 hours of taped or transcribed interviews with agents, friends of McCoy, and others directly involved in both cases.

I have not tried to diagnose or psychoanalyze Richard or Karen McCoy. Neither is this a rehash of tired old D. B. Cooper theories.

More than twenty never-before-released links in the *modus operandi* of the two cases are startlingly identical. Most convincing, however, is the disclosure of two personal items that Cooper inadvertently left on the plane before he jumped, objects that members of McCoy's family later independently identified as Richard's.

All names, dates, and events are factual and are written as they happened back in 1972, with one exception. Out of respect for his family, the name "Maurice Slocum," a pseudonym, is used to protect the identity of one of the FBI agents mentioned in this story. Otherwise, this story is true. It begins in a small town in Utah on Friday morning, 7 April 1972, a few days after Easter.

The Hijacking Begins
7 April 1972, before Dawn, Provo, Utah

Long before the sun had found its way through the frozen peaks of the Wasatch Mountains to the east of Provo, Richard McCoy had stored his luggage in the old gray Plymouth Fury parked at the curb and was backing the Volkswagen out of the driveway. Karen, quickly zipping four-year-old Chanti's snowsuit, picked up little Richard and hurried both children into the Plymouth.

Karen later explained the plan: "Take separate cars south to Spanish Fork. Leave the Volkswagen there and drive together to the Salt Lake International Airport. Then later that night when Richard and the money were safely on the ground I would pick him up, drive him to the Volkswagen, and lead interference for him in the Plymouth in case there were roadblocks. Richard had talked and planned for months how to hijack an airplane," she added, "but I didn't really think he would do it. It never dawned on me when we left the house that morning that within thirty-two hours it would be under around-the-clock FBI surveillance."

The McCoy house, as they drove away that Friday morning, looked exactly like its neighbors behind the line of bare-limbed horse chestnut and sycamore trees that arched over the street: they were all small, square, two-bedroom bungalows built in the early or maybe the late forties, with matching concrete front porches and slate-colored, over-sized, pitched roofs; they were all made of dark red brick held together with oozy gray mortar. Overgrown pyracantha bushes lining either side of the houses had licked most of the metal-gray paint from the worn wooden windowsills. On the south side of each of the houses, two narrow strips of concrete, separated by unmowed bluegrass and dead weed stems, led to single-car, frame garages in the back.

Provo, Utah, is the home of Mormon-church-owned Brigham Young University, where the number of children per family is twice the national average, the divorce rate is half, and one out of every sixteen people in town either teach, take classes, or do odd jobs for BYU. Provo is a predominantly white, Mormon community, where, except for a few athletes or international students, a person can grow up, marry, have children, and pass on without ever getting to know a black person, a Catholic, or a Jew. Provoans are law-abiding; they normally do not hijack airplanes.

Interstate 15 north links Provo to Salt Lake City. Toward the south, the direction Richard and Karen were driving, it follows a winding, fertile valley with 11,877-foot Mount Nebo visible on the left, perched just above apple and cherry orchards. To the right, Utah Lake goes on for miles, furnishing irrigation water to the small townships—many with names from the Bible—of Goshen, Salem, Mona, Nephi, and Spanish Fork.

"At Spanish Fork," Karen reconstructed, "Richard parked the Volkswagen in Central Bank's parking lot at about six-forty-five A.M. and rode with me north to the Salt Lake City airport." They argued most of the fifty miles over the divorce proceedings Karen was threatening to file—who would get custody of the two kids, how much of Karen's hard-earned money had been spent on airline tickets, guns, and disguises.

"You're a dreamer, Richard!" Karen screamed from the driver's seat of the Plymouth that morning. "You don't intend to go through with this thing! You're crazy. And you're just throwing my money away!"

At the Salt Lake International Airport, Richard dragged his two pieces of luggage from the trunk, kissed the kids through the open rear window, and promised Karen he would call her from Denver at exactly two o'clock if everything was going as planned. "Toodle-oo, Richard, toodle-oo," Karen mumbled angrily, lifting her pale blue eyes to the rearview mirror and flipping the old Fury into drive.

Richard arrived at Denver's Stapleton International Airport at 12:30 that afternoon. It was Friday, 7 April 1972, and a totally different airport from the one he had seen a week earlier when he flew over to make his practice run. It was like the New York Stock Exchange on Monday morning: standing room only, everyone talking, only a handful of people listening, and of course, no one listening to him. Businessmen in a futile attempt to make connections after a long Easter weekend, caterwauling threats "never to fly this SOB airline again," flashed gold-colored credit cards, VIP certificates, and showed signs of cardiovascular blowouts and nervous breakdowns. Young, exhausted mothers walked wailing babies. College students and grandparents returning from Easter vacation fumbled for their loved ones' hands. All of this producing an ambiance not unlike the sinking of the *Titanic*.

Stapleton had become a mess because of O'Hare Airport in Chicago, hundreds of miles away. O'Hare had been closed half the night owing to the arrival of thirteen inches of new snow. It was still snowing. Air traffic in and out of Chicago had been curtailed by 70 percent. When O'Hare gets a chest cold, every other airport in the world consumes large quantities of old-fashioned barroom cough medicine. Ticket-counter personnel were frantically punching computer buttons in vain efforts to reroute passengers through peripheral destinations. Hostile passengers, who had earlier left the counter in frustration, were now drifting back again, cutting in at the head of the line.

Richard picked up his two pieces of luggage and went immediately to Stapleton's United Airlines counter to pay for the ticket he had reserved a week earlier under the name James Johnson. He was disconcerted by the long line, but the Los Angeles plane didn't leave until 2:30 P.M. He surely had enough time to get his ticket, check his luggage, and change clothes in the terminal restroom.

He was standing in the short line, but it never went anywhere. Then it closed completely, and the five or six people in it were sent to the long line where all the promises, threats, and high-powered negotiations were going on. He paid for his ticket with a crisp new fifty and a ten-dollar bill at exactly 2:00 P.M. Ticket agent Borg Sveland folded the bills into a container which he placed in a pneumatic tube (not so different from the one at J. C. Penney's that Richard had seen as a child back in Raleigh, North Carolina). "It seemed like hours passed," Richard said, "before that same little apparatus kicked out a one-dollar bill." United Airlines Flight 855 was scheduled to depart Denver en route to Los Angeles, California, from the B-4 loading area at 2:30 P.M.

"I had promised Karen I'd call her at exactly two P.M.," Richard told me. "But I could see I wouldn't have time to call. I was running for the men's room with this small handbag to change clothes, when I heard the name Johnson being paged. . . . James Johnson, they announced, was wanted on the telephone. I was sure something had gone wrong at the other end and Karen was calling to tell me to ditch the whole thing." It was another James Johnson they were paging—not Richard at all—but he had lost a good ten minutes trying to locate the airport page phone before finding that out. It would not be the last irony of the escapade.

He made it to the restroom and quickly changed from his well-worn conservative brown suit into dark blue double-knit slacks, navy blue oxfords with a bright beige band across the toe, and a shirt with loud green flowers on a cream-colored background and a wide collar. A dark, wide, navy blue necktie went untied under his royal blue, red-striped sport jacket. Mirrored sunglasses completed his outfit. Richard took off for gate B-4 where Flight 855 was now rescheduled to depart at 3:10 P.M. He sat alone in the crowded loading area with a small blue and red plaid suitcase in one hand and a manila envelope in the other.

"Richard has always felt like an outsider," explained his younger brother Russell, "especially when he was living at home. Old men around Kingston and Cove City said Richard may never be just right, you know, with his parents being first cousins and all."

Richard wasn't visibly deformed when he was born on 7 December 1942, in Kingston, North Carolina, but the cord under his tongue was too tight for him to speak clearly. That had to be cut, leaving him with a slight lisp. Then they had to scrape scar tissue from his eardrums so he could hear as well as other kids. But those problems, they thought, probably didn't have anything to do with his parents being first cousins. Old-timers around Cove City said Richard Floyd McCoy, Sr.—he went by Floyd—probably wasn't his real father in the first place. After all, everybody knew that Richard Edward Holland, a well-to-do sawmill owner, had fathered Russell, Myrtle McCoy's second son, while Floyd served in Belgium in World War II.

Russell was eighteen months younger than Richard. He was a captain in the U.S. Army and a helicopter pilot like Richard, with stories of his own to tell about the war in Vietnam. "I think Richard's troubles started when he was in the third grade," said Russell. "As I remember, we had just moved from Highland Park, New Jersey, to Arlington, Vermont, and I remember the other kids laughing at us because of our southern accents. Richard had just been put back the year before in school, but don't misunderstand me. He wasn't dumb. We were just different. I remember him being harassed by somebody every day of his life when he was little. Richard was labeled an instigator or troublemaker in school because he was quick to lash back at people."

It was when the family moved down south to Cove City, where the McCoys had lived for generations, that the two boys learned for the first time that Floyd and Myrtle were first cousins. They had married young, Myrtle running away from home to join Floyd at his army base.

Russell married when he was about twenty. On his wedding day he learned that Holland was his natural father. Myrtle had worked as Holland's bookkeeper at the sawmill in 1943 while Floyd was in Belgium, but had dated Holland long before she married McCoy. "You can imagine what a surprise it was," Russell said, "for Mom's husband to come home after two years in Belgium and find he had another son. Of course, a great deal of family irritation developed at that time and in later years, which eventually ended up with our parents getting a divorce."

Russell remembered being spanked by Floyd, then seeing his mother point her finger in Floyd's face and shout, "That boy may not be your boy, Floyd McCoy, and you might not like him being around here! But he's my boy—and from this day forward, you'll never again lay a hand on my son." "And he never did," said Russell. "Instead, he took it out on Richard. And no one ever did anything about it."

So Russell grew up with his middle name the same as his biological father's, and Richard grew up wondering from which one, exactly, he had gotten his first name. "This not knowing, I guess, has nagged him all his life," said Russell. "He'd call me long distance, even after we were grown, and go over and over how he had begged Mother to tell him. And how he never got a simple yes or no. Richard said she told him she wasn't sure herself."

At 2:45 P.M., passenger-service personnel opened the door to

Flight 855. First in line, Richard handed over his one-way ticket, which he carefully held only by the tips of his right thumb and first finger, and hurried to his seat, the right aisle seat in the last row.

The stewardess seemed familiar. She was. "It was the same crew I had flown with earlier that morning from Salt Lake City to Denver," Richard recalled. "In fact, I was sitting in the same row of seats. If this plane, I thought, was the same one, my fingerprints would be all over it." His concern about fingerprints on the ticket would be a wasted effort.

While the other passengers were boarding, Richard went straight to the aft cabin restroom. He had calculated the timetable: "Less than five minutes to put on my dark makeup, wax and curl my mustache, then there was the wig. That darn wig. Karen had cut it short and dyed it black, or at least tried to—leaving it hard and stiff. I had a can of hair spray with me, just in case, and felt it would work. The idea, of course, was to get the wig over my ears. These ears of mine would be the one thing, I knew, witnesses would later remember. Scotch tape had worked before to keep my ears from sticking out so far from my head, but this time I decided to use one of Denise's headbands under the wig." Richard was working away, a hand towel wrapped around his neck to prevent water and hair spray from running into his makeup, when a loud male voice announced from the ceiling loudspeaker, "Has someone aboard United Flight 855 left a manila envelope in the boarding area?"

Richard froze. The unsealed envelope contained hijack notes he and Karen had tapped out on Denise's typewriter. "What on earth do I do now?" Richard thought to himself. "Do I dare claim them or not? Someone probably opened the envelope looking for a name and read the notes. If someone did, and I step up to claim them, you can bet I'll be marched off Flight 855 in leg irons and handcuffs at gunpoint. And if I don't, airline security will have to read them and then everyone on the plane will be led off at gunpoint."

He decided to take the chance. Stewardess Diane Sugomato had walked down the aisle and was holding the envelope over her head near the back seats. Richard edged partway out of the restroom door and waved to catch her eye, coughing and gagging as though he were already motion sick. He could feel blue-black water from the dyed hairpiece cutting through heavy tan makeup as he mopped and concealed his face with a fistful of blue and white United Airline towels.

Snatching the envelope from her outstretched hand, he immediately disappeared again behind the bathroom door.

Only seconds passed before loud knocking resounded off the flimsy bathroom door. The huge 727 suddenly lurched forward just as the toilet seat slammed shut. A man's authoritative voice ordered, "Get out of there at once. We're ready for takeoff." Richard unlocked the door and snaked his way past Second Officer Kent W. Owens to seat 20D. Wearing a fresh layer of dark shiny makeup, a waxy-looking wet hairpiece, and a bright blue and red sport jacket, Richard looked as if he'd been dressed that morning by the cast from *West Side Story*. But despite this series of hitches, Richard was calm. Thirty thousand feet above the ground, racing west at six hundred miles an hour, the big Boeing 727 and its eighty-five unsuspecting passengers were about to become hostage to the eighty-sixth.

Bob Lawless, a contractor from Denver, occupied the window seat, 20F. His brother-in-law and employee Mike Andria sat in 20E next to Richard. Lawless would later be first on a long list of witnesses interviewed that night by FBI agents in San Francisco. He and Mike had seen a stewardess knock on the rear restroom door, then call for help from one of the aircraft's officers. As the passenger in seat 20D crammed his zippered blue and red plaid suitcase under the seat in front of him, Lawless noticed his "dark brown wig, collar length, that just covered his ears. He was white, I think, but dark complected, possibly Spanish, five feet ten inches tall, a hundred sixty pounds, wearing mirror-type sunglasses. As we left the ground, I watched him unzip the suitcase and take a large manila envelope out and put it in the back pocket of the seat in front of him. Then I watched him slip something bulky out and hide it under his heavy, blue and red sport jacket. The 'Fasten Your Seat Belt' light went off, and the man is back in the bathroom again. Not more than a couple of minutes and he comes back, takes out a black ballpoint pen and scribbles something on a yellow three by five pad. His right hand, I remember, was steady and clean as he wrote. Like a businessman or schoolteacher."

Mike Andria said that he initially paid very little attention to the flashily dressed man in the aisle seat. "But not long after we were in the air—I guess it was the closeness of our seats or the rubbing of elbows that got to me—I instinctively knew that something just wasn't right. Anyway, that's about the time I begin to feel a little bit uneasy." About twenty minutes out of Denver, the captain announced minor hydraulic problems. Nothing serious, he said, but the plane would land in Grand Junction, Colorado, in a few minutes for repairs.

Suddenly, the man in the aisle seat leaned toward Andria and whispered, "That's not why we're stopping in Grand Junction." Andria later recalled, "I could feel something hard push against my ribs. When I looked down, I could see the nose of a black forty-five–caliber pistol and what I felt sure was a hand grenade." McCoy handed Andria a yellow 3 x 5 card that read, "This is a hijack. Move forward and get a stewardess." Several minutes later, Diane Surdam came to the rear of the plane. McCoy handed her a white 5 x 7 envelope. Typed on the outside was "GRENADE-PIN PULLED PISTOL-LOADED." It contained two pages of typed instructions, the pin from a World War II pineapple grenade, and a live .45-caliber cartridge.

Captain Gerald Hearn had been suspicious about the dress and behavior of the man in 20D since takeoff and had radioed back to Denver to learn that the passenger held a one-way ticket and used the name James Johnson. He had then radioed ahead to Grand Junction, where FBI agents would be waiting. But it was too late. The nightmare of all stewardesses, passengers, and pilots had just become a reality on Flight 855.

Captain Hearn's descent into Grand Junction stopped when Diane Surdam handed him the manila envelope. He was climbing again as he read the instructions, poorly typed on a manual typewriter. Surdam had told him the hijacker wanted the instructions returned, so first and second officers Ken Bradley and Kent Owens scribbled down notes of the details of his demands and instructions, the procedure they would continue to follow as additional notes and instructions typed on federal aviation flight-plan forms came up to the cockpit. Richard would have had easy access to these forms. The first note, according to the crew's reconstruction, read:

WE HAVE A GRENADE, THE PIN HAS BEEN PULLED. WE HAVE PISTOLS, THEY'RE LOADED. WE HAVE C-4 PLASTIC EXPLOSIVES. IT'S A LONG WAY TO THE GROUND.

WE ARE TAKING THIS PLANE TO SAN FRANCISCO, NOT LOS ANGELES! SECURE PERMISSION TO LAND

ON RUNWAY 19, AT EXACTLY 4:30 P.M. PACIFIC STAND-
ARD TIME. WE ARE FAMILIAR WITH THE AIRPORT
AND WILL KNOW IF WE ARE BEING TRICKED. HAVE A
FUEL TRUCK WAITING WITH 6 HOURS OF JET FUEL,
ONLY TWO PEOPLE ON THE TRUCK. AFTER LANDING,
ALL VEHICLES WILL BE PARKED ONE HUNDRED FEET
FROM THE NOSE OF THE PLANE, ON THE LEFT SIDE.
WE WANT $500,000 IN CASH—DIFFERENT DENOMINA-
TIONS. FOUR COMMANDER PARACHUTES WITH STOP
WATCH AND WRIST ALTIMETER—GET THEM FROM
PERRY STEVENS EQUIPMENT COMPANY IN OAK-
LAND. THE STEWARDESS I GAVE THESE NOTES TO—
I'LL CALL HER "JANE"—WILL BE THE ONLY ONE
WE'LL TALK TO. YOU WILL READ QUICKLY AND
RETURN ALL NOTES TO ME. DON'T TELL THE PAS-
SENGERS WHAT'S GOING ON. HAVE EVERYTHING
READY WHEN WE LAND IN SAN FRANCISCO!

Stewardess Diane Surdam left the cockpit with a new name and the
lonely, dangerous assignment of go-between. Surdam, the newest,
but not the youngest of the three stewardesses, was tall, her eyes
were a soft brown, and her charcoal-colored ponytail fell just past her
waist, where it was held together with a shiny, white ribbon.
Although she was not yet thirty, her soft reassuring voice and unfal-
tering composure kept her passengers' apprehensions subdued.

Richard McCoy knew his threats had worked when Captain
Hearn's second announcement crackled over the intercom: "This is
your captain again, ladies and gentlemen. Grand Junction tells us
they're a little too small and not equipped to handle a 727. Our
problems, I assure you, are minor, so there's nothing to worry
about. But we'll do as we're told; we'll set her down and have her
looked at a little later in San Francisco."

Richard McCoy was a throwback, a latter-day Jesse James, riding
a juggernaut through the sky at six hundred miles an hour. And
within minutes the best-organized posse in the annals of law enforcement would be saddling up to come after him.

"Richard deliberately volunteered to fly gunships," Karen
McCoy recalled. "Combat ships, not MEDIVAC helicopters, where
they rescue wounded soldiers." During his second tour of duty in

Vietnam as a Green Beret, Richard piloted the army's C-13 combat helicopter over hostile territory on more than twenty-five missions. On 12 August 1967, while participating in a search and rescue operation in the jungles near Ap-binh-Hoa, a light observation helicopter lost power in heavy ground fog and was forced to set down. A second American crew flying an armed OH-23G helicopter was sent in to make the rescue from the air as there wasn't room to land. Richard was piloting a third 'copter, giving backup protection. He could see the battalion sergeant major standing on the bubble of the downed chopper waving his arms as the rescue helicopter descended. Suddenly it too lost power and fell to earth, catching the sergeant major in the rotor blades. Both helicopters burst into flames.

It was getting dark, but there was enough light from the flames of both aircraft that Richard could see more than a hundred Viet Cong troops snaking through heavy elephant grass some three hundred yards away. "It had to be done, and it had to be done quick," the commanding officer's report read. Richard forced a landing place next to the downed 'copters, his rotor blades cutting through tree limbs as he made his descent. On the ground, he found only two survivors, both hysterical. There wasn't time to sort through the dead. The three of them scrambled for Richard's C-13 workhorse. Richard could feel his helicopter buck as the rotor blades cut through heavy foliage on their way out. The sky was dark, a somber background for the explosions of enemy ground fire and fuel tanks erupting. On 26 November 1967 he received the Army Commendation Medal for Heroism.

Then, on 29 April 1968 he received the Distinguished Flying Cross for yet another rescue. The citation read:

> WARRANT OFFICER MCCOY distinguished himself by exceptionally valorous actions during the early morning hours of 8 November 1967, while serving as a Helicopter Pilot with the Air Cavalry Troop, 11th Armored Cavalry Regiment, in the air over a Vietnamese Popular Forces compound at Xa Duy Can, 7 miles northwest of Tanh Linh, Vietnam. Upon hearing that the compound was in the process of being overrun by a large Viet Cong Force, Warrant Officer McCoy volunteered to fly his aircraft to the scene in support of the friendly forces, in spite of poor visibility due to thick ground fog and intermittent cloud layers, and a complete lack of tactical maps for the area. Flying by instrumen-

tation and radio alone, Warrant Officer McCoy located the compound and came under automatic weapons and small arms fire. With the position of the compound marked by a flare and the firefight marked by tracer rounds, Warrant Officer McCoy began a series of firing passes, launching rockets directly into the Viet Cong positions until all his ammunition was expended. Due to his courageous flight and highly accurate fire, the enemy was completely routed, leaving 20 bodies behind. Warrant Officer McCoy's outstanding flying ability and devotion to duty are in keeping with the highest traditions of the military service and reflect great credit upon himself, his unit, and the United States Army.

"It took me awhile," Karen continued, "to figure out that Richard had to have the excitement. He didn't want to kill anybody, I don't think, and he didn't want to die. He just, pure and simple, wanted to hear those big guns go off. He said he used to lay awake at night, wait to hear the bell ring. He would just take off on a dead run. Be the first one out there in line to go. He just had to have that excitement. As if he was trying to dare death to come."

When Richard returned in 1968 from this second tour of duty in Vietnam, he still wanted to go back. "Our marriage has never been what you would call rosy," Karen hesitated, "but . . . well, I don't know, I guess you could say we were getting along fairly well until he wanted to go back and I couldn't understand this. Why he had to go back to Vietnam."

Karen described her husband as "one of the most honorable, honest, and religious men I've ever known in my entire life." In Vietnam, he baptized one of his buddies under fire. He would fly out on Sundays with his helicopter, collect the Mormon boys, and hold services.

"Richard," Karen said, with possibly the first tears she'd shed in years, "is what I call—and I've never said this to his face—my hero." She managed the next words between deep sobs, "An American hero."

Richard was a certified American hero, no question about that. Karen liked that about him. She also liked his looks. His nose was set just off center, and his scarred high cheekbones gave him the look of a middleweight. He was handsome, in a rugged, uneven way. He had deep-set blue eyes, and his arms were long and muscled. There was always something exciting about Richard McCoy.

Karen, at twenty-seven, had both brains and backbone to go with her good looks and had learned resourcefulness early. She grew up in Canton, Ohio, and was only eight when her father died. Her mother, given to severe bouts of depression and alcohol abuse, became an added responsibility. Karen grew up running the house and caring for her younger sister, Denise. As a high-school junior, Karen suffered from severe headaches and depression that eventually led to psychiatric treatment. She became a Mormon in her teens along with Denise and their older brother, graduated at the top of her class, and was awarded a partial academic scholarship to Brigham Young University.

Richard first came to Provo in 1962 and enrolled at Brigham Young University as a freshman. Then he dropped out for a two-year tour of duty as a Green Beret in Vietnam. Wounded in 1964, he was awarded the Purple Heart and spent the next year at home in North Carolina recuperating. In 1965 he returned to Provo, reentered BYU, and met Karen Burns. They were married that summer. In August 1967, he reenlisted on condition that he go back to Vietnam, and, after a year of intensive training, he did. "It was the excitement, I guess," Richard told me. "The risks you take in combat, knowing death is always one step away."

2

The FBI's Man:
Russ Calame

At 3:50 P.M., thirty minutes after Flight 855 turned away from Grand Junction, the FBI office in Salt Lake City received word from Grand Junction that a commercial aircraft was being hijacked and would be passing over Utah en route to San Francisco. Russell P. Calame, special agent in charge (SAC) of the district office, sent two special agents, Harry Jones and Charlie Shepherd, to the control tower at the Salt Lake International Airport.

Russ Calame's FBI assignments sent him to the Salt Lake City Division as its SAC in May 1969. This assignment was a reward, a relatively peaceful assignment in a great location. Calame and his family all liked the Rocky Mountain West. At that time, the Salt Lake City Division was responsible for the state of Utah and, over the years, had experienced relatively few criminal cases. There was no way, however, that Calame or his agents could have foreseen the string of kidnappings, extortions, bank robberies, and hijackings that would come one after the other over the next three years. At age forty-eight, Calame could have retired in the summer of 1971, but candidly admits, "I just couldn't bear to retire. We were having such great success with our cases and law enforcement relations." As it turned out, had he retired, he would have missed "the best of my twenty-five years with the FBI." I met Calame about May 1969, when Agent Charlie Shepherd brought him over to my office.

Calame was a tall, slender man in his late forties with flecks of gray sprinkled naturally through his thick, dark hair. Although outwardly not a tough guy, Calame, I could tell, was deadly serious about his work, his family, and especially his country. A rumor out of his own office described him as "hardworking and the luckiest guy on earth," but the adjectives I would have used—more correctly— were driven, organized, and a master of people. A special agent in charge like Calame, represented, more often than not, the cream of the Federal Bureau of Investigation.

To become a special agent in charge of a field division, I knew that Russ Calame must have had ten to fifteen transfers—"going through the chairs," as the agents put it. I knew he must also have an insider's knowledge of bureau politics and workings, had reached his position against extremely keen competition, and shared with other SACs three common elements: power, power, and power.

The SAC of a field division was responsible for every phase of the operation: personnel, training, public relations, weapons, criminal and civil cases, motor vehicles, administration, and discipline. Calame had complete and total control over his agents' lives. A regular field agent could be reassigned by his SAC or sent packing based on the SAC's recommendation. J. Edgar Hoover's organization, backed with knowledge, training, and discipline, created unity, cohesiveness, and loyalty to the system that resulted in immense commitment to get the job done.

The strength of Hoover's system, however, was also its weakness. Not all special agents in charge of field offices were hard workers, capable, bright, or even well rounded. As in any other large organization, some had made it to the top of their chosen ladder and there retired, in effect, without bothering to submit a letter of resignation. If a SAC was weak or derelict, chased women, or drank too much, the organization would still protect him, even though he became an "unmentionable" to outsiders.

Calame was one of the bureau's finest, one of those whose intellect, integrity, and years of dedicated service had helped shape the image that criminals feared and school kids stood and applauded. He had just started his freshman year of college in 1939 when he met Mary Harter, a Des Moines girl, tall and slim with bright, curious blue eyes and golden hair the color of an Iowa autumn. They went together their entire college careers and married a few days after Calame graduated from Officers Candidate School and was commissioned a second lieutenant on 8 July 1943. When I met Mary, five children and twenty-five years later, her hair was more the color of winter, but she was still a tall, handsome woman who had found her identity, not as the wife of an agent in charge but through her own efforts. Calame never talked about the hazards of his job with his family, but they read the newspapers and followed his radio and television broadcasts. Along that same line, he had never really talked much about his three and a half years in the army and mentioned to me at one of the government get-togethers that his youngest daughter came up to him one day while she was in junior high school, saying she'd been looking at an old photo album, and had he ever been in the army? Somehow, she had only associated him with the FBI.

Calame had hired on with J. Edgar Hoover as a special agent not long after World War II and completed his training at the FBI Academy in Quantico, Virginia, in 1947. His first assignment was the bad side of Chicago; successive assignments took him to Philadelphia and Scranton, Pennsylvania; FBI headquarters in Washington, D.C.; Houston, Texas; Omaha, Nebraska; Cincinnati, Ohio; FBI headquarters a second time; and then to Salt Lake City, Utah. When he was transferred from Houston to Omaha as the deputy chief of division, the *Houston Press* carried his photograph and an article accusing him of spending much of his time with hoodlums, bank robbers, swindlers, and Murphy men. They said other nice things about him and pleaded with him to stay, but Hoover had ordered him to Omaha, and that was that.

Calame and I talked about the weather, how long he'd been in Salt Lake, first impressions of the city, and our jobs. Within a few minutes, we'd worked our way around to the living legend, J. Edgar Hoover. I probed a little, "Pretty hard fella to work for, I hear." I may have leered a little bit to show that I already had my own opinion of Mr. Hoover, or Caesar Tiberius, as he was often called in the federal system.

Calame, his gray Stetson resting on his knee, did not leer back. He cleared his throat. "I've always been very proud of being selected by Mr. Hoover as one of his FBI," he said earnestly, "and my feelings about Mr. Hoover personally run deep." Whether you liked Calame, I thought, depended on whether you liked the bureau. Because that's exactly what Calame was—FBI through and through. "I have always found Mr. Hoover to be sincere," Calame continued, "forthright and gracious, even when he is pointing out some weakness or deficiency which has come to his notice. Mr. Hoover has always made an honest effort to be fair and just with all his personnel.

He stays on top of a situation unbelievably well, and when he has some corrective instruction to give, he tells you about it in direct terms and leaves no doubt in your mind what he expects in the future. When you get to know me better, Mr. Rhodes," Calame concluded, "you'll then understand Mr. Hoover and the Bureau better."

I couldn't have agreed more. I also felt as if I'd been spanked. But Calame had one more speech before he was finished. "Mr. Hoover has instilled in me a desire for justice in all things, and I believe if I seek justice in all my endeavors, surely justice will serve me."

I had trouble understanding that day how a law enforcer in his latter forties could still possess such trust and optimism. How strange it seemed to meet someone in the "Me Generation" of the sixties who not only made speeches about, but lived by, a set of principles, consecrated through nearly fifty years of FBI excellence. But I also had a new awareness, after meeting Calame, that Salt Lake City was Hoover's way of showing Calame his appreciation for twenty-some years of calmly chasing top-ten fugitives, armed bank robbers, and confidence men.

Calame's reward—Utah. It's a strange state. Its image—or part of it—for over a century has been of bearded white men in tall black hats tinkering around with an old and often-envied social phenomenon known as polygamy. I've heard that a major airline back in the 1960s used to advise passengers, while taxiing into the Salt Lake terminal, that they were now in Utah and to set their watches back a hundred years.

While the politically conservative and traditional Mormons represent only 55 percent of the population in the Salt Lake Valley, they occupy 95 percent of the seats in the state legislature and 100 percent of Utah's congressional seats. The other 45 percent of greater Salt Lake's nearly 800,000 inhabitants are a mixture of Catholics, Lutherans, Unitarians, and ex-Mormons. Less than one-half of 1 percent of Utah's population is black. Between Mormons and non-Mormons, social, political, and religious issues of varying weight and importance become a part of daily life in newspaper editorials, TV talk shows, and demonstrations at the Capitol Building.

First-time visitors to Salt Lake City are generally not disappointed when they get a look at its wedding-cake architecture around Temple Square and the long line at Snelgrove's, where ice-cream worshippers gather. Brigham Young, who led the Mormons to Utah in 1847, gets the credit, at least in folklore, of personally laying out the city. From the uncompromising block of Temple Square, he laid off streets running in the four cardinal directions, each one wide enough to let two yoke of oxen pulling a covered wagon turn around without backing. The streets are still as wide and clean as they were then, but skyscrapers, malls, and glass office buildings loom above them.

3 The Ransom
7 April 1972,
2:25 P.M., San Francisco

In twenty minutes Flight 855 would be landing in San Francisco. Following Richard McCoy's orders, Stewardess Diane Surdam escorted passengers from the nineteenth and twentieth rows to the first-class cabin, calmly instructing them not to tell others about the gun they'd seen or the green pineapple-shaped hand grenade with the pin removed. She then returned to the rear and, as instructed, sat down quietly beside McCoy.

To the left and one row in front, one passenger had not been moved forward—in compliance with another of McCoy's instructions. The man still sitting in row nineteen, William Coggin, was in his early twenties, six feet two inches tall, weighing two hundred pounds, with long, thick brown hair. Joe Gonzales of the California Department of Corrections had planted him in 19B a few minutes before regular passengers were permitted to board. The passenger in the window seat, an older man, had climbed incuriously over both of them. Coggin had been arrested a few days earlier on a fugitive warrant in Denver, Colorado, and was on his way to become Prisoner #B33739 at San Quentin State Penitentiary. He had previously escaped from Duel Vocational Institute at Tracy, California, where he was serving a long sentence for an even earlier escape from Santa Rita Correctional Facility, Alameda County, California, in July of 1970.

Gonzales, unarmed, had occupied the aisle seat next to Coggin. He didn't pay much attention to Richard in 20D, but when Coggin obviously did—with smiles, nods, and subtle hand gestures—he thought Coggin was planning to distract him and make a run for it.

The guard ordered him to "sit down and shut up," but Coggin had sniffed it out before anyone else. He watched the transformation of Richard McCoy from pale to brown and suspected that McCoy was packing a gun or other heavy object under his coat, since he was using his right elbow to help support the object.

When the passengers had moved to the first-class cabin, McCoy quietly slipped into the seat across the aisle directly behind Coggin and dropped his gloved hand on Coggin's right shoulder. Startled, Coggin twisted around. McCoy's eyes were hidden behind over-sized, mirrored sunglasses. His thin, curled lips formed an unintentional smile. "Young man," he whispered, "today's your big day. After the ten o'clock news, everybody in the country will have seen your face on television." Coggin said nothing. McCoy held a yellow pad where Coggin could read the note: "GO UP FRONT, THE CAPTAIN WANTS TO SEE YOU!" Coggin would be the courier; he would bring the money and parachutes aboard in San Francisco.

At 2:25 P.M., Pacific Coast time, the San Francisco Federal Bureau of Investigation received a call from the FAA indicating what had happened in the Colorado skies five minutes earlier. Until then, it had been a routine Friday: a bank robbed that morning in the suburbs, another one in the Tenderloin District of downtown San Francisco during the lunch hour. Two suspects were already being held in the noon robbery and witnesses had identified one of them. A skeleton crew, as usual, was already scheduled to work over the weekend. FBI agents had to put in a minimum of fifty hours a week anyway. Those high man-hours, the arrests, and the conviction statistics were J. Edgar Hoover's ammunition when he went up against the Congressional budget committees.

With the phone call, the tempo quickened. Flight 855 was due to arrive at 4:40 P.M. Norm Merckle, with the FAA at the San Francisco International Airport, was glued to his radio, his communication link with Captain Hearn. San Mateo County Sheriff Earl Whitmore began assembling his SWAT team, trained in hostage tactics, who would work with the FBI. Because air piracy is a federal crime, the bureau was calling the shots.

SAC Robert Gebhardt did not need to refer to Mr. Hoover's antiskyjack plan of 1970 as he swung into action. He ordered every available FBI agent in the Bay area to report for duty according to his prearranged group assignment, either at the San Francisco Airport or to the FBI office in downtown San Francisco. Gebhardt set up a command post in the planning area of United Airlines offices. The assault team of several crack marksmen were already picking out locations on the chilly terminal rooftops, cradling high-powered rifles equipped with infrared laser scopes, giving them the capacity to pinpoint a target even at night.

Aboard the plane, Harry Huffaker, M.D., returning from Denver to his Honolulu medical practice, was sitting in first class when Stewardess Surdam finished moving the passengers forward. Quietly approaching Huffaker, Surdam asked if he had supplies to handle a medical emergency. "We hope you are not called on, Dr. Huffaker," she said softly "and you probably won't be, but we have a man in the rear of the plane with a hand grenade. The pin has been pulled, and we are at this very moment under hijack."

"Yes, of course," Dr. Huffaker told her. He had the usual things a doctor takes with him in the overhead luggage compartment. "But I'm afraid," he added, "I wouldn't be much help to you or anyone else if that hand grenade blows up back there with this plane full of people."

Suddenly Surdam moved toward the rear of the plane. A tall man in the ninth row, aisle seat, to her right, was half-squatting in the aisle, focusing a small 35mm camera with an oversized flash attachment that he had borrowed from a stranger next to him. A young, well-dressed salesman for the M&M Candy Company, he had just learned from another passenger of the drama taking place in the back and was taking appropriate steps. "Nothing," someone said later, "that any other enterprising young salesman intent on making the cover of *Look* or *Life* magazine wouldn't have done." Although by now nearly half of the passengers were aware they were being hijacked, they sat quietly. As the would-be photographer fiddled with the focus, a gloved fist in the back holding a dark green grenade raised, then lowered. Suddenly Surdam was in front of him deftly plucking the camera away, her voice still pitched softly and soothingly, "No pictures in the plane, please. Let's have the camera, sir. You'll have it back when we're allowed to depart! Thank you."

FBI offices all over the western United States were on the alert. Back in Salt Lake City, Calame was going over the details of his own antihijack plan. He had had several of his best agents labor over it for weeks when Hoover had sent word to each agency to develop one in 1970. By December of 1970, Utah's plan had been approved back at FBI headquarters.

Basically, the plan identified the most advantageous positions for the maximum number of agents and equipment, stage by stage as the crime progressed. Because the Salt Lake City FBI had jurisdiction over the entire state of Utah, the plan also covered the Ogden and Provo airports, which had runways capable of handling most commercial aircraft.

Team One would operate out of the airport control tower, providing around-the-clock contact with the victim airline, the Federal Aviation Administration, and its regional control facilities. FAA regional control has the responsibility of tracking all aircraft on skyways between their point of origin and their destination. When the hijacker directs the pilot to a new destination, Team One relays those changes immediately to all affected field divisions. FAA regional monitoring concerns all aircraft and naturally handles much more traffic than a single airline monitoring only its own planes. Covering both the airport tower and FAA air-route traffic control center is good insurance that nothing will be missed.

Calame's plan called for two men on Team One: Harry Jones and Charlie Shepherd. Harry Jones was a scholarly, balding agent of about forty. Respected and well organized, Jones had earlier been given the difficult assignment, under Calame's supervision, of drawing up Utah's antihijack plan. His partner Charlie Shepherd considered himself responsible for countering Harry's mild image. "Harry's still," Shep would say, "probably the toughest man in the office, next to me. Best man I know of to kick a door down with."

Charlie Shepherd, known to his friends as Shep, was different in a lot of ways from Jones. Shep operated more on intuition, like a frightened colt that instinctively rears and kicks just before a thunderclap or the sight of a rattler. A high-class, well-paid street fighter for the people of the United States. Wounded during the last days of fighting on Iwo Jima, Sergeant Shepherd of the 4th Marine Corps Division had been awarded the Purple Heart and sent home to heal. Hoover may have seen him during the late forties carrying the ball for the University of West Virginia or watched as Shep ran back punts during the two years he was in the pros, because it wasn't long before he was teaching self-defense and firearms to new agents at the FBI Academy at Quantico. At just over six feet tall and 185 pounds with black, thick wavy hair, Shep, with Mr. Hoover's blessing, had played a bit part in *The FBI Story*, filmed at Quantico during the late fifties, which starred Jimmy Stewart. "The first year I taught at Quantico," Shep said, "I wouldn't have traded jobs with Mr. Hoover himself. By 1960, the third year I'd been there, I'd have traded jobs with the devil to get out of there." But firearms came naturally to Shep. During those three years he taught at the academy, his quickness and steady hand made him into one of the best shots in the bureau.

In 1958, the television program *You Asked for It*, sponsored by Skippy Peanut Butter, went on location at the FBI Academy. *You Asked for It* was an evening, family-oriented show where viewers wrote in and described some strange, odd, or otherwise unbelievable feat they had heard about, asking that it be brought to television. Trick shooting—over the shoulder and behind the back—was what they were after this time, and they wanted the best. With drums rolling, Shep stood flatfooted, leveling a .38-caliber police special in his steady right hand back over his left shoulder.

"Are you ready, Agent Shepherd?" the show's host asked.

"Ready," Shep said, squinting into the diamond ring he wore to find the target behind him as the cameras hummed.

Hoover never acknowledged he had seen *You Asked for It*. But he did indicate that he had seen something similar. In a letter dated 29 September 1960, just before Shep transferred to Salt Lake City, Mr. Hoover wrote:

Dear Mr. Shepherd:

It is a distinct pleasure to commend you for your outstanding feat in splitting a bullet on an ax blade which was captured on film by photographers of the National Geographic Magazine for inclusion in an article regarding the FBI.

Despite the fact that the indoor range was in semi-darkness, you performed this achievement time after time until a most dramatic series of photographs was obtained. This is indeed excellent and you should be very proud of your efforts. Your marksmanship is noteworthy and certainly a credit to you and the Bureau. I want you to know of my appreciation.

Sincerely yours,
J. Edgar Hoover

Team Two, the communications and logistics group, would set up in Calame's third-floor office to provide special agents, technical personnel, and clerical staff. The choice of locations was based on the simple fact that Calame's office had the best possible communications with FBI headquarters in Washington and all other FBI field offices. Calame's assistant, Vic Schaefer, would head this team. Agents in that group would keep a minute-by-minute log of activities, maintain constant liaison with local law enforcement agencies, coordinate the information flow to identify or locate a suspect, establish and maintain roadblocks if needed, furnish personnel for a ground-search in areas where a suspect might have landed, and chase down specific leads as they came in from other field divisions or from the public. Personnel assigned to this group would also review teletype information coming in from various FBI offices, divide it into logical groupings, and research in office files. Usually there would be about ten or twelve men on this team.

Each field division had been previously assigned a primary frequency to use on major cases like this with its field agents. In the case of static from neighboring FBI offices or other unexpected interference, they would switch to an alternate frequency. Adjoining FBI offices, however, always have at least one common frequency that both can utilize if the distance is not too great.[1] To provide first-rate communications to the area around the affected airport, radio equipment transported to the assembly point or other field command center always includes at least one portable base station which generally had a greater wattage than the hand-carried radios.

Team Three was the action squad. Stockpiled in a vault in Calame's office were duffel bags of equipment and supplies: ammunition, lights, cameras, .308 Remington rifles with scopes, .870 Remington twelve-gauge shotguns, a 25-watt suitcase-radio unit, two pairs of airline coveralls, body armor, field glasses, Mace, and tear gas. Designated agents of Team Three would pick up the equipment and hurry to their assembly point or designated duty station. The assembly point for the action team at the Salt Lake City International Airport was the steam plant just north of Terminal 1, away from routine airline traffic in case the skyjacker started shooting or set off a bomb. Team Three would be looking for an opportunity to board the plane, search it, or make an arrest. Because absolutely no action was ever taken without the joint approval of the special agent in charge, the airline official in charge, and the airport authority, liaison and communications had a high priority.

The plan also designated office space inside Terminal 1 as a press room with an agent in constant attendance. He not only helped keep the public informed of what was going on but also kept news people corraled. The city police, sheriff's department, and highway patrol all had supporting roles—primarily closing off access roads to and from the airport and restricting public access to the steam plant.

[1] Unfortunately, none of the FBI frequencies are completely secure from eavesdropping. The news media have sophisticated scanners which automatically run through a radio spectrum of frequencies and stop when they find a conversation in progress. The FBI uses code words or double talk, when necessary for the safety of a kidnap or extortion victim. Other occasions call for radio silence. In rare cases, usually counterespionage, they use a full code—rare because using a full code is cumbersome, requires preassigning arbitrary or fictitious names to subjects, suspects, and locations, and demands time-consuming translations. Even the more common surveillance jargon must be memorized and understood to the letter by the entire operative agent personnel.

For example, in a delicate surveillance, arbitrary names and numbers could be assigned to the principal subjects, streets, and activities. By numerically adding three to each street and four to each avenue, Fifth Street would be transmitted over the air as Eighth Street and Fifth Avenue would become Ninth Avenue. Another way to sow confusion is by simply advancing the first letter of a street or avenue two letters up the alphabet. Thus, Cinderella Avenue would be transmitted as Einderella Avenue.

4 McCoy's Rehearsal: D. B. Cooper

America's first rock-solid airplane hijack for money took place on 24 November 1971, Thanksgiving Eve. A lone male Caucasian who gave his name as Dan Cooper bought a one-way ticket at Portland, Oregon, for the twenty-five-minute flight aboard Northwest's Flight 305 to Seattle, Washington. Cooper settled down in seat 18E, the middle seat in the last row on the right. Soon after the Boeing 727 was airborne, he showed a bomb to Stewardess Florence Schaffner and told her to read what was typed on the outside of a white 5 x 7 envelope:

> MISS—I HAVE A BOMB HERE, AND I WOULD LIKE YOU TO SIT BY ME.

He was holding two copper wires connected to a battery and eight sticks of what looked like dynamite. And he was, in the words of another of the three stewardesses, Tina Mucklow, "as cool as a cucumber." Then he dictated the following instructions to Schaffner:

> I WANT $200,000 BY 5:00 P.M. IN CASH. PUT IT IN A KNAPSACK. I WANT TWO BACK PARACHUTES AND TWO FRONT PARACHUTES. WHEN WE LAND, I WANT A FUEL TRUCK READY TO REFUEL. NO FUNNY STUFF, OR I'LL DO THE JOB.

Cooper instructed Northwest's Captain William Scott to circle SEA-TAC Airport until Northwest confirmed that $200,000 in twenty-dollar bills, four parachutes (two back, two chest), and a wrist altimeter were ready to be brought aboard. The FBI counted and recorded the serial numbers of ten thousand twenty-dollar bills and, by 5:45 P.M., three full hours later, told Flight 305 it could land.

Although the refueling truck was ready, the FBI was not. The stall would last the larger part of two hours. Passengers and crew members described Cooper as dark-complected. Some estimated his age as young as thirty, others as old as fifty-five. They agreed that his hair was short and shiny black. He wore mirrored sunglasses, had noticeably big ears, and was of medium build—about five foot ten, 160 to 170 pounds. He wore a dark brown suit with narrow lapels. Cooper wore what they described as either long underwear or thermal gear that covered his socks.

Cooper chain-smoked Raleigh filter tips from the moment the no-smoking light went off. Tina Mucklow, sitting in the aisle seat beside him and lighting his cigarettes, noticed a yellowish discoloration on the first two fingers of his right hand, where he was holding his cigarette. She thought it must have been a nicotine stain. Russ Calame theorized later that it was probably from applying heavy makeup to his face.

Just before takeoff, Cooper carefully examined the money and the four parachutes, then surprised Captain Scott by allowing his thirty-five passengers and two of the stewardesses, Florence Schaffner and Alice Hancock, to leave the plane. Cooper was smiling as he watched Florence and Alice collect their personal belongings. "Then suddenly," Alice would tell the FBI, "he reached his hand into the canvas money bag [weighing almost twenty-one pounds and stenciled SEATTLE FIRST NATIONAL] and offered each of us a packet he said contained $2,000. . . . 'Here, you take it,' Cooper said, 'since I never gave you a tip for being nice to me.'" Both women, startled, refused the money, then later, realizing that it might have had Cooper's fingerprints on it, wished they had thought faster.

At 7:30 P.M. Flight 305 left the SEA-TAC runway with instructions to fly toward Mexico City, some two thousand miles south. Captain Scott sent word back to Cooper that the distance would require at least two interim fuel stops. But Cooper had no intention of going to Mexico. He had Tina Mucklow take up a typed federal aviation flight-plan form to the cockpit, instructing Scott to fly southeast, following flight path Victor 23 south along Interstate Highway 5, in the direction of Reno, Nevada. Mucklow brought the flight plan and note back, per Cooper's order.

Only minutes after their takeoff from Seattle, Cooper asked Mucklow to help him open the rear exit door leading to the aft cabin stairwell. Later he had to be told how to release the rear stairs. Aside from these two items, according to Scott, Cooper knew more than most about aviation. Cooper correctly used "interphone" rather than "telephone," was familiar with other flying terms, and instructed Scott on the flight plan to maintain an altitude of 10,000 feet, lower his flaps fifteen degrees, and continue his air speed at 170 knots—or roughly 195 miles per hour.

At about 8:12 P.M., along Interstate 5, somewhere in the vicinity of LaCenter, Washington, north of Portland, Cooper walked out the rear door, sat for some moments on the rear stairs, and suddenly disappeared with the $200,000.

But Cooper left behind two telltale pieces of physical evidence which the FBI, for the next twenty years, would keep a secret from the press, from the public, and from a long list of D. B. Cooper impostors who over the years would be interviewed one by one and eliminated. In preparation for his jump, Cooper removed his narrow, dark clip-on necktie and milky mother-of-pearl tie clasp and left them on seat 18E. FBI agents searching the Cooper plane in Reno found them. Six months later in Utah, the tie and tie clasp took on new importance in the Richard McCoy investigation.

Overnight, Cooper became a folk hero. His hijacking had required intelligence, daring, specialized skills, and above-average strength. The FBI was familiar with some of these characteristics in America's criminals who specialize in confrontational crimes like kidnapping and armed robbery. But D. B. Cooper was in a class apart. A ballad of how he had outfoxed the feds hit the airwaves, fan clubs sprang up, T-shirts bearing Cooper's name were sold as souvenirs, and pubs and restaurants opened with neon signs bearing the name of this new Robin Hood.

5

Ground Wait in San Francisco
7 April 1972, 4:30 P.M.

On board McCoy's hijacked plane, Captain Hearn cut the huge rear jets, lowered his wing flaps about forty degrees, and made a twenty-degree bank over Oakland in preparation for his descent into San Francisco. Flight 855 would touch down at exactly 4:30 P.M. as instructed.

As the 727 pitched to the right, Richard McCoy from seat 20D could see Oakland clearly. Even at 8,500 feet it looked cold, and it brought back only bad memories. "As a student pilot," Richard told me, "I had practiced take-offs and landings in and out of Oakland's airport hundreds of times. That was in 1970, Mr. Rhodes. We were there almost a year while I was getting my fixed-wing pilot's license. We had a tough time those nine months we were there. Karen had her sister, Denise, with her. So there was a lot of tension. Chanti was only a few months old." A burr of resentment crept into his voice. "Karen could have worked. She already had her undergraduate degree. What's more, Denise could have babysat. But not Karen. She said she was going to be hired and paid as a professional or she, just pure and simple, wouldn't work. Our marriage has not been what you would call stable, although I never wanted a divorce until she wanted one." So far, the things Richard could control had come automatically—almost without thinking. And that probably had been his salvation, because somehow, in spite of their never-ending arguments over money and kids, Richard still couldn't seem to get Karen out of his mind. The sight of Oakland below had triggered the memory of seven years of frustration and disappointment with a wife who usually went her own way. And yet when they were apart, her absence, to him, was almost overpowering. That, more than anything else, it seemed, was their own personal tabloid: a legacy of feeling alone, even while together.

"Our wedding day was not," as he put it, "what we had planned it to be." Richard and Karen had planned a quiet family celebration in Louisburg, North Carolina, in an ivy-covered Mormon meeting-house that August of 1965, but an argument between Karen and Myrtle "got loud and nasty," according to Richard, "and our wedding plans had to be kept secret."

In July 1972 I got to hear Richard's mother's side of the story.

"It was a Friday," Myrtle McCoy said, in a Smoky Mountain drawl. "I had just gotten home for supper when the telephone rings, okay? Well, I just about went to pieces when Richard told me he was in Louisburg, a little town outside of Raleigh, and had just said 'I do.' Well, it upset me terribly, Mr. Rhodes, because I knew he didn't know what he was doing. He didn't know that much about the little Burns girl and nothing at all about her family."

Myrtle McCoy was a big-hipped, narrow-waisted woman in her late forties or early fifties, a Southern belle of sorts, with sparkling brown eyes and wavy, home-permed auburn hair. Her ancestors had been North Carolina tobacco growers and sawmill operators, and she had inherited a little money from what there was to pass down from her father. But accompanying that soft, sugar-cured Southern accent was a cold, calculating determination.

"But if you'd be kind enough," Myrtle said, studying me suspiciously from across the desk, "to permit me to back up a little, I'll try to answer any questions you have about any members of my family. As best I can remember, it was 1965, just before school ended down at Brigham Young. Richard called and was just overjoyed about this new girl he'd met. Oh, he said, she made all A's in her studies and was such a good cook.

"Well, Richard's daddy and Russell were ever so thrilled he'd found him a new girlfriend. Me, now, I didn't feel that way back then, and I can't truthfully say as I feel that-a-way now." What Myrtle wanted was somebody like Dorothy Porter, a local girl who was engaged to marry Russell. They had known each other since high school; and Dorothy, according to Myrtle, "wasn't a bit outspoken, could cook and knew exactly how to take care of a man."

At Myrtle's instructions, Richard promised to visit Karen's home and learn more about her family background. As soon as school was out, he and Karen would visit her family in Ohio, then his home in Raleigh. Myrtle was out that June evening when Richard drove up with Karen Burns, introduced her to Floyd, and got her settled.

"I found nothing the matter with the girl's looks," Myrtle's story continued to uncoil. "She was a pretty little blue-eyed, blonde-headed child, so I greeted her as nice as I knew how and gave her a room upstairs where she even had a bath of her own. But she wasn't happy from the minute she walked in that front door."

One focus for Karen's unhappiness was how quickly Richard and Russell's fiancee, Dorothy, hit it off. "They loved to dance together," remembered Myrtle, "and, of course, that enraged Karen Burns. She'd run up to her bedroom and bawl until supper time."

Myrtle's affection for Karen did not increase as Karen confided her girlish feelings about Richard: "She says," Myrtle recalled, " 'Mrs. McCoy, I've met a lot of nice boys in college and dated a lot too; but Richard is the first boy I've ever met that I can tell what to do and he does it. Richard,' she said, 'always had extra money to spend around campus and then there was his shiny new car.'

"Well, that car, I said, didn't belong to Richard McCoy. It was Russell's. Then I let her in on another family secret. The bank account that so impressed her down in Provo, Utah, I said, is in both Richard's name and my name. When the account gets low he notifies me and I transfer a little more money in. Richard, I assured her, was allowed just so much a week while he was in school; and now that they were living in my house, they'd both have to work and help support themselves."

She did not report how Karen took this announcement; but if she was hoping it would discourage Karen from marrying Richard, she was disappointed. When Richard called from Louisburg with his announcement, "You could have knocked us over with a feather!" exclaimed Myrtle. "Daddy and I both just went all to pieces. We didn't want to be there when they came home, so Daddy and I packed the car and drove back to a little farm I have." They returned the next evening to find Richard "all smiles" and "a wonderful supper" that Karen had cooked for them.

The supper could have been a happy reconciliation; but whether from bad luck or design, it deepened the wound. "Without a word," Myrtle went on, "we all sat down to eat and Daddy as usual asked the blessing. All of a sudden Karen Burns jumped up from the table, brushed past Daddy, and ran upstairs just screaming and bawling. Richard jumped up right behind her and said, 'I hate both of you,' and hurried upstairs behind her.

"I looked at Daddy, and he just sat there shaking his head. We didn't know what we'd done wrong. Well, I'd had enough; so I go upstairs an' listen at their bedroom door. All I can hear is Karen sobbing and trying to catch her breath while Richard's telling her: 'Everything's going to be all right, I promise. Honey, please don't cry. Honey, please hush.' Well, I didn't know what to think! So I knock on the door and stand there until Richard finally opens the door, and I can see Karen stretched out across the bed just squalling like me and Daddy had taken a stick to her.

"When she finally catches her breath, we find out it was all because Daddy hadn't—now listen to this—asked Richard to bless the food since it was Karen's hand that prepared it. Daddy and me just looked at each other and went back downstairs."

When Myrtle informed them that they needed to find work, Richard hired on at a sewing-machine company; but Karen cooly informed Myrtle that, as a college graduate, "I don't intend to work for nobody for no ninety-eight cents an hour like you're doing." Myrtle huffed at the memory, "Here I am killing myself for the same ninety-eight cents an hour, and it didn't bother her in the slightest to sit down at my kitchen table and eat off my ninety-eight cents."

Karen became more accommodating briefly—while she was planning the big church wedding with her whole family present—and worked long enough to buy clothes and accessories to set off the floor-length wedding dress with raglan sleeves she had worn at their secretive wedding in Louisburg. Then she made addressing wedding invitations a full-time job, meanwhile wheedling Myrtle to allow her fifteen-year-old sister Denise to come take part in the wedding.

According to Myrtle, "Karen and Richard had a wedding we'll never forget. That little Mormon church there in Raleigh was just packed with people. As soon as the bishop pronounced them man and wife, Karen and Richard walked out of the church and down the stairs, arm in arm. All of Richard's friends had the car decorated with old pots and pans and old shoes and toilet paper and every ribbon they could find in all of North Carolina."

Myrtle's eyes glinted as she recounted how Richard's friends sprang a shivaree on them and drove off with Karen "just kicking and screaming. A couple of hours of that girl and they were glad to get back to my house and let Richard have her."

The next day, Sunday afternoon, the wedding party continued at Spring Gardens, a resort outside Raleigh. When Richard drove down too close to the riverbank, "like boys will do," nodded his mother indulgently, Karen, again screaming, leaped from the car, and began hitchhiking back to Raleigh in her bathing suit, "showing off in front of everybody," her mother-in-law added disapprovingly.

The wedding and the reception were very elegant, Myrtle averred, even though "Richard wasn't earning a lot of money and Karen absolutely refused to work where they were not going to pay her for her brains." Karen and Richard continued living with Myrtle and Floyd until just before Christmas 1965 when they moved into a one-bedroom apartment because, Myrtle was convinced, "Karen didn't want Richard's people anywhere close around him. She was the most jealous and possessive girl I ever saw in my life."

The apartment was only a block away, but Richard and Karen never invited Myrtle to visit. When she stopped by on her own, one glance showed her the sparse furniture, the tiny bath, and the complete lack of closets. Then Richard reenlisted. A combination of circumstances drove him to it. He had a flare-up of an ear fungus that had developed earlier in Vietnam, and the nonmilitary doctors didn't know how to treat him. Furthermore, Karen was about three months pregnant with Chanti, and they had no money. "With his back to the wall," Myrtle said, "Richard did what all the other McCoy men did. He went back into the army."

He took helicopter training in Texas while Karen lived with Myrtle and Floyd, "crying over the telephone and carrying on till finally, as usual, Karen got to go to Texas," sighed Myrtle. He was later posted to Fort Rucker, Alabama, for six months of advanced training. Here Chanti was born. "We hoped the baby would settle Karen down some and keep her from being so overbearing," Myrtle sighed. "Maybe after all these months of Karen's tantrums and Richard's trying to adjust to them, finally now things would begin to get better."

When Richard was commissioned a warrant officer, his brother Russell, by then a second lieutenant, received permission at Richard's request to swear him in. Floyd pinned one bar on one shoulder and Karen pinned on the other.

Richard had rented rooms at the base guesthouse for Russell and his wife, Dorothy, and his parents. Before the evening dinner party for graduates and their parents, Richard and Russell got in Russell's car and drove off "to swap war histories and tales they'd heard about each other. Like brothers, they wanted to be alone for awhile." When Karen discovered that Richard was gone, she hustled Chanti into the front seat of their Volkswagen bus "and just runs full blast all up on the curbs," Myrtle continued with mournful relish, "and gets behind Richard and Russell and practically sits on that horn. She had no regard for who she might be disturbing. She followed them all over the base just blowing the horn."

The men, embarrassed and angry, returned to the house to get dressed. While Russell was trying to fasten Richard's stiff collar, Karen screamed that she was taking Chanti and their belongings and returning to Ohio.

"Another one of Karen Burns's little fits," said Myrtle, shaking her head. "Well, Richard stops dead in his tracks, looks her in the eye, and says, 'Well, go right ahead! If that's what you want, sister, that's what you oughta do.'"

Karen backed down enough to get dressed and go to the reception; but on the way, she got in an argument with Russell and slapped him. Richard grabbed Russell's arm as he started to hit her back. "But by the time we arrived at the reception, which was a buffet-style dinner party," Myrtle marveled, "Karen had calmed down and you would never have thought she'd had one of her spells just a few minutes earlier. She smiled and greeted everyone as if nothing had ever happened. After dinner, Richard and Karen walked out on the dance floor and danced the first dance." But when Richard asked Dorothy for the second dance, "that's when the commotion starts all over again. Karen gets tears in her eyes, begins to swell up as if she was going to throw another fit, so everyone jumps up, grabs their coats, Richard took her arm, and we all ran for the cars."

Richard's car was already packed for the leave-time drive back to Raleigh, so Russell volunteered to drive Richard, Karen, and Chanti while Richard slept. With their headlights shining through Richard's rear window, Myrtle and Floyd had a ringside seat to the next act in the circus. "Here we go, Mr. Rhodes," explained Myrtle, "with Russell driving Richard's car and Richard sitting next to him in the front seat and Karen sitting on the ouside holding Chanti. Karen gets jealous over Richard and Russell leaving her out of the conversation;

42

and just as we come flying down this big hill, we can see Karen reach over and grab the steering wheel from Russell and try to jerk the car off the highway. Then she begins pawing and scratching at both Richard and Russell. All of a sudden, the car comes to this screeching halt on the shoulder of this blacktopped two-lane road. Karen crawls out of the front seat with that little baby in one arm just screaming and kicking at both of them. We pulled in behind them and sat while Karen stood there, threatening to throw little Chanti under the wheels of the first truck that came along. And lo and behold, here comes one of those big P.I.E. trucks just flyin' with this big trailer swinging around on the back. Richard grabs Karen and the baby from behind, locks them in a bear hug while Daddy and me sit with our eyes shut. They screamed and argued at each other out on that highway until finally Russell got out and said, 'Here, if you two want to kill yourselves, be my guest,' because he was riding with us.

"Richard got in behind the wheel and drove in front of us for awhile. Then they'd slow up and get behind us for awhile. We could tell they were still arguing. The next morning at our house in Raleigh, Karen walked in the front door with Chanti just like nothing had ever happened and told us what a lovely time she'd had. How much she enjoyed our company."

About two months later, with Richard on his way to Vietnam again as a Green Beret helicopter pilot, Karen took Chanti back to Provo and enrolled again at BYU. "It so saddened us all to see Richard go," Myrtle shook her head. "Her and Richard would pick up again, start having it out where they left off as soon as he got back from Vietnam. I don't know whether they loved each other or not, Mr. Rhodes, but it wasn't healthy. You could see right from the beginning that something terrible was bound to happen."

By the time all four wheels had touched the ground in San Francisco, Stewardess Surdam had unfastened her seat belt and, with her usual composure, was walking down the aisle past a planeful of frightened passengers to the captain's cabin, carrying another white 5 x 7 envelope. The instructions inside read:

NOW—GO TO THE END OF RUNWAY 19. PARK FACING NORTH NEXT TO THE BAY. FUEL FOR SIX HOURS. ONLY TWO PEOPLE ON THE FUEL TRUCK. ONLY THREE MEN UNLOAD LUGGAGE. PUT IT ON LEFT

SIDE OF PLANE. ALL VEHICLES PARK ONE HUNDRED FEET TO THE LEFT. HAVE STEPS BROUGHT TO FRONT EXIT DOOR. MOVE ALL PASSENGERS TO FORWARD SEATS. THEY USE FORWARD RESTROOM. EVERYONE STAYS ON PLANE. RETURN NOTE TO ME.

Captain Hearn taxied to the far end of runway 19, then swung the tail section around, so the nose pointed toward the terminal with the tail section next to the bay. All three jet engines fell silent.

"I could see both sides of the plane clearly," Richard said. "The tail section was practically over the water, so the only blind spot for me was in the front. I could see three baggage men hand-carrying the luggage, but carrying only one piece at a time—slowly, from the right belly of the plane, around the nose and stacking it as I had told them to do, on the left. But the long stall, I could see, had already started. All three baggage handlers wore blue UAL coveralls with red and white trim. I noticed one man wore brown leather work boots; the other two were wearing low-cut black street shoes, the kind an FBI agent in disguise should never wear. I believe Stewardess Surdam saw them before I did and hoped I hadn't noticed."

The driver of the fuel truck was sitting, legs crossed, making no effort to refuel. Richard could see camouflaged figures scurrying along terminal roofs and watched intently as high-powered rifles took dead aim at the last small window on the right of the plane. With a vacuum between the double panes of hardened glass, a rifle shot from three hundred yards was not a serious threat, but Richard kept watching. As a third-year law enforcement student at Brigham Young University, Richard had set his sights on working for the FBI and had already passed the written tests for the highway patrol. It could have been him out on the roof, scoping in on a criminal. "I could imagine myself next to them, Mr. Rhodes, taking steady aim along with the others. With my background, you see, in flying, parachuting, and my knowledge of weapons, I would have been a natural for that type of case."

The exit doors were still locked. The stewardesses had not made their usual exiting announcements. Suddenly a tall, gray-haired man in his late fifties, wearing a dark three-piece banker's suit, stood up in the aisle and scanned the back seats. Glaring at Diane Surdam, he snapped, "For God's sake, girl, what on earth is going on here? I have a business meeting in Los Angeles later today! If you people can't get me there, then for God's sake, let me off this thing and I'll hire someone else to!''

Richard gently nudged Miss Surdam from behind, nodding permission to her unspoken question, to have Captain Hearn make his long-delayed announcement to the eighty-five passengers. Once again, she made the trip to the cockpit, then returned.

Captain Hearn's voice, like Miss Surdam's, was calm and cosmetically reassuring, intended as much to soothe the hijacker as the passengers: ''We have people aboard this plane, more than one, we think, who want to use it for a while. Want the plane for their own personal use. They have asked for a sizable amount of money; and we can assure them now, that it's on its way. They are armed, so stay calm. Please stay in your seats and make no effort to interfere in any way. United Airlines is doing everything it can to get the money and other things they asked for aboard, so it shouldn't be much longer. Thank you and please bear with us.''

SAC Gebhardt had alerted Wells Fargo Bank on California Street—also prearranged—about the ransom demand a little before 3 P.M. By 4:15, the manager, John Montang, finished counting for the third time the two hundred stacks of bills laid out on a large, dark oak conference table in the safety deposit area: two hundred thousand dollars in one-hundred-dollar bills, fifty thousand dollars in fifty-dollar bills, two hundred thousand dollars in twenties, and fifty thousand dollars in tens.

Montang escorted Special Agent James Blanton through three metal-latticed, locked gates to the safety deposit area, where they both waited for the United Airlines personnel to arrive and recount the money. It was United Airlines, not the federal government, that was being held hostage. United Airlines must decide whether to comply with the ransom demands. Robert Barden, Flight Operations Officer for United Airlines, arrived minutes later. By the time the money again was counted, dusted, and serial numbers recorded, it was 5:25 P.M. Blanton and Barden left, each carrying a leather United Airlines flight bag—one brownish tan, the other black.

Both men then climbed into Barden's 1970 yellow Volkswagen while four agents in two unmarked bureau cars, facing in opposite directions, watched from across the street. Then they pulled out into the heavy downtown traffic behind Barden as he led the way out to Van Ness, then to Highway 101 and the airport, some thirty minutes away.

Perry Stevens, owner of Stevens Para-Loft in Oakland, was already home in Hayward when the FBI reached him. Stevens was also a jumper, and from the explicit instructions, he was pretty sure that the hijacker was an experienced jumper and probably a free-faller as well. He quickly drove back to the loft where he packed two sports packs with orange and white panels. Both were light and easy to maneuver. Attached to each chute was a bright orange nylon sleeve containing a pilot chute approximately twenty-two inches in diameter when fully inflated.

Stevens then packed two white reserve chutes and two Northstar altimeters mounted on black velcro wristbands. Then the agents handed Stevens radio transmitters and watched as he rigged them to each of the four chutes, resealed each chute, and recorded the serial number. A Coast Guard helicopter from Hamilton Air Force Base shuttled the four chutes to the planning area at the airport, where Special Agent John Breslin had taken possession of the two United Airlines flight bags from Blanton containing half a million dollars. Throwing both bags and chutes into the back of a light blue United Airlines station wagon, Breslin, wearing UAL coveralls, crept cautiously to the end of runway 19, hoping to somehow get aboard Flight 855.

The Coast Guard was also standing by with two C-130 tracer planes. These two Hercules craft, packed with FBI agents, would follow Flight 855 once it left San Francisco.

It was now almost seven o'clock, nearly dark, and Flight 855 had sat at the end of runway 19 a little more than two hours. Yet it hadn't even been refueled, and Richard knew that would take at least thirty to forty-five minutes. He tapped Miss Surdam angrily on the shoulder and snapped, "Jane, go tell the captain this instant he has until eight P.M. to get the money and parachutes aboard—not a minute longer. Tell the pilot we mean business!"

Intently, calmly, Miss Surdam went to the cockpit with a message for the pilot. Neither the FBI agents looking down from the control tower nor the manager of United Airlines could see Captain Hearn's set jaw or his uniform, dripping with nervous perspiration, but the intensity in his tired, raspy voice would have convinced anybody that he had had enough. "Looks like we're going to have to leave you people," he radioed up to control. "We may have overstayed our welcome already. Our man in the back is getting nervous and I'm afraid he may do something we may all regret."

Breslin, sitting in the light blue station wagon, received radio instructions to deliver the money and parachutes to the left front of Flight 855 and leave the area immediately. A set of wheeled metal steps were quickly rolled into place. In an effort to move things along, Richard gave Captain Tom Davis, an off-duty United Airlines pilot deadheading from Denver to Los Angeles, permission to help Coggin carry the parachutes and money bags aboard. It took two trips.

As Tom Davis came up the aisle, McCoy leaned out, pointing the black automatic at him. "That's right, friend," Tom Davis repeated the hijacker's words to the FBI. "Set it right here by me, in the aisle." Davis obeyed and returned to his seat. Still holding the grenade, McCoy tucked the .45 into his waistband while he inspected both bags.

It was now 7:30 P.M., and even though the San Francisco sky was suddenly pitch-dark, nearly ten thousand yellow runway lights lit up the tarmac like a huge football field. Outside, cold winds from the bay chilled the ground crew, who rubbed their reddening ears with their hands as they refueled. Inside the plane, only a few overhead reading lights were on, illuminating the passengers anxiously facing the forward exit.

Next came the part of Richard's plan he dreaded most: offloading the passengers. "I knew all along there were FBI agents swarming the place, posing as airline personnel, working themselves near enough to the plane to totally encircle it. Getting eighty-five to ninety passengers and all their personal belongings off that plane without an FBI agent slipping on, hiding himself between the seats or in the stairwell. . . . This is a good time, I remember thinking, a damn good time for somebody to get killed."

Richard passed a handwritten note over Diane Surdam's shoulder to her:

EVERYBODY OFF NOW EXCEPT STEWARDESS[ES]. THEY STAY PUT. GET THE HELL OFF THE GROUND. BE QUICK ABOUT IT. USE THIS RUNWAY.

"The thing about that last note," Richard said regretfully. "I forgot to get it back. I guess I assumed she'd just bring it back. But she didn't." Instead, taking advantage of the confusion and Richard's distraction, Diane Surdam folded the note and slipped it into her bra. He paused, then added analytically, "I was all by myself, you see; but it would have been much easier with two people. The note, Mr. Rhodes, by itself, if the FBI will admit it, didn't mean a thing by itself. On the other hand, when they knew who to match the handwriting with—why it was as good as a written confession."

As the captain's announcement crackled over the intercom, the anxious passengers filled the aisles. Richard nodded at Diane Sugomato, jerking his head for her to leave, too. He had realized, belatedly, that, when he isolated the crew in the cockpit while he jumped, five people wouldn't fit. Sugomato's departure would lessen the congestion.

Within seconds after the last passenger had hurried down the steps, Hearn was pivoting the plane's nose to the northeast. Diane Surdam quickly closed and locked the forward exit door and sat again in front of Richard with Marjorie Newby, the stewardess from the first-class cabin.

SAC Robert Gebhardt and Sheriff Earl Whitmore had concealed themselves in a Coast Guard hanger at the end of runway 19 soon after Flight 855 landed, waiting for a slip-up or mistake, anything at all where they could pass the word to rush the plane. But nothing ever came. Watching from runway 19, they tracked the big plane, half the length of a football field, as it climbed north by northeast in the direction of Reno.

Gebhardt's only satisfaction was the relief and happiness on the faces of the uninjured passengers as FBI agents escorted them to a debriefing area. The good news would come later when Russ Calame, waiting in Salt Lake City, would report that Gebhardt's stalling had worked. It had thrown Richard and Karen off their schedule and forced them both to commit critical errors. That and Diane Surdam's quick thinking. Within hours, the note resting against her skin would be on its way to the FBI Laboratory by air courier, a key element in the airtight case against Richard McCoy.

6
Déjà Vu: Another Salt Lake Hijacking
May 1972

"It's his state of mind that bothers me, Mr. Calame," was the way the captain of Western Airlines Flight 407 put it one late afternoon on 8 May 1972, one month after the McCoy hijacking. "He's holding a handgun in the ribs of one of my stewardesses, then waves it around back in the aft section. I have us about fifteen minutes out of Tampa where we'll be making our last stop for fuel. Should be on the ground about an hour so you'll have time to talk to him then, if you feel it's safe. Might be safer on the ground," the captain added, "than up here at twenty-six thousand feet. You know, in case he flips out."

"Absolutely, Captain," Calame said from his third-floor office at the Salt Lake City Federal Building. "Couldn't agree with you more. But keep this in mind. When you leave that runway in Tampa, your next stop will be Havana. Then we're too late to try to talk him down."

This was actually Utah's fourth hijacking case; but it was the only one in which the perpetrator would end up spending time, first in a Cuban prison, then in an American one.

Agents in the Salt Lake FBI office were still catching their breaths that May from a six-month series of major crimes: the Cooper hijacking; the McCoy hijacking; the Donald Lewis Coleman hijacking out of Chicago; the kidnapping of twelve-year-old Nick Galanis; a million-dollar extortion attempt against United Airlines; a $500,000 extortion attempt against a prominent religious leader; a $500,000 extortion attempt against a Las Vegas casino; plus the usual run of frauds, embezzlements, and robberies. Then Western Airlines Flight 407 was highjacked by a man using the alias of John Harris, who boarded at Salt Lake City.

It was late afternoon when the FBI first received notification of the hijacking. SAC Calame issued instructions through the radio dispatcher and telephone central that all agents were to work that night and scheduled the initial briefing about the hijacking for 6:00 P.M.

"All right, people," Calame said, settling the agents down. "Let's get this show on the road, since we don't have time to burn. Operations personnel for Western Airlines have notified us and other offices concerned that this afternoon about three-fifteen P.M., a white male boarded Flight 407 at Salt Lake City. About the time they were over the Utah-Nevada border headed toward Los Angeles, this man stuck his hand into a blue carry-on bag and came up waving a three-fifty-seven Magnum. He told the stewardess to tell the pilot, 'We're going to Cuba! So get up there in the cockpit and tell the pilot to gas up in Los Angeles and then take off for Havana tonight.'

"So," Calame continued, "here's what we know at this time about the hijacker: male, white, dimple cheeks, about twenty years old, about six foot two, a hundred seventy pounds, light brown hair, blue eyes, extremely nervous, no indication he is on drugs, has made remarks leading the stewardess to believe he's bitter over the U.S. involvement in the Vietnam War. He's also made veiled threats against the President, so the Secret Service is interested. Glenn Weaver, Special Agent in Charge of the Secret Service here in Salt Lake, is on his way to our office now.

"The hijacker is described as wearing faded blue jeans, a red plaid shirt, and carrying a small, blue, canvas bag aboard. We've already sent Jones and Shepherd out to the airport to maintain liaison with Western. Western, in turn, has checked on the passenger data and determined there are sixty-one revenue and four nonrevenue people aboard. Further, they have had their personnel checking and determined that a young white male using the name John Harris got aboard at Salt Lake City without furnishing an address and bought a one-way ticket for Los Angeles. This young man looks like our best suspect, but let's also check out the whereabouts tonight of any persons with the name John Harris living in the area; further, we will split up the names of male passengers and pin down their description and something of their life-style. We'll make assignments now and then, after that, we'll take up any questions or suggestions."

There should have been red flags flying at the Salt Lake International Airport earlier that windy afternoon with bold, black inscriptions: BEWARE! WARNING! ENTER AT YOUR OWN RISK! While airlines and air terminals had been besieged for the past several years by threats, bombs, and close calls, very little was being done to protect the passengers.

By 1969, a brand-new social phenomenon began dominating Walter Cronkite's six o'clock edition of the news: "And again tonight," was the way he'd put it, "another American passenger plane, on its way to Miami, was taken over by two men and a woman purporting to be Cubans, who forced it to land in Havana. So far, no one has been injured, and no ransom has been asked for."

It should have been familiar. It happened thirty-eight times in 1969 between the United States and Cuba. "Buy a ticket to Miami and spend three glorious days in Havana," said the quipsters. "Fly now," the saying went. "If you're caught, pay later." Most of the hijackers that year, the Justice Department told us, were unhappy Cubans, lonesome for their homeland. Another theory was that Castro himself rewarded his own people to embarrass the United States and leave the impression that the American system was coming undone. All, however, were not Cubans. Many were angry American boys who chose this form of protest against their country's policies at home and in Vietnam.

On 9 March 1972, President Richard M. Nixon had ordered the immediate implementation of existing FAA security regulations on screening passengers and monitoring carry-on luggage. This included the use of magnetometers—already available but being used only in a few of this country's larger air terminals. Earlier in 1970 and 1971, many major airlines hired armed guards to ride their international flights and a few domestic flights—but to protect expensive cargo, not necessarily the passengers. By mid-1970, "sky marshals" in teams of two, pulled from the ranks of the Treasury Department and U.S. Customs, along with some military personnel and a few FBI agents, could be found aboard flights originating or passing through risky terminals like Miami, Atlanta, Houston, and New York City. But airlines were competing with each other for the half-million daily passengers and had taken the position that uniformed guards, body searches, long waits, and ominous pieces of electronic equipment would only inconvenience and unnecessarily frighten the honest traveler.

By 10:30 P.M., agents were drifting back, having covered their assignments. As each made his verbal report, it was clear to Calame that John Harris was the prime suspect. They'd checked out the local men named John or J. Harris: too old, the wrong color, or in bed asleep. Furthermore, family members or neighbors of the other male passengers aboard gave convincing portraits of legitimate citizens. But the passenger John Harris had no address, no phone number.

While the agents were running down all leads, Glenn Weaver had set up an open line with the Secret Service in Washington, D.C., which did not conceal its interest in getting an identification on Harris. Local law enforcement files, University of Utah officials, and others interested in aggressive Vietnam protesters turned up many names and photographs of student marchers. Several were close matches, but nobody was clearly the man on board Flight 407.

Flight 407 had now left Los Angeles and was on the ground in Dallas with agents at the airport looking for an opportunity to board the plane and subdue the hijacker. Western advised the FBI that if there was no opportunity at Dallas, then they would refuel the plane at Tampa before lifting off for Cuba. Calame had contacted the FAA in Washington, D.C., and made arrangements to patch a telephone line through to the plane on the ground at Tampa, if necessary.

Around 11:00 P.M., Calame called another conference of the case agents to order. "We're almost out of time," Calame told them with a quiet intensity. "Somewhere along the way we've missed something. This young man didn't just sit in his room bellyaching about the Vietnam War and Nixon. He must have talked to people about it, or written an article for a school paper, or even marched in a demonstration. Think of the demonstrations you've covered against the Vietnam War, campus activist groups, bombings, military sabotage—even minor ones." Calame picked up the description sheet. "Now, let's go over the details of his description carefully while everyone tries to visualize the appearance of this guy. A white male, between twenty and twenty-five years of age. . . ."

As the details went on, so did a memory. Agent Bill Geiermann's head jerked up. "Boss," Geiermann said to Calame, "I interviewed a local kid a year or so ago, a student up at the University of Utah. He was in a demonstration against the Vietnam War. Let me review my closed files in that category."

"Get on it," Calame nodded. "Take three or four men. If you

52

find you need to get into other classifications, let's put some people on that too."

A little after midnight, Geiermann, a tall, thin introspective man with horn-rimmed glasses, entered Calame's office grinning from ear to ear. "I think we're onto something," Geiermann said. "Michael Lynn Hansen, white male, six feet two, weight a hundred seventy pounds, long, light brown hair, blue eyes, dimples, date of birth, 10-18-'50. That would make him twenty-one. Vietnam War protester. We have pictures of him marching at the State Capitol Building and later the same day down here in front of the Federal Building. I interviewed him back in November of nineteen-seventy after the Kent State demonstration." Geiermann remembered that he lived with his mother up Emigration Canyon.

The plane would touch down in Tampa in a few minutes, and the airline personnel could only stall on the refueling for so long. Calame sent Bill and Shep out to the house. If he wasn't there and his mother didn't know where he was, they were to bring her back to the office.

"It could be anyone's son, Mrs. Hansen," Calame said sympathetically, sitting in one of the brown leather straight-backed chairs in front of his desk facing a slim woman in her late fifties.

"Sounds like Michael, though, doesn't it, Mr. Calame?" she said huskily.

"Yes, I'm afraid it does, Mrs. Hansen," Calame said. "Selling his car yesterday, like you said. He'd have money for plane fare at least, wouldn't he? When he left the house this morning, or actually yesterday morning, it's almost one o'clock now, but when he left this morning, Mrs. Hansen, did he give you any indication where he was going, or say when he would be home?"

"You must understand, Mr. Calame, I work for the telephone company and generally get home around six in the evening, so I just expected him to be there. He's twenty-one now, practically a grown man. A fine young man, I think, too. So . . . I'm sorry, Mr. Calame. What was your question?"

The FBI case report later sent back to Washington headquarters described Mrs. Hansen as calm and cooperative, about five-feet-two inches tall, approximately one hundred and ten to fifteen pounds. It neglected to say that she had still been wide awake at 12:30 A.M., that her eyes were red and swollen, or that while she sat in Russ Calame's office, the tip of her tongue traced circle after circle after circle on her thin colorless lips.

"Have you seen a change in him recently?" Calame repeated patiently. "Anything that would lead you to believe he could do something like this?"

"Well," she said, paused, then went on, "as you already know, he's against the war in Vietnam. He's against Nixon. Against most things, I guess you could say. Except picketing and marching and such. But this thing today just kills me. Of course, maybe it's not him!"

"We should know in a minute or two," Calame said, removing his rimless reading glasses and trying to rub eighteen hours of who did what from his bloodshot eyes. "As soon as we're able to talk to him, then we'll know. I'll ask you to talk to him first, Mrs. Hansen." Calame put the glasses back on and looked into her anxious eyes. "Tell him you love him, that you're behind him, that maybe it's not too late to work this thing out."

Captain Adams's transmission from Florida crackled through the open telephone receiver. "Adams here, Captain Adams," the pilot shouted. "Am I reaching Salt Lake City, Utah?"

"Yes!" Calame answered, "yes, indeed you have. FBI, Salt Lake City. Go ahead, Captain Adams."

"We're on the ground in Tampa, Mr. Calame. Refueling. Could be here another thirty to forty-five minutes. I've been on the radio with your agents here in Tampa. They're standing by, hoping they find a way to come aboard, but it doesn't look good. Our boy in the back seems to have calmed down some, Mr. Calame, so like I told your counterparts here, we want to avoid pushing him over the edge if we can. Agreed?"

"Agreed," Calame shouted into the small brown conference box. "Yes, of course we agree, Captain Adams; but like I said before, we're reasonably sure we've identified your man as Michael Lynn Hansen. We have his mother here in the office now, and she's agreed to talk with him."

Mrs. Hansen moved in front of the brown box while, in the aircraft, Captain Adams spoke into the intercom, "Ladies and gentlemen, this is your pilot, Captain Adams. We have a mother in Salt Lake City, Utah, who has been patched through to us. She's terribly afraid her son Michael is aboard and is concerned about his safety. If we have a Michael Lynn Hansen, H-A-N-S-E-N, date of birth 18

October 1950, with us, will he please make himself known to one of the stewardesses?"

Seconds passed. Then Adams's voice crackled again in the brown box. "I'm terribly sorry, Mr. Calame. You and your men have done a heck of a job, and it's the Hansen boy all right—but he's out in the aisle again, cursing and waving that gun around. He told me to tell his mother it was too late to turn back now. 'Tell her I'll send her a postcard from Cuba,' he said, 'if they let me.' "

I remember the Michael Hansen case, mainly because in 1975 the United States Department of Justice drew up a prisoner-exchange treaty with Cuba, and Michael Lynn Hansen was one of the first to be released from a Cuban prison and sent back to the United States by Fidel Castro. My probation officers reconstructed the crime Hansen had committed and the three years he had spent locked in a Cuban prison.

Originally, Hansen was housed with other young hijackers in a minimum-security work camp just outside Havana. Disillusioned with Castro's communism, he was caught twice going over the fence. His next stop, maximum security, could have been his last stop but for a well-received monthly check to the warden from his mother and father. Back in the U.S., Hansen was prosecuted for air piracy by his own government and sentenced to ten years. Once on parole, he absconded, and for the next several months was a federal fugitive. Arrested and convicted of robbery in the State of Oregon and for escape in Fargo, North Dakota, he wasn't released from custody until well into 1987.

Night Flight to Utah
7 April 1972, Evening

Back aboard Flight 855, still flying with McCoy's gun in its back, Captain Hearn gathered his forces for the next challenge. Turning the controls over to First Officer Ken Bradley, he would spend most of the next three hours on the radio with Commander Dale Schmidt and FBI agents aboard the two Coast Guard tracer planes. Second Officer Kent Owens took up his position on one knee peering unnoticed through a small crack where the cockpit door had not closed flush with the doorjamb. A small fisheye hole in the cockpit door, installed on all 727s after the D. B. Cooper hijacking, had been earlier taped over by their hijacker.

"Soon after we took off in San Francisco," a weary Captain Hearn later told agents in Salt Lake City, "the plane seemed to hesitate—to oscillate for a second or two. Then a red light lit up on our instrument panel, indicating that the aft cabin exit door had been opened. At twelve thousand feet, the plane automatically began depressurizing."

Kent Owens watched Surdam and Newby adjust the oxygen masks that had fallen from overhead recesses. They looked innocent and young. They looked like sacrificial victims.

It was a little after nine in Salt Lake, after eight in San Francisco. United Flight 855 had been in the air almost twenty minutes. After a cup of black coffee and a two-hour briefing with Charlie Shepherd and Harry Jones in the control tower, Russ Calame hurried back across the tarmac to a waiting National Guard helicopter. He spread out a polyethylene-covered map of Utah and began making black grease-pencil circles over Ogden, Provo, and Hill Air Force Base.

"It's the waiting that I can't stand," Calame muttered to Major Tom Brewer, the pilot. "It's terrible just sitting here. Wanting to get in the thick of things, and knowing if you move too fast you can play right into the perpetrator's hands and take yourself out of action before the hunt ever gets started. It's a lot like chess, Tom. As hard as it is on the nerves, the game we've got going right this minute with our perpetrator requires patience. Years of discipline and making the right moves—that's what we're counting on, Tom. Things change by the minute up there," Calame pointed out. "The nose of that 727 moves five degrees north, suddenly we're out of the picture, and Seattle's in. The nose moves five degrees southeast, and suddenly Phoenix and Albuquerque are on alert. Just that quick, Tom." Now, it was Salt Lake's turn while, all over the western United States, FBI agents were on alert and had been since a little after 3:00 P.M.

Diane Surdam carried up another set of instructions to the cockpit, again carefully typed on a flight-plan form. The instructions designated not only the route but also the speed, flying times, and several visible navigational fixes. Just short of Reno, Flight 855 obediently turned southeast toward Coaldale, Nevada, at an airspeed of 180 knots, altitude 14,000 feet. Captain Hearn also had instructions to notify the hijacker five minutes prior to reaching Coaldale and the other fixes. The other notes had spoken of "WE." This one read: "I KNOW YOU HAVE CHASE PLANES FOLLOWING. IF I SEE ANY, I WILL DETONATE EXPLOSIVES—AFTER I BAIL OUT."

Richard then had Diane open both flight bags again so he could double-check the money. It was his first chance to get a good look at it. "I practically had to choke myself to keep from screaming," he later told me. He wondered if it would all be there. Or if some or all of it would be fake. But it looked real, and there was enough to be at least close to a half-million dollars. "This was when I first realized what I had actually pulled off. I remember thinking, what would Karen think of me now! You can't imagine, Mr. Rhodes, how many bills it takes, even with fifties and hundreds, to make a half-million dollars."

He had Diane Surdam close the bags, then made a final check of the front end. "I crouched down and slipped up the aisle with this small pen-size flashlight in one hand and a loaded forty-five automatic in the other, and made a quick check between the seats to show myself an agent hadn't slipped aboard while all those passengers jammed the front door trying to get off. It would have been easy to do. Then I took a quick peek in the forward bathroom and galley where the first-class stewardess had prepared the meals. Everything, I thought, looked good to me."

The second pretyped FAA flight-plan form sent Flight 855 toward Tonopah, Nevada, then to Wilson Creek, and then east toward Milford, Utah. Flight 855 was heading east but zigzagging north and south. Richard had planned these changes deliberately "to keep the FBI off my tail." He could visualize them setting up on the ground "with dogs, spotlights, and helicopters." At Wilson Creek, he sent the two stewardesses up to the cockpit with one last order: When the plane reached Milford, they would find the next instructions in the pocket of seat A, row eight.

In one of the rear restrooms, Richard shaved off his mustache and sideburns, an exhausting chore with the oxygen mask off. Then he changed back into his brown tweed suit pants and white shirt. A freezing blast of air from the open rear door forced him to hurry into his olive-green thermal jumpsuit and a pair of black-laced jump boots. Richard explained all of these details to me seriously, working hard on remembering. "My intention originally, Mr. Rhodes, was to throw out all the Perry Stevens chutes. I'd made maybe thirty or forty jumps with my own chute, carried aboard in my luggage in San Francisco. I intended to use it as my main chute. I had another one I'd borrowed from Larry Patterson, a small sport chute. I wanted it because of the altimeter on it. About two weeks earlier, I took it and the altimeter up in a National Guard plane and preset it at thirty-five hundred feet, just in case I bumped my head on the tail section, blacked out, or just flat fell apart at the last minute.

"But like I said, a lot of things went wrong that day that I didn't expect. During our climb out of San Francisco, the empty plane lifted up with such ease and pitch—and I still don't understand it now—but somehow it must have triggered the preset altimeter and Patterson's chute suddenly pops open in the plane. Maybe at thirty-five hundred feet, I don't know. It almost knocked one of the stewardesses out of her seat. Anyway, I tried to repack it by stuffing it back in the sleeve, but I was ripping my fingernails until they cracked and bled, and by that time it was getting too late anyway. I had no choice. I had to use one of the Perry Stevens chutes as a backup because of the load I had to jump with. It didn't look as though the seals had been broken, so I grabbed one and thought, 'What the heck. Maybe the FBI hadn't had time to bug all four of them. Maybe none of them.'" The chute Richard McCoy was about to jump with was number 171, and it was bugged just like the others.

Richard had had two big green army duffel bags brought aboard in his luggage in San Francisco. In one bag, he packed everything he didn't intend to take home—an old suitcase, a flight bag with the red and blue sport jacket, the shoes, wig, mirrored glasses, makeup, and the rest of the mod clothes. About fifteen minutes east of Wilson Creek, Nevada, he uncranked the rear stairs and booted it out along with one of Perry Stevens's chutes. "If you've bugged these chutes," he remembers thinking, "this should give your chase planes something to do while I'm trying to get this stuff on the ground."

Tailing Flight 855 was Lieutenant Commander Dale Schmidt, piloting one of the two Coast Guards C-130s that had been circling San Francisco. The Hercules was slow, straining even to stay in radio contact with the Boeing 727. There were a dozen agents aboard, led by Leon Blakeney, who had formerly worked in Salt Lake City. They were the backup team. In case the hijacker jumped or forced Flight 855 down at some remote airfield the ground agents couldn't reach, they'd land as close as possible and become the first-line team. A second chase plane was also laboring along in the hijacked plane's wake.

"It was a perfect night," as Hearn later described the weather to the FBI, "clear enough even at fourteen thousand feet to follow the physical characteristics of the ground's surface, the mountains, the lakes, Interstate Highway Fifteen, and that had helped us tell where we were most of the time."

A moment after McCoy jettisoned the chute, Schmidt spoke sharply into the microphone, his words a military staccato: "Captain Hearn, we're still with you! I show us presently at thirty-eight degrees latitude, one-fifteen degrees longitude, about ten minutes north and twenty-five minutes west of Wilson Creek, Nevada. Sounds like we're picking up what could be a beeper from those chutes you took aboard. Take a look, Captain. Wouldn't surprise me if you've lost your passenger back there. I'll send the backup plane down"—he sounded almost cordial—"to take a look, if it's alright with you. But for the time being, we'd really like to cozy up a little closer, drop a few flares, and take a look around the area. You feel comfortable with that?"

"Hearn here. No, no," Hearn came back, "don't do that yet. I don't think that would be such a good idea right now. Of course our man wants it dark back there, but we think we see shadows moving around in the back. From all we can tell, he's still aboard. We're looking over a note now where he says he can detonate the plane from the outside after he jumps, so let's give him a little more time, Commander, to do whatever it is he's going to do."

The last two hours had dragged by for Calame and his agents in the National Guard's big green Hueys. As Charlie Shepherd and Harry Jones intercepted information, they fed it piecemeal to Calame. The helicopters had a seating capacity of twelve, but the safest number, depending on the weather, altitude, and the amount of extra equipment, was somewhere around six. Compared to other military 'copters, the Huey warmed up fast, didn't require much idling time, and, as Major Tom Brewer told Russ Calame, "is pretty much ready when we are."

In the second 'copter were Jim Stewart, Jim Downey, Clair Empey, Lynn Twede, Joe Cwik, and another agent from Team Three. Stewart and Downey both sat perched in the gunner door like hunting dogs, waiting for Calame to finally give in, pull his long legs through the open 'copter door, buckle his seat belt, ditch that big respectable Stetson, and give the word to take off.

"There's been an unweighting, Tom," Calame announced, knowing that Stewart and Downey were intercepting the same transmission, "around Wilson Creek, Nevada. Hearn says he felt an unweighting in the back of the plane. Like something heavy either jumped or was pushed out."

Then they heard that a chase plane was picking up beeps. "One of my concerns all along, Tom, has been he might force one or more of the stewardesses to jump first," Calame continued thoughtfully. "He asked for more than enough chutes, didn't he? Stewart and Downey, I'm sure, want to get in the air and get after him, hoping I'll send their crew on over to Wilson Creek. But it's two hundred miles over to Wilson Creek, Tom. Then two hundred miles back. Counting time on the ground, once they get over there, even by helicopter, that's six or eight hours. If I give them the green light, and we find our perpetrator is still up there on the plane, they've taken themselves out of action for the rest of the night."

So Calame's order was, "No, not yet, men."

His decision was not a popular one in the next helicopter. Stewart wanted in! Now! Let's do something, Boss. Stewart's voice could be heard over the whacking sound of the idling rotor blades: "Let's . . . get . . . this . . . son . . . of . . . a . . . bitch . . . in . . . the . . . air . . . Boss!"

Stewart and Downey were two of a kind. They needed to be in the action, sniffing out tight situations by instinct, recognizing in each other the same characteristics. Jim Stewart had transferred into the Salt Lake City office a few months before Calame did. He'd grown up in South Dakota, gone with the FBI in 1960 right out of law school, and, after a couple of years working Indian cases in Albuquerque and Farmington, New Mexico, was transferred to the Oklahoma City office. That's where, according to others, he really began to take to the bureau. Stewart taught firearms and self-defense to local law enforcement officers and could have been part of the local FBI palace guard.

But Hoover himself had ordered Stewart's transfer to Salt Lake City for disciplinary reasons. It had all started when the SAC, in Oklahoma City, allegedly had too much to drink one night at a local law enforcement conference and ran his hand up a local meter maid's uniform. Stewart and four or five other agents who were there defended the boss and refused to testify against him. Hoover accepted the SAC's resignation from the bureau and transferred the agents. It became a permanent black mark on the record of an outstanding, high-profile agent who more than once had caught Mr. Hoover's eye.

On 15 January 1964, Mr. Hoover had written Stewart a letter expressing his "sincere appreciation" for the role he had played in arresting Thomas Asbury Hadder, a fugitive then on the FBI's ten-most-wanted list. "As a direct result of the alertness you and your fellow agent demonstrated in recognizing an alias used by the subject, Hadder was located," Mr. Hoover had continued. "Thereafter, you assisted your fellow agent with much skill and effectiveness in taking him into custody. Also noteworthy was the thorough and diligent manner in which you handled your duties during the course of this investigation. It is my pleasure to commend you."

Did Stewart appreciate it? "Jerry Scott—my 'fellow agent'—and I got letters of commendation," observed Stewart with a thin, sarcastic smile, "but the boss got a cash bonus. God, Scott was hot. 'Here's what I think of Mistah Hoova's incentive program!' he told the boss; and in front of everyone in the office, he stood there and tore the damn letter in a thousand pieces. I should have too," Stewart murmured regretfully, "but I didn't."

Something I saw in the FBI was a not-so-perfect side that I'm sure Calame would never have admitted to. Hoover, I believe, unintentionally bred into the bureau a narcissistic side that encouraged withholding information on active crimes from local law enforcement on the assumption not everyone could be trusted. But the same attitude leaked down until FBI offices didn't share information with each other—and often agents in the same office played lone hands. Some of this secretive approach to information was simply wanting to look big in Mr. Hoover's eyes when a transfer came around. But greed probably was the more dominant reason. Cash bonuses, ranging from a hundred to several hundred dollars, arrived in the Salt Lake office like Christmas packages from Mr. Hoover during Calame's thirty-seven months. Yes, the local bureau had earned them with grade-A work, and nobody was anxious to see the flow slow to a trickle. This practice, I thought then and still do, provoked local resentment of the FBI and often impeded interagency cooperation.

So Stewart and Scott got letters of commendation, the boss and others in the office got cash bonuses, and Scott got transferred to Philadelphia, not exactly his first office of preference. He quit the bureau not long after that.

I decided, after I got to know Jim Stewart better, that the Oklahoma City office must have been the place where he, like every other new agent, discovers an esprit de corps that makes them religiously devoted to the FBI. The Oklahoma City office had a nickname for Stewart, "The Shadow," because he stayed out of the limelight. A half a dozen years later, over the meter maid incident, his faith in the FBI faltered but never quite failed. Stewart's reputation for lingering in the shadows had followed him all the way to Salt Lake City, but

Russ Calame liked self-starters. Relying mostly on what he saw, not what he heard, Calame made Stewart his legal officer.

As it turned out, Calame could have unleashed Stewart's helicopter and still had plenty of time to call him back, because just then Hearn told Captain Dale Schmidt that one of his stewardesses had reported shadows moving in the back of the plane. Hearn had to believe his hijacker had thrown one or two of the bugged parachutes out near Wilson Creek to confuse things.

Hearn and his crew did not mention that the lumbering 727, even with a fifty-mile-per-hour tailwind howling out of the west, was barely staying airborne. Obediently traveling at 180 groundspeed knots, they were moving dangerously slow. "Maintaining an altitude of fourteen thousand feet for a plane the size of a Boeing 727," Captain Hearn later told the FBI, "would have been near impossible without that tailwind."

The long, depressurized fuselage was lighted by only one small signal light centered between the two rear bathrooms. At 14,000 feet the air was cold and thin. Oxygen masks swung dimly over empty passenger seats. Richard pulled on the rest of his outfit—a black skydiver's helmet and black leather gloves—then packed the second green duffel bag. It weighed about seventy pounds. The half-million dollars must have weighed forty pounds alone, Richard estimated. Then there was his brown suit coat, the green pineapple grenade, the .45-caliber pistol and Patterson's chute.

It was nearly 11:00 P.M. when Captain Hearn received his final set of instructions, found in the pocket of seat 8A by Diane Surdam according to plan. The last note outlined a route north to Delta, then to Fairview, then to Provo, Utah. There, he was to turn southeast toward Price and Grand Junction, Colorado.

A shadow darting across the aisle up front frightened Richard. Then, he recalled, "I realized it was only the stewardess. She stood about the eighth row, hugging herself in the dark; and I could tell she was cold and tired and wished this thing was over. She was afraid, too. We had been at this thing nearly ten hours."

The aft stair door had banged open and shut for most of the trip. Inside the aft door was an instrument panel that released the rear stairs. Richard had chosen a Boeing 727 to hijack because it was the safest to jump from. When fully extended, the rear stairs dropped at a forty-five-degree angle toward the ground. At two hundred miles an hour, the airstream held the stairs almost parallel to the ground, and Captain Hearn could feel the tremendous pull the second Richard lowered them.

Richard used D rings—the kind of snap rings mountain climbers favor—to fasten both metal handles on the duffel bag to the metal rings on the front of his parachute harness. "There was no way that darn bag could get away from me," he recalled, reliving the moment. "I stood there in the open door for what seemed like hours with that cold wind banging me in the face, yet I could feel my hands sweat. Then I positioned the bag, which was about three feet long and three feet around, between my legs, took a deep breath, and took my first step outside." The stairs suddenly dropped about two feet, throwing him and the clumsy bag forward. Richard clutched the handrail, wrapping both arms around it, wondering if the teetering stairs might slam shut, folding back into the plane with him still on them.

It was bitter cold. His eyes were watering. One of the big jet engines was just a little behind and above the rear door, and its roar was deafening him, shaking him on the stairs. He groped for the penlight he had tied with a two-foot string to the zippered cigarette pocket on the left arm of the jumpsuit. It was gone. He fumbled helplessly on the stairs for it and found it, just as it was about to fall.

He scanned the sky for chase planes. Nothing. Below was a continuous string of lights along Interstate 15 between Salt Lake City and Provo. Slowly, the stars began to rotate, and he realized the pilot was making the thirty-degree bank he had ordered just before Provo.

Midnight Jump
7 April 1972, near Provo

Utah is considered a rural state. Nearly 70 percent of its 1.5 million people reside along the Wasatch Front, a chain of valleys following the Wasatch Mountains from Logan in the north to Provo in the south. Utah's four northern counties sometimes have snow deep enough to cover an automobile for months at a time. Bitter northeast winds can often howl down out of the canyons, snapping off frozen telephone poles like kitchen matches and whipping small frame houses around on frostbitten foundations. Twelve to fifteen feet of snow accumulates in local ski resorts until late spring or early summer; then, almost without warning, there can be a torrential cloudburst, dropping as much as two to three inches of warm rain in a single hour, turning the snow into runoff that comes gushing out of the mountains, uprooting aspens and pines, tearing out bridges, and flooding downtown Salt Lake City. Yet Utah is still more than 90 percent desert. Twenty-five miles west of Salt Lake City, on the bare floor of prehistoric Lake Bonneville, the earth swells and cracks under 120-degree temperatures. Raging duststorms send tumbleweeds flying through a hidden sky and turn the sunsets a greenish purple.

But on 7 April 1972, fresh evening lights rising from Salt Lake City and Provo dotted the desert like a garden of young stars. The moon's narrow reflection from Utah Lake seemed sympathetic, and a thousand snowy seagulls swirled and circled above the lake as if weaving a thick feathery haze.

"Two weeks earlier," recalled Richard, "I had flown over that exact Milford-to-Provo area at night in a small four-passenger National Guard plane at twelve thousand feet and knew exactly which landmarks I was looking for: Utah Lake, I-Fifteen, Provo's business lights and then the Spanish Fork airport where Karen was to meet me. I warned her earlier that morning that, if I wasn't there by ten-thirty, I was either dead or in jail.''

Karen furrowed her brow, remembering. "I really didn't know for sure that he had done it until about five o'clock that evening while I was driving home from work. I was listening to the news on the car radio. It shocked me so much I had to pull over and stop." When she started the car again, she was faced with the job of acting normal in front of Denise and the children. They ate out that night. Then she set out at about 8:30 P.M. to pick up Richard. She hadn't listened to the news deliberately to keep Denise from hearing it, so she didn't know that Richard's schedule had been delayed two hours. She drove down a little side road that led to Spanish Fork's tiny airport and caught the nine o'clock news. Flight 855 had barely taken off from San Francisco.

"Here I am, just sick. Well, I had two choices. I could go home or I could stay. I was frightened to death and I couldn't leave him so I stayed. Every time a plane would fly over I'd jump out of the car and get all excited. When the ten o'clock news came on, they figured he was over Nevada, so I thought in about an hour he would be here. Then the eleven o'clock news said he was now over Utah, and about that time I heard these planes coming over, but they swung around over Provo like they were heading up the canyon toward Price. Well, right or wrong, I thought, I'm here, so I've got to stay now.

"Every half hour or so, lovers come flying by in their old trucks and that's about it. All of a sudden [about midnight] I see ten million cars coming from every direction." Karen had no excuse for being in a place where people only went in pairs. She sat petrified, when suddenly there was a break in the traffic. She pulled out smartly onto the road, drove into Spanish Fork, and checked on the Volkswagen in the bank parking lot. It was still there, so she drove home.

That was one of a series of things she regretted. But not getting rid of Denise when Richard had asked her to was close to the top of her list of regrets. As it turned out, Denise was home alone when

Robert Van Ieperen called. With that phone call, the crime started to unravel.

Richard, riding the rear stairs ready to jump, was nowhere near the Spanish Fork airport. Captain Hearn's bank was way too shallow. Flight 855 was approaching the mountain pass that leads toward Price when Richard finally came to his senses, wedged the bag between his legs, took a deep breath, and bailed out feet first. "The first sensation I remember was like falling off a bank building, Mr. Rhodes," Richard said. "The second was a rush of cold air that practically tore my head off. I had free-fallen at night only about three times before—not all good jumps—but nothing at all like this."

He stemmed—arched his back as high as possible—so that the wind hitting his front would start slowing him down. Leaving a plane traveling two hundred miles an hour meant that his free-fall speed was about a hundred and twenty miles an hour. The duffel bag had worked loose from his legs and began pulling him onto his back. A wave of nausea and weakness swept through him. "I remember thinking, 'Simmer down,' but I was too weak. Everything was coming so fast I went black. I'm guessing, but I must have been unconscious twenty or thirty seconds.

"When I woke, there was no sensation of falling at all—just a breathtaking stream of cold air getting stronger and stronger. The bag began floating out of control around behind me on my left, offering more resistance to the wind than I was. Trying to position myself in the direction the bag was going, I stemmed left and could now feel myself going faster. I had the feeling I was still plenty high because I could see two military planes coming up on me with these gigantic spotlights searching around."

He had barely time to realize that the chute must be bugged before another wave of nausea hit. Both chase planes were circling and dropping flares, so he knew he couldn't open his chute. The tug of the huge bag was spinning him against the wind, increasing his dizziness and nausea. He knew that he might be too weak to open the chute if he waited any longer. Using his left hand, he forced his right arm chest-high and yanked the release handle. It was stuck. He pulled as hard as he could. "I remember thinking," he drawled, "that if this thing don't open pretty soon my funeral could be as early as next Tuesday." Still, nothing happened. Finally, he yanked with both hands, dizzy, panicky, and desperate. His back chute suddenly popped open, but the velocity of Richard's spinning twisted the parachute lines, winding him right to the top of the canopy. "It was like being wound up in a kid's swing," he remembers. "I started slowing down at the top, then stopped completely, then almost as fast as before, I came winding back down. I'm Mormon, Mr. Rhodes, you know that, but that's what it must feel like to get good and drunk."

Magnesium flares on small parachutes floated along Interstate 15, hanging over Utah Lake like Mardi Gras lanterns with blues, greens, and deep reds sparkling in the sky. These flares and the Provo airport lights made the sky bright enough for Richard to read the altimeter, but he was too dizzy to focus. Cars below seemed to be "spinning around as if they were on ice." He guessed that he was still several thousand feet high, hoped he was headed for the east side of the freeway. On the west side, he risked landing in Utah Lake. He had brought along a ten-foot lead rope, intending to tie it to the duffel bag and let it hit the ground first, but the bag was too heavy and clumsy.

He was close enough now to see traffic stopped at a dozen road-blocks along the freeway and all the side roads. "I knew the FBI was down there waiting." Richard paused before continuing. "I could see I was heading into freeway traffic," Richard went on, his voice serious and unanimated, "and moving way too fast so I turned my body into the wind which slowed me down a little. I was floating now, probably two or three hundred feet above the freeway and heading straight for a cow pasture."

Still dizzy and sick, he had good control those last few feet and landed almost softly on the plowed ground, holding up a sprained right ankle so that his left foot absorbed most of the shock. (Richard had told everyone that he had sprained his ankle in a skiing accident.) "I just laid there on that big duffel bag full of money, Mr. Rhodes, for at least ten or fifteen minutes with the parachute canopy blowing around over me. It was such a great feeling, I remember, to be back on the ground, because you see, Mr. Rhodes, ever since I was a little boy I have been deathly afraid of heights."

When Richard looked at his watch, it was a little after 11:30 P.M.

At 11:27 P.M. Captain Hearn had reported in: "Our hijacker, gentlemen, is no longer aboard Flight 855. We figure he jumped at eleven-twelve P.M." Just after Provo, the noise level had momentarily become much louder, probably because the stairs jackknifed shut when Richard jumped, then opened again. Hearn tried several times to make contact with the hijacker on the interphone, then sent Second Officer Kent Owens to the rear. No one was there. He found the rear exit open, the aft stairs outstretched, whistling shrilly against the wind.

Calame's voice over the radio was calm, almost laconic. "Our perpetrator has left the plane. He's now in the air somewhere over Provo." They had been on alert for almost nine hours. Like Calame, most of his men were practical. They screened out emotional highs and lows automatically as potentially dangerous. But that night, each time the nose of Flight 855 zigged north or zagged south, someone cursed under his breath, rechecked his weapon, or looked for the hundredth time at his wristwatch. Now, both Hueys coughed, strained, then leaped from the airport tarmac, their bellies full of FBI agents.

Hearn swung Flight 855 around just before Price, Utah, still accompanied by Captain Dale Schmidt, reaching the Salt Lake International Airport at 11:47 P.M., and taxied to a stop at the steam plant for debriefing. For nine hours, the crew aboard Flight 855—with clear heads, flawless accuracy, and vivid descriptions—had prepared Calame to make quick, sound decisions as information was fed to him. "Now it's up to you fellows," Captain Hearn was heard telling FBI agent Jim Theisen.

Roadblocks stretched sixty-five miles along I-15 from Salt Lake City south to Payson. A steady stream of brown-clad regular and voluntary law enforcement officers, two hundred or more, were being called in to man roadblocks, conduct house-to-house searches and work Utah Lake's marshes with bloodhounds.

"A million cars," Karen said, shaking her head. "A million cars out that night driving around in a town no bigger than Provo."

Jutting out from the dash panel between Calame and Brewer was a radio console with various channels for monitoring transmissions and communicating with ground personnel. "What I want you people to do," Calame told Provo resident Loftis Sheffield, as Brewer circled once over the Provo airport, banked, and dropped, kicking up dust and dead leaves, "is find out from Sheriff Dick Chappell and Chief Jess Evans where they have their roadblocks. And where the Highway Patrol has theirs. Another thing I need to know is exactly where our other helicopter is and who's running things down there on the ground."

Stewart and Downey crackled their "ten-twenty" back to Calame while strong April winds and high waves tossed their Huey around as it hovered over the surface of Utah Lake, four miles west of Provo. Below them, a hundred small white parachutes from the magnesium canisters bobbed lifelessly in the water. Holding hands to form a human chain, Stewart and the others suspended all of Jim Downey's 155 pounds above the water while he looked for traces of the hijacker, dipping down to retrieve torn pieces of cloth and empty canisters, sputtering when he went under the whitecaps that sloshed through the inside of both open 'copter doors.

Richard had anticipated the FBI stall in San Francisco and half-expected chase planes. Both had been elements of the earlier D. B. Cooper hijacking. But he hadn't expected the stall to set a chain of ill-starred events in motion. Even as he was falling to earth, fate had taken a hand and, in Richard's house, Denise was picking up the ringing phone.

"Hello?" she said.

"Yeah, Karen, this is Van. What's going on?"

"Oh, hi, Van. No, this is Denise. Karen's not home."

"Actually, Denise, it wasn't Karen I wanted in the first place," Bob Van Ieperen said, "I wanted Richard. Tell him to get his face out of the television and come to the phone."

Van Ieperen was a tall, bent-over man who, although he looked much older, was about Richard's age. He was calling from the Highway Patrol office in South Salt Lake where he worked as a dispatcher.

"Richard's not here either, Van," Denise said. "I think he had duty with the guard in Salt Lake tonight. At least, that's what Karen said."

"Have him call me when he gets in, will you Denise?" said Van Ieperen excitedly. "He's gonna flip when he hears what's going on. There's been an airplane hijacking over Provo. We think the guy's already jumped with half a million bucks. Richard's gonna love it, Denise. Have him call me the minute he gets in, okay?"

Van Ieperen, too, was a Vietnam veteran and a good friend of Richard's. Although not in good health, he still flew helicopters with Richard for the Utah National Guard. On weekends, when Richard had the money, they parachuted together at the Alta Parachute Club just south of Salt Lake City.

When Denise Burns ran for the telephone the second time, it was exactly 12:05 A.M. on Saturday, 8 April. She could hear radio calls squawking in the background. "He's not back yet?" Van Ieperen shouted impatiently.

"No, he's not," Denise said, "and that's scaring me, Van."

"Well, has Karen showed up yet?"

"No," Denise said, in a waiflike half-whimper, "but she told me when she left . . . Oh my God, Van! You don't think Richard did it. He couldn't possibly do something like that, could he?"

"Denise, I'm gonna have to put you on hold for a minute," Van said. "I've got a newspaper reporter on the other line, calling from California. Now hold on, I need to talk to you." A minute passed, not more than two, and Van Ieperen was back on the line. "Denise, have you seen Richard at all today?"

"Why no, I haven't, Van," she said, "but you're scarin' me. They both left early this morning, way before I got up. I think they took both cars. I got off work about four this afternoon and the kids weren't home yet. So then Karen came home at five with the kids and says she's got to hurry down to Grant's to pick up some hair spray. And acted kind of funny when I said, 'Well, why now? I want to go eat.' So then I said, 'Well, okay, if you have to, go on; and when you get back, me and you and the kids can go get a hamburger. It's Friday,' I say, 'so let's don't cook.' But Karen says she can't. 'I'm going out to dinner with Richard tonight,' she says, 'after he gets out of guard.'"

Van Ieperen said nothing. He knew that the National Guard office was closed, that no maneuvers were scheduled for that night, although he and Richard were both supposed to report for duty the next morning. Meanwhile, Denise was hurrying on, "So I say, 'Well, I want to go out to dinner too!'—like that. I tell her she can go with me and the kids, 'and then you can go with him later.' She finally says okay, but she didn't act like she wanted to. She was picking her face, Van, and seemed extremely nervous about something. But I didn't, you know, think anything about it at the time"—Denise's voice was tense and childlike—"because she's cross with me and Richard a lot. But now I don't know, Van."

"The airlines are offering a $50,000 reward for the hijacker's head," Van Ieperen said. He sounded relaxed and amused. "Maybe we ought to turn him in, Denise, and split it."

"Van," breathed Denise, "I'm just scared to death it's Richard. Now that I think about it, it all fits."

There was a short silence, then Van Ieperen asked why she thought that.

She continued, speaking with breathless urgency. "He's talked to me about stuff like that before—like helping him. He had it all planned out once," Denise persisted, "where he wanted me to call the airlines. This was several months ago. He wanted me to call some airlines and tell them there was a package of instructions in a locker and a bomb on one of their planes. Another time—and I don't know why I'm telling you all this—but he wanted me to pick him up out in the Nevada desert. I said, 'Whoa! I'm not going to set out there in the middle of no place by myself. Then have the police come pick me up.' "

"Well, if it's Richard, Denise," Van says, "he didn't jump this time over Nevada. He bailed out about five miles south of your little red brick house. A good crosswind and he might come crashing through that big front window. Wham! like that."

"Van Ieperen, you're scarin' me! You mean he's really in the air, coming down right now?"

"That's what I picked up on my patrol radio a couple of minutes ago between an FBI agent and somebody."

"If this is just a joke of some kind, Van . . . "

"No, it's no joke, Denise. I just hope if it's Richard, his leg's healed. He's gotta have everything going for him to make it, because we've got roadblocks set up along I-Fifteen and all the side roads clear down to Payson. FBI agents and deputy sheriffs sprawled out on the hoods of their patrol cars all along I-Fifteen with searchlights, shotguns, and thirty-caliber rifles, pointed straight in the air. Sheriff's even got bloodhounds searching the lake area. Boats, too, in case the guy lands in the water. On top of that, the FBI has two National Guard choppers circling the marshes where they think he might come down."

"Van," Denise gasped with excitement, "I think it's Richard; don't you? God, I wished you hadn't called me. God help me, I wish you hadn't. Here I sit with these two little kids all by myself and no idea where their mother or father is."

"Maybe it isn't Richard at all, Denise," Van said, not very convincingly. (Later, Van Ieperen would say that even after his phone calls to Denise that night he had a hard time convincing himself that Richard, a nice guy, would hijack an airplane.) "Maybe we're just making a mountain out of a molehill. Maybe he and Karen'll both walk through the door in a minute like nothing ever happened. Either way, have him call me, Denise, when he does, just for the heck of it."

"I will, Van," Denise quavered fearfully, "but you've got to promise me something, Van—that you won't tell Richard what we talked about. He'd kill me if he knew I'd been sittin' here all night blabberin' my big mouth off to you."

She had a point. As *Time* magazine later wrote about Richard, "With friends like his, who needs enemies?"

In my opinion, that assessment included sisters-in-law. Richard's mother, Myrtle, had her own description of Denise: "The spittin' image of Karen—chunky, big blue eyes, pretty, with short silky blonde hair." At one point, Myrtle had welcomed newly wed Richard and Karen as well as Denise into her home in Raleigh, North Carolina, for a stay of undetermined length. Myrtle soon regretted her action. "Cute, but spoiled rotten," was her characterization of Denise. "A sophomore in high school, and you could hear that girl sucking her thumb all over the house. Even worse, she had a little baby blanket she drug around behind her." It was right in the middle of tobacco season, so Myrtle hustled Karen and Denise away from the television set and out to cut tobacco. When Richard drove Karen and Denise out to the field, Karen got out of the car, tried to jump across a little irrigation ditch, and sprained her ankle. Richard swooped her up, carried her back to the house, and stayed there with her for the rest of the day. It was the first and last of Karen's tobacco days.

"But you couldn't keep Denise away from those sweating old farmhands with a baseball bat," said Myrtle, smiling wryly at her own naïvéte. "I remember thinking, she just must like getting out in the fresh air. Then one of the local farmhands, a boy named Junior, looked up at me one evening when I was ready to pay him for the day and said, 'Miss Myrtle, I won't be helping you no more.' So I asked him why. He said 'Miss Myrtle, that Denise is crazy. She tried to make me take my pants down today and get me on that baby blanket of hers. I told her, 'No, Denise, I darsn't.' 'Then I'm going to take them off for you,' she told me. 'Miss Myrtle, that girl tried to rape me, and I don't think my momma'll let me work for you no more.' When I told Richard about what the boy said he turned Denise's backside in the air and spanked it good and red.

"The very next weekend, like nothing happened, Denise was back in the fields and the same thing started all over again. This time a married man named Johnny Ray walked up to me and said, 'This has to be my last day if Denise stays around here. Your little blonde-headed tobacco hand, Miss Myrtle, is doing her damndest to get one of us men in the penitentiary. But it ain't going to be me!'

"So that's the way that long hot summer of 1965 ended," Myrtle said.

9

Hiding Half a
Million Dollars
Saturday, 8 April 1972, Provo

Richard could hear dogs barking and helicopters whup-whupping over the marshes only a mile away as he pried himself off the duffel bag. He was about forty yards from I-15, not far from an empty hay shed. He had no way of contacting Karen. Even if she was still at the airport, that was three miles away. He had some road flares in his jumpsuit sleeves, but he could have his choice about whom to sur-render to if he lighted them.

He made two trips to the barbed-wire fence and got his gear over it. There he discovered a round metal culvert that ran under the road. It was dry, a perfect hiding place for the money and the bugged chutes.

"It seemed like I was forever making it, Mr. Rhodes," he said, "the mile and a half into Springville. My leg was killing me, and every time a car came by, I had to dive in these wet ditches along the side of the road. I hobbled through wheat fields, over railroad tracks, crawled a lot on my belly because there were police every fifty yards. Then there was this helicopter circling with searchlights. Once I thought they spotted me."

In Springville, near midnight, the only place open was the Hi-Spot Drive-in. They were cleaning up for the night when Richard bought a Coke, paying for it with a United Airlines twenty-dollar bill. "I was afraid to call home," Richard said, "thinking Denise may have one of her boyfriends there, so I found this hippie-looking kid there and said, 'Hey man, this your car?' He said it was, so I told him I'd give him five dollars if he'd drive me to Provo. It was only about four miles, but I would have given him fifty to take me home. He said it was actually his dad's car and he had to head for home. I said, 'Five dollars will buy a lot of gas, man,' so he finally took me up on it. We didn't talk much on the way. I told him I had been at a girlfriend's house and my friends went off and left me.''

He got out about three blocks from the house and checked around back. Karen's car was gone. When Denise let him in, she exclaimed, "Have you heard the news? Some guy jumped over Provo with half a million dollars!''

Richard, feigning surprise, remarked, "No, I haven't. Where's Karen?''

Denise, glancing down, saw the jump boots clashing curiously with his suit pants and, her mind obviously whirling with possibilities, commented, "Oh, she's just out visiting somebody." Then, bursting with news, she added, "Van Ieperen called twice. He thinks you did it, Richard! Wants you to call him!" Then, unable to resist the temptation, she demanded, "*Did* you do it, Richard? You know you can tell me.''

About half an hour later, around 1:15 A.M., Karen walked in the back door.

"Here Richard is, sitting there in the kitchen as cool as a cucumber. I just about fainted. I thought sure he was dead. Denise was sitting there, too, dying to know if he did it and he wouldn't tell her. Then Denise brought up the phone call from Van Ieperen . . . ''

"Who called whom, Karen?" I interrupted. "Did Denise call Van or was it the other way around?''

"Van Ieperen called Denise, Mr. Rhodes," she answered with malicious promptness. "And I can prove it. When I got my little old phone bill that month, there were no phone calls made from this house to Salt Lake that day. So Denise can't go out and say, 'I get the fifty-thousand-dollar reward for catching Richard,' because you have to start the thing and she didn't.''

Karen could not resist a remorseful replay of what-ifs. "If I'd been home when Van Ieperen called like Richard told me, I'd have simply said, no, Richard's sleeping, or studying, but definitely couldn't come to the phone. And if that reserve chute of Patterson's hadn't opened in the plane, they'd have gone on to Denver before they knew he was gone." She was saving the big what-if for last: "But had I got rid of Denise like Richard asked me to . . . I can't believe she's my sister. She's so stupid. Richard told me time after time: 'I don't care what you do, Karen,' he'd say. 'Help me or don't help me; but if you don't do anything else, just please get rid of Denise.' Of course I didn't listen, and if it hadn't been for Denise, they would have never caught him. But if he'll admit it, her living with us was his idea to get her out of the house."

"What are you talking about, Karen?" I asked. "Whose house?"

"My mother's," Karen said. "She was just making life hell for Denise. Trying to run her life. Wanted Denise to stay home and take care of her. It bothered Richard so he invited her to come stay with us. She was lazy and wouldn't help. Yet she just worshipped Richard. When she had problems she went to him. Not me. And she's a heavy drinker too, Mr. Rhodes."

"Really?"

"Drinks every night before she goes to bed. Someone bought her a full fifth so she wouldn't open her big mouth and tell everything she knew just after Richard was arrested. She drank half of it, and it didn't even faze her. Now can you imagine, this is the same little Denise Burns that sucked her thumb until a year ago? Sucked it and had sex with every boy that was willing until we finally put her in college. She failed the entrance examination at BYU, so we borrowed some money and she borrowed some money and we started her up at Ricks College in Idaho. She got a federally insured loan, went through $2,000 the first semester, and came home. This was the summer of 1971 and she thought of nothing but boys the entire time she was up there."

"Did Richard go into detail with you, Karen," I wanted to know, "about how he took the plane over up there?"

"Not *detail* detail, Mr. Rhodes. But if you've ever heard Richard tell a story, it was fascinating. Denise wouldn't go to bed that Friday night, so Richard and I go in the bathroom to have some privacy and he takes a bath. When I got him alone, I said, 'Richard, for goodness' sake, tell me! Did you really do it?' And he said, 'Yeah,' really cool.

"When I asked him about Van Ieperen, he said, 'Karen, I've told you. Don't worry about Van Ieperen. We're friends. He won't say anything. Believe me.' Well, hell, Van Ieperen was running his mouth off to the FBI while we were talking."

Richard told Karen where the money was and insisted that they go after it that night. Karen was shocked to learn that there was "half a million dollars laying in a ditch along the road and all these millions of cars driving by," but the thought of going out again terrified her. Richard insisted, so about 2:30 or 3:00 A.M., they set off.

Did they see any searchlights, police dogs, helicopters? I asked. "No," she said. "Nothing." First they drove to Spanish Fork and picked up the Volkswagen. Everyone had gone. Karen followed Richard, pulling over at the spot he indicated and watching while he piled the duffel bag in the Volkswagen trunk, leaving the chute in the culvert.

"Did you watch him load it, Karen?" I asked.

"Oh, yeah!" exclaimed Karen. "This could be very damaging, Mr. Rhodes, couldn't it, if the FBI knew? They'd probably throw me in with him, wouldn't they?"

I didn't answer. Karen continued with her story. They reached the house, cut both engines, and rolled the Volkswagen into the driveway so that there would be no noise. Together, they carried the money into the house. Richard had been up almost twenty-four hours by then. He was groggy with fatigue and irritable. In the back-yard, he had dug a posthole and lined it with a three-foot section of stovepipe. A half-million dollars wouldn't fit in it. "Didn't even come close," Karen shook her head. It was dark. Richard was mad. She suggested driving into the mountains and hiding it somewhere. Richard refused. So they threw everything in a big cardboard box and put it in their walk-in closet.

"My fingerprints are all over everything," Karen recalled. "Would you know, Mr. Rhodes, if they found any of my fingerprints on any of that stuff?"

"On any what?" I asked.

"On any of the money," Karen said, insistently, "the hand gre-nade. My fingerprints should be all over it."

"Could be," I told her, my voice unhurried and reassuring, "but it isn't you they're after, Karen. So don't worry about it."

"You're probably right," Karen mused, her sharp blue eyes focused on nothing. "They think, poor little girl with those two little kids. That husband of hers probably pushed her into it."

After the evening flares and smell of burning magnesium Friday night, Saturday morning's sky over Provo was a clear azure. Russ Calame and Tom Brewer had watched the sun rise over the Wasatch

Mountains from their big green helicopter, hoping to find a parachute and a duffel bag, half-expecting a dead body washed ashore along the lake. Their whirlibird kicked up small rooster tails as it tilted forward, dropped, then touched the runway about fifty yards away from the cluster of local news people and the handful of UPI reporters just west of the Provo airport's main terminal.

Calame was tired, unshaven, but imperturbably calm in his dark gray suit and his light gabardine trench coat as he adjusted his Stetson and walked forward to talk to the press. He explained, in methodical detail, that the batteries in the bugged chute transmitters would last only a few hours, "so we feel sure they won't be any help to us this morning."

D. B. Cooper's name had come up, of course, already. FBI agencies were phoning in all the possible aspects for this hijacking from all across the country. It was on Calame's mind as he continued, "What we hope is, we didn't get stung last night like that Cooper fellow did about five months ago up around Portland."

Then he worked steadily through the other options. "Of course, what we can't rule out is the possibility that someone was down here waiting for him and whisked him out of the area. Or that he managed to slip through a roadblock. Maybe he just laid low until they took them down around two o'clock. The things you miss," Calame said, "or overlook in a situation like last night in the dark, is unbelievable. The San Francisco and Salt Lake City agents have debriefed the crew aboard Flight 855, and while their description of the perpetrator varies considerably, they are all together on when and where he went out: over Provo at eleven-twelve Mountain Standard Time last night. So we at least know he was a stone's throw from us last night just before midnight."

What Calame didn't tell the press was that Santa Claus could have driven his reindeer through those roadblocks totally unnoticed. Friday night's roadblocks in Utah County—despite how they looked from the air—were a sieve. Those south of Provo, around Mapleton, were for some strange reason stopping only vehicles going south, away from the area. North of Provo, the roadblocks stopped only vehicles coming into Provo. In either case, some were only searching vehicles carrying mustached men. And, best of all for Richard, the police removed the roadblocks after a couple of hours.

That same Saturday morning, forty-two miles north, in Salt Lake

City, just after seven o'clock, Ben Anjewierden, a Salt Lake deputy sheriff, parked his car on Emerson Avenue just below Thirteenth East and waited for Bob Van Ieperen. Both were close friends of Richard McCoy, both worked in law enforcement, and both were on their way that morning to join him for National Guard duty. They sat for awhile in Anjewierden's car, discussing the morning *Tribune*'s account of what they had both learned firsthand the night before.

"Know who I think did it?" Van asked Ben.

"Who?"

"Richard. Richard McCoy. Sounds a lot like Richard," Van said. Anjewierden eyed him skeptically. "Exactly half a million dollars, which is what we all agreed was as much as one person could jump with. And Provo! How many people do you know in Provo that have the guts and training to do it? And Denise was home alone last night till close to midnight. She told me she thinks he did it."

Anjewierden's reaction was "You're crazy, Van. Even if Richard could, he wouldn't."

Ironically, that's exactly what Lieutenant Bob Reid of the Utah Highway Patrol had told Van Ieperen at a roadblock between Springville and Provo a little before two o'clock that morning when Van laid out the case for him. "Forget your friend McCoy and get back to work," Reid had snapped.

Van Ieperen didn't appreciate the rebuke. Still stinging over it the next morning, he told Ben to turn the car around and drive back to Van's house. From there, Van Ieperen called Calame's third-floor office. Before nine, he was telling his story to Special Agent Jim Theisen.

Calame took Jim Theisen's phone call at the Provo Airport just before nine. He and every agent in his division had worked around the clock, and it was time to split them up, send half home for some sleep, and get ready for the long haul.

"Theisen's call didn't at first look that promising," Calame recalled. "College student, law enforcement major, Mormon Sunday-school teacher, father of two. That doesn't sound like a skyjacker, but it was the best lead we had and not far up the street, so I buttonholed Lynn Twede and Clair Empey as quietly as I can and we beat it up to McCoy's house.

"Most people I've run into," he added reflectively, "when you tell them you're FBI, if they have nothing to hide, they generally let you in. They may say, 'Give me a minute to put the dog in the bathroom,' but generally they try to be decent about it. Providing, of course, they're innocent."

Denise Burns, who slept on the couch by the front door, answered the 9:30 knock wrapped in a blanket, opening the door a cautious crack. "And this guy stuck his hand in the door with a *badge*," she breathed, "and says 'It's the FBI, lady,' like that, and wanted to know if Richard was home." Denise, by instinct, instantly said no, but she lost without a struggle to her curiosity and promptly opened the door. "Well, I have always been interested in law enforcement, Mr. Rhodes," she explained, "and Richard would come home after class and tell me really interesting facts about sex crimes and things." Fortunately for Richard, she remembered that he had also warned, "'Denise, whatever you do, remember, you don't have to say nothing and you don't have to let no one in without a search warrant.'" She remembered this good advice, but it barely slowed her down as she volunteered the information that Richard was at the National Guard depot and answered their other questions, flirtatiously parrying their request for a photograph.

Richard had, in fact, left about 5:00 A.M. that Saturday, after barely two hours of sleep, driving the Volkswagen to Salt Lake City, where his National Guard unit had duty at the airport.

By then, the noise had awakened Karen, who was calling Denise. Leaving the three agents at the door, Denise hurriedly conferred with Karen, who refused to talk to them. Calame and his men left, and Karen ordered Denise to get dressed and take the children for a reconnoitering walk around the block. At first, Denise said, she saw nothing unusual around the neighborhood. Then she noticed "this blue ordinary-looking car sitting across the street and down a little ways. I act like I don't see it, and then when I turn around real quick, suddenly it's gone. I think, well now, that was kind of funny."

Karen then sent her and the kids to a little grocery store on Third South for some ice cream. Standing in the sidewalk in front of the neighbor's house and conferring in a low voice were the same three men, a tall man in a dark gray suit and a gray Stetson, one in a flight suit, and another in green insulated coveralls and a heavy work shirt. This third man was wearing a gun conspicuously at his side.

"Now, Mr. Rhodes," confessed Denise, "I have always been petrified of policemen. Always. So I says, 'Listen, you guys. I know what you're doing. I know your techniques. Richard McCoy is also a law enforcement officer—I mean, a police major at BYU. He's studying to be an officer. And he has kind of told me my rights and that I don't have to say nothing to you or anybody else.'" Patiently they repeated that they only wanted to talk to Richard. Denise repeated that he was with his National Guard unit. As soon as Denise walked back in the house, Karen told her to go to the Albertson's supermarket on Fifth West and call the Chuck-A-Rama in Salt Lake City for its menu the night before. Denise claims, at that point, "I began to put two and two together when she wanted to know what they had had the night before, and it about scared me to death." Refusing to take the children, Denise hurried out to Karen's Plymouth. The same blue car and at least two others were back. An agent asked where she was going. In a rare fit of restraint, Denise didn't answer, but when the blue car followed her to Albertson's, she became too frightened to make the call. "So I bought some toilet paper and hurried out, knowing they could see everything I did. When I got to the car I could tell it wasn't the same men that had been at the house. I just gave a big sigh because the others scared me."

"Did you ever find out what the Chuck-A-Rama had to eat the night before?" I asked.

"Never did, Mr. Rhodes. Just couldn't get myself to pick up the receiver."

When I interviewed members of the McCoy family in July of 1972, Karen was angry at Denise, Van Ieperen, her own mother, her mother-in-law, me, and the entire federal government, all at the same time. And Myrtle didn't care very much for her, either.

Denise was not as bright as Karen or Myrtle, but she had less fire coming out of her nostrils. "You were at Albertson's, Denise," I began. "You told me earlier about driving to Albertson's that Saturday morning to pick up toilet paper and call Chuck-A-Rama for Karen. You'd just come out," I said, "of Albertson's and here stand agents Jim Stewart and Bob Schamay. So then what happened?"

Denise blew at her blonde bangs. "They both hurry over to my car and Jim Stewart says, 'We would like to talk to you a few minutes, if you don't mind.' I said, 'I don't say nothing! Why don't you leave me alone!'" Then they tell me Richard is a suspect in the hijacking. They start asking me about fifty questions at once; and every time, I say, 'Well, I'm sorry, but I don't say nothing.'

"Now they were very nice to me. But all I wanted to do was get away from them. I am not, you have to understand, the kind of person to be rude and turn my back on people and leave. They ask if they could sit in the back of my car, and I say, 'No sir, I know that's one of your little tricks too.' So I says, 'Sorreeee, but I've got to go!' Stewart's hands are still on my car windows when I just take off like hell. I had to get out of there, Mr. Rhodes."

By the time Denise got back home, Karen had burned the notes Richard had had Diane Surdam take up to the pilot. "My little service for mankind," Karen called it. "I think that's called destroying the evidence, isn't it, Mr. Rhodes?"

"Sounds a lot like it to me, Karen, but while we're on the subject, tell me a little more about those notes. Who typed them? What'd they say, if you remember?"

"Well," Karen replied, "at first I wanted nothing to do with it, so Richard typed the first draft. He asked me to read it over and approve it. I wasn't that much help because I didn't know that much about hijackings or being a pilot. Then we got in this big fight, so I think, what the hell, and go ahead and type them up for him on sweet little Denise's typewriter, put them in envelopes and more or less forgot about them. To Richard, it was like a big game. He gets up one morning and tells me he's going to Denver. The FBI, I'm sure, would have a field day over that, too. He used an assumed name out of Salt Lake and flew to Denver. A practice run, to get the feel of it. When he came back I said, 'Well, if you like it that much, you can take another flight to L. A. and do your little job.'

"Frankly, I was getting a little irritated but it was all planned and ready to go. I don't know if I will ever say this in public, but he had it so well planned, that except for the jumping out of the plane part I could have done it myself. It just wasn't that hard. If the public knew how easy it was, the airlines would have two a day instead of two a month. Well, that's neither here nor there, but I did burn the notes. I don't regret what I did. They have enough evidence now, without the notes. But that would have been the crowning touch."

While Denise was driving back from the supermarket, Karen was fending off two agents at the door that Saturday. They were not, as she tells it, sweet: "'Where's your husband, ma'am? Where were you? We want answers, hear? You better cooperate!' Well, tough luck! I know my rights! 'If you have nothing to hide . . .' one of them said. Well, I did have something to hide. I had a half a million good reasons not to tell them. Hell, they really got mad. But they left, and Denise came home. She was bawling. She should get the Stupid Glott of the Year award. You just talked to her, Mr. Rhodes, so you know what she's like."

"Yes," I said, "she's a lot different than you."

About an hour later, Jim Stewart was back. Karen, with reluctant admiration, called him Mr. Smooth. Nor were his good looks lost on her. But when he asked for a photograph of Richard, she stonewalled again. Richard wasn't running for office, she told them. They could take their own picture if they wanted one of him.

Stewart replied, "We will, Karen, as soon as he comes down from flying."

Karen snapped back, "Fine, I'll be there too, Jim Stewart, when you have your little talk." She added, "And I could tell he knew he'd just made one big, big mistake letting me know. Oh, he was very smooth and handsome, but I'm always very leery of people like him."

A little after noon on Saturday, according to Denise, Karen doped the kids up on some sleeping pills, loaded them and her into the Plymouth, and headed for Salt Lake City to find Richard at his National Guard unit. She was still smarting over Stewart's comments about taking Richard's picture. Four unmarked FBI cars fell into procession behind her, so "just for meanness," Karen signaled right, then suddenly turned left, did a U-turn in noontime traffic on Provo's busy Center Street, and then headed to Salt Lake City on I-15 at ninety miles an hour.

As she took the airport exit toward Richard's National Guard unit, she saw three of the four cars peel off behind her at the preceding exit, the main downtown exit. "I think, 'Whoa! They know something I don't!' so right in the middle of this main airport highway, I about kill ten people switching lanes and turning around again in the middle of the highway." Her segment of the procession ended up at the Federal Building on State Street and Second South. Denise stayed in the car and watched the sleeping children, while Karen followed smooth-talking Jim Stewart through three locked doors and up to Calame's third-floor office.

Richard was sitting across the desk from Calame while Shepherd and a team of interrogators prowled the bullpen, firing questions at him: "Where were you yesterday, April 7th, Richard, between eight in the morning and midnight?" someone would say. "You weren't at guard," another one would jump in. "We know that. You weren't at home. We can prove that. You had phone calls Friday night and weren't home. You weren't with Karen. We know that. You might as well level with us." "We have a handwritten note here," the next one would say, "from Flight 855 that one of the stewardesses kept. We're sending it and some writing from your military records back to FBI headquarters tonight for comparison." One question right after another.

Karen must have felt undiluted admiration for Richard as he told them, very calmly, "Look, I know I don't have to say anything and you know I'm not, so either charge me or release me." "He was so cool," Karen said, "I couldn't believe it. So when I walked in, I said, 'Well, I just thought I'd come and have my husband take me to lunch.' Everybody just stood there looking at each other until finally Agent Shepherd said, 'Well, Mrs. McCoy, I guess we have nothing else to ask.' So Richard got up and says, 'It was nice talking to you guys,' and we leave."

Richard had almost instantly deduced that Van Ieperen had fingered him, but the FBI wouldn't give him the satisfaction of confirming his guess until later. Richard was pleased to see Karen, but "Oh my God, was he mad at Denise! When he opened the car door," Karen said, "he began to swear at her. 'You dumb bitch!' he said, then to me, 'That woman is so repulsive, Karen, I can't stand to even think about her.'"

With the FBI cars still following and Richard still swearing furiously at Denise, he headed straight for his guard unit at the Salt Lake airport where he had left the Volkswagen earlier that morning. Van Ieperen was flying Senator Frank Moss around in a helicopter, but Richard got him on the radio and told him in a quiet rage, "Thanks, big mouth."

Van responded weakly, "I don't know what you mean, Richard."

"Yes, you do, big mouth," Richard pressed.

Van gave him a "ten-four" and cut the connection.

Denise took baby Richard and drove Karen's Plymouth back to Provo, where she found three FBI cars still sitting out front. Then Denise began waiting for Richard, Karen, and Chanti. Karen told a ludicrous story when they showed up much later, about 7:00 P.M.

The Volkswagen had run out of gas on the freeway. Their FBI tail simply parked behind them and waited while Richard walked two miles off the freeway to a gas station and back.

Denise's curiosity once more got the better of her. "I says, 'Listen, Richard'—I was very blunt with him—I said, 'if you don't tell me right now whether you did it or not and I find out later, so help me I'll rat you in.' I said, 'I've just got to know.' He said, 'You rat on me and I'll kill you, Denise, understand?' Then he turned to Karen and said, 'I want her out of here.' I don't know for sure what I said, it startled me so.

"About half an hour later he said he was sorry. As if to apologize, he began to tell me about it. He never came right out and told me he did it. He told me how he used my headband to pin his ears back, about the stewardess he called Jane—then we saw her on TV standing with the captain—how they had to bang on the toilet door to get him out while he was still putting on his makeup.

"I said, 'How much did all this cost you, Richard, plane tickets, clothes and all?' He told me, 'Less than five hundred dollars, but I have to get rid of this watch so that'll be more.' Karen said, 'Why the watch, Richard? I gave you that watch,' and he tells us the stewardess kept looking at it. Karen said she didn't care, he should keep it. It was an expensive watch, she said, a Bulova Accutron, and it keeps good time too.

"The pilot appeared on Channel Five television saying, 'The crime was ingeniously planned, except for the note,' and I said, 'What note is the captain talking about, Richard?' and he said, 'The ones we did on your typewriter,' and I said, 'Oh great! On my typewriter! Now I'm mixed up in this thing, too.' "

It was almost ten o'clock by then. Denise was starving and insisted they go out to eat. Richard refused, said he was tired, gave Karen some money, and told them to bring him back some hamburgers. Just as Karen and Denise were getting ready to walk outside, a brisk knock sounded on the door and a pair of agents politely asked whether there was a typewriter in the house. Karen, cutting off Denise's denial smoothly, said, "Never mind, Denise. I'll give them the typewriter." Richard signed a release, and Karen, to Denise's unfeigned admiration, handed over not Denise's, but her own old-model typewriter.

Later, when Denise and Karen returned from eating, Denise told Richard she was afraid to sleep on the couch and asked if she could bring her blanket and sleep on the floor next to their bed. Richard said yes.

That was a little before midnight on Saturday night.

About half an hour later, at 12:30 A.M., Sunday, 9 April, Palmer Tunstall, a handwriting expert in the FBI lab, picked up the phone and called Russ Calame—"one of the most welcome telephone calls I've ever had," Calame later told me. He had not been asleep very long, and he'd been awake for a long time before that, but the news brought him instantly awake.

Just before midnight Friday, Calame's men had begun a meticulous and painstakingly careful search of United Airlines airplane #7426, Flight 855. Special agents Walt Anderson, Art Riege, Don Bechtold, Charles Middleton, and several others recovered the hand-lettered note retained by Stewardess Surdam, an envelope, cups, napkins, the headrest cover from the hijacker's seat, cigarette butts, *Mainliner* magazines, air-sickness bags, airplane emergency cards, 727 instructions, FAA Form 7233-1, a pilot's preflight checklist, and a piece of mirrored glass that was on the aft staircase.

The agents also dusted and lifted latent fingerprints and, with the permission of United Airlines, cut the seatbelts from the six seats in Row 20, bagged them, labeled them neatly, and flew them by courier to the FBI Laboratory or the FBI Identification Division—depending on the type of examination desired—in Washington, D.C. Samples of McCoy's printing from his military records in St. Louis, Missouri, were already on their way.

Tunstall's conclusions, crackling over the phone at 12:30 Sunday morning, were succinct. The hijacker's hand-lettered note and the lettering on Richard Floyd McCoy, Jr.'s, military records had been created by the same person. Within hours came the second call Russ Calame was waiting for. The FBI Identification Division told him that two latent fingerprints found on the back of a *Mainliner* from Seat 20D and four from an envelope were positively identified as the fingerprints of Richard Floyd McCoy, Jr., Army Service Number RA-14796789.

There was now probable cause for an arrest, given the handwriting comparison, the matchup of fingerprints, and William Coggin's unhesitating identification of a photograph of Richard McCoy in San Francisco. While he dressed, Calame called his dispatcher to set up a conference.

In Provo, the shift changed. Agents watching the McCoy house went off duty. Another crew went on. A phone call woke Mary Edmondson and Louise Praught, two of the bureau's clerk-stenographers; they were dressed and waiting by the time a car called to bring them to the office. Another car brought C. Nelson Day, the U.S. attorney who would authorize the warrant of arrest to Calame's office. Agents Lote Kinney and Bill Geiermann were preparing the application for the warrant to search the Volkswagen, the 1966 Plymouth Fury, and the house at 360 South 200 East, Provo, Utah. Day signed the warrant of arrest a little before 2:00 A.M. Sunday, but the search warrants had to wait until the U.S. magistrate could read the application for the warrant and put the affiant under oath. All of this happened a little after 1:00 P.M., Sunday afternoon.

The Arrest
Sunday, 9 April 1972, Provo

"They're harder to see at night," remembered Karen McCoy. "Harder to see than ordinary people. With the lights off in the living room that Saturday night, we could see cars moving back and forth and then they would park at both ends of the block. But we couldn't see anyone in them. Richard must have known it was just a matter of time, because he went to bed about midnight without saying a word. I couldn't sleep. I just lay there trembling next to him. Thinking tomorrow would be Sunday, Sunday someone might not live to tell about. Wondering what would happen to the kids. And thinking how close we had actually come. I must have drifted off around four thirty, because at five the next morning—bam! bam! bam! They practically tore the door down getting in. I can remember Richard stepping over Denise as he jumped out of bed and went running barefoot for the living room. I could hear loud voices coming from the next room, and then I heard the soft clicking sound of handcuffs.

"When I finally came to my senses, I wrapped a robe around me, grabbed the baby, and ran out into the living room. That's when I saw Richard sitting on the couch with his hands cuffed behind his back and his head down between his legs. Four or five FBI agents were standing over him with their guns drawn. The big cheese, Special Agent in Charge Calame, wearing the gray Stetson hat, was looking down at Richard reading him his rights.

"Looking back now, I should have made them break the door down. Stuff was strung all over the place. The gun and grenade were in one place, the typewriter and notes were in the kids' room, and then the half-million dollars. Well, where do you hide a half-million dollars in a house this small?''

The FBI agents drove Richard to Calame's office in Salt Lake City, where he was charged by complaint with violating Section 1472(i), Title 49, U.S. Code, Aircraft Piracy, and Section 1472(j), Title 49, U.S. Code, Interference with Flight Attendant. (Later, the federal grand jury indicted him on one count of aircraft piracy.) He was rushed before U.S. magistrate A. M. Ferro, where he was advised of the charge, the penalty, and his right to counsel, then ordered to be held in jail without bond. At a little after eight o'clock, they let him call Karen. He was fine, he told her, asked about the kids, Karen remembered, ''and then said, 'be sure and take care of everything.' He said, 'Ev'ry-thing,' Mr. Rhodes, like that, so I knew he meant for me to hide ev'ry-thing.''

Salt Lake City's *Deseret News* started off that Sunday morning with a UPI story about a cataclysmic earthquake in southern Iran, which, according to a witness, had hit like the end of the world on Judgment Day. Judgment Day in Tehran was mild compared to Judgment Day in Provo, Utah.

Sunday mornings in Provo for the past 125 years meant, for Mormons, attending a full day of church services in which they are urged to follow the dictates of their faith and to turn from sin. Now, someone in Provo had actually sinned, had been caught at it, and was being carted away to be punished. Inside 360 South 200 East, Karen was hissing frantically at Denise, ''Denise Burns, you have got to get up, get yourself dressed, take these two kids of mine to the babysitter's, and help me hide all this stuff.'' Outside, the neighborhood had taken on a toy-balloon atmosphere. Youngsters, perched high on their fathers' shoulders, pointed at the house from across the street. Photographers, television crews, and a front yard full of curious onlookers had to be held back by some FBI agents while the rest sat waiting for the green light from Calame, shovel in hand and anxious to start digging cavernous holes in the McCoy yard.

When Denise and Karen got back from dropping the children off at the babysitter's, they had already had one screaming match in the driveway and Karen had threatened to turn Denise in to the FBI. Denise had caved in.

Back in the house, Denise's first action was to start wiping away at her typewriter keys.

"Denise," snapped Karen viciously, "what do you think you're doing with that typewriter?"

"Cleaning my prints off it," responded the frightened Denise.

"Stupid!" Karen snarled. "It's *your* typewriter. Whose prints would they expect to find on it?"

Denise hadn't thought about that.

"I wasn't very nice about it, Mr. Rhodes," Karen admitted, flipping her head back. "But I had to scare Denise into helping."

"And the house was still surrounded, was it?" I asked.

She nodded. "They didn't have their search warrant yet. And they knew they weren't getting in my little old house without a valid search warrant."

"What time are we talking about, Karen? Before noon or after?"

"Just about noon, Mr. Rhodes."

"All right, now, go ahead with what you were going to do."

"Well, basically, we took everything out of all the boxes we could find. Clothes, toys, and then we went down to the bottom of this big cardboard box and took the money out. It was all there for them: the grenade, the gun, sunglasses, gloves. And of course we had to do this very quietly because they were sitting around all over the yard.

"We didn't know how much time we had before they came charging in like the Light Brigade. As it turned out, we had several hours. If I had to do it over, I would have cleaned the gun. But then what good would that have done? Burned the gloves. But what for? Sweet little Denise helped me put some of the money in this three-foot-long stovepipe. There was a little crack in the corner of the window where the drapes didn't fit so she would duck every time she went by. When she got her hands on the money, she was so nervous she jerked some of it half in two on the end of the stovepipe."

They covered the end of the pipe with a plastic sack. The sack fell off, spilling money. Richard kept calling, chatting coolly and unconcernedly but hinting clearly to Karen's sensitized ears that the FBI was about ready to search the house.

Karen dug out the two cardboard boxes that their phonograph speakers had come in and shoved the money into them. "We tried to hide them as high as we could in the room adjacent to the kids bedroom, but we knew it was really a waste of time."

Between Richard's calls from Salt Lake, calls started coming from

California, North Carolina, and New York. Karen smiled mirthlessly, "Here we are still stuffing the grenade and gun in the money box and telling people on the phone, 'I'm sorry, but we don't know what you're talking about.'" The doorbell was ringing, too. Karen made a call of her own, one to Sister Mathews from their local Mormon ward. (Mormons call each other Sister or Brother.) To the terrorized Denise, that was the final nightmare. "Karen had called Sister Mathews because she felt she was starting to fall to pieces. Karen threatened to kill herself," Denise said, "because her life was over without Richard McCoy and she had driven him to do it, and all she wanted to do now was just die. Sister Mathews said, no, she shouldn't, and of course talked to her in a sensible manner like anybody would. Me, I was too upset to say anything so I left the two of them alone." Karen left with Sister Mathews, ordering Denise to guard the house until she saw the search warrant. It came within minutes after Karen left. Denise abandoned the house to Jim Stewart and scurried over to the neighbor's house where Karen was drifting off, the doctor's tranquilizing shot taking effect. "She just laid there," Denise recalled, "on the couch saying, 'My life is over. My life is over. They've got the wrong person in jail,' she'd say. 'I belong there, not Richard. All over, gone forever.'

"So I thought the FBI had the case all wrapped up. Looked like it to me. They found the money and other incriminating stuff. Then all of a sudden they—Stewart—start working their way around me, asking me questions about where he landed, who was with me when Van Ieperen called, and I said no one, I was alone babysitting the two children, then I say, 'Whoa, I gave it away, so you guys I don't say no more.'"

"What time Sunday was this, Denise?" I asked.

"About two-thirty or three in the afternoon."

"Where was Karen when Stewart talked to you about what you were doing that Friday night?"

"Okay, Mr. Rhodes, Karen went to the hospital. A Dr. Robert Crist came and took her to the Utah Valley Hospital. She was held in Room 374, under another name, Karen Adams. Because she was still threatening to kill herself."

The lead story in the *Deseret News* that Monday morning read:

RANSOM FOUND—MINUS $30
PROVOAN IN JAIL ON AIR PIRACY CHARGE

FBI agents have recovered $499,970 of the $500,000 ransom paid to a skyjacker who parachuted from a United Airlines 727 jetliner over the Provo area late Friday.

The money was in a cardboard box and was among several items seized Sunday by agents armed with search warrants who combed the apartment [*sic*], yard and two automobiles belonging to Richard Floyd McCoy, Jr., 29, 360 S. 200 East, Provo.

McCoy is being held in the Salt Lake County Jail without bail on federal charges of air piracy and interfering with a flight attendant.

He was arrested about 5:30 A.M. Sunday as he was leaving his home to attend a Utah National Guard drill. He offered no resistance to FBI agents.

The FBI had been watching the house since Saturday afternoon on the quiet, tree-lined residential street about two blocks from downtown Provo.

The stake-out of the house apparently was based on information first supplied by McCoy's sister-in-law and a good friend of McCoy who is a Utah Highway Patrolman.

The same edition also carried a press release from Special Agent in Charge Russ Calame:

An inventory of evidence seized at the home of Richard Floyd McCoy, Jr., 29, Provo, charged in a $500,000 skyjacking of a United Airlines plane was provided today by the FBI. The list included: a blue and white parachute, black parachute harness and a military type flight suit . . . a green military canvas bag, a black crash helmet, a brown coat, a silver colored man's wrist watch and . . . two . . . electric typewriters. A cardboard box containing various items of clothing, a pistol, a holster and a black glove was confiscated.

Almost as an afterthought came the final item: "Also found was $499,970 in U.S. currency, most of it still wrapped in bank bands."[1]

---

[1] The missing $30 was never located, but could probably be accounted for in the bill Richard used to purchase a drink at the Springville Hi-Spot and the money he gave Karen and Denise for supper Saturday night. Other money in the house was not inventoried.

 # The Judge: Willis W. Ritter

Because aircraft piracy was a federal crime, Richard McCoy would be tried in the United States Court for the District of Utah, presided over by Chief U.S. District Judge Willis W. Ritter.

Judge Ritter inspired a lot of different feelings in people, most of which, I think, were variations of terror. Even I, who was probably as close to him as anybody on this side of the grave—or the other, for all I knew—and really liked the old judge, never made the mistake of forgetting that Ritter was a landmine and that the slightest tickle could set him off. I'm not sure why Ritter liked me. It wasn't so much that I was Catholic, like him, as it was that I wasn't Mormon. More, I suspect, because I wasn't a Republican. I was from Harry Truman's home state of Missouri, and, as Ritter used to tell people, "That's grounds enough to trust a man, even if you can't believe anything he tells you."

In 1962, not long after I'd finished college and left Houston, I was standing before Judge Ritter's bench, along with the defense attorney, the prosecutor, and the defendant, a young man in his late twenties up on a charge of dealing heroin. It was my job as probation officer to make a brief background report prior to sentencing. One of my pious points was his prior experimentation with lysergic acid diethylamide, or LSD, the hallucinogen of choice for the "Me Generation." Reeking outraged morality, I heard myself say, "By the early age of seventeen, Your Honor, this man was already experimenting with LDS."

Ritter looked up. "Experimenting with what, Mr. Rhodes?"

Behind me, I could hear belly laughs being swallowed by men facing as much as forty years in prison. LDS is the acronym for Latter-day Saint, a shortened form of the official name of the Mormon church: the Church of Jesus Christ of Latter-day Saints.

"Your Honor," I said, "I misspoke myself." I waded gamely into that sentence again and I'll be damned if it didn't come out "LDS" again! By now those muffled belly laughs had turned into what resembled grand mal seizures.

"Your Honor," I began for the third time.

"No, no, Mr. Rhodes," Ritter said, "that's enough for one day. It isn't really that important whether this young man was experimenting with LDS or LSD. Just the slightest exposure to either one and a man begins to hallucinate."

I wouldn't say that my faux pas started any great and glorious friendship, but Ritter did have a sense of humor, and I got along with him as well as anybody else.

During the weeks following Richard's arrest, he received visits and phone calls from lawyers as far away as New York volunteering to represent him pro bono (without charge). But for one reason or another, he rejected all offers and asked Judge Ritter for court-appointed counsel, paid for by the federal government under the Criminal Justice Act.

Ritter didn't mind that and emphasized to his court clerk, John Brennen, "I want a lawyer in this McCoy case, John, that has knee action and fluid drive. With the death penalty at stake, this case is going to end up before the Supreme Court, and I can't afford to have this thing botched up. There's been an incessant drumfire of scurrilous and malicious plotting back there to run me off this bench. So I want a good lawyer appointed in this case. The best trial lawyer we've got around here." Brennen appointed David K. Winder.

Winder was a Stanford Law School graduate, just under six foot three, athletic, in his late thirties. Born into a wealthy Mormon family, he leavened his dress and manner with apologies to the poor and less fortunate. Winder had caught Ritter's eye as an assistant United States attorney during the mid-sixties prosecuting criminal cases, but had since joined the prestigious law firm of Strong and Hanni as a full partner.

Dave and Pam Winder were vacationing with their three children in San Diego when the clerk of court reached him by telephone.

When Ritter's voice burst on the telephone line, it came like a cloud-burst on a tennis match. Summer clothes were suddenly stuffed into suitcases, reservations for leisurely dinners overlooking Mission Bay were canceled immediately, and the family Mercedes headed north-east again.

On 26 May 1972 Assistant United States Attorney Jim Housley stood and advised the court that Richard McCoy was present for arraignment. Judge Ritter had the clerk read the charge. Dave Winder then reminded the court that prosecution witness Dr. Eugene Bliss, director of psychiatric services at the University of Utah, had examined McCoy and that the court should hear him on the question of competency before a plea could be entered.

Dr. Bliss, a short, wiry man whose thick, black hair was always in his eyes, took the witness stand that day. He was succinct and easy to understand. Ritter liked that. Dr. Bliss found Richard to have above-average intelligence—the capacity to formulate intent and under-stand the charges—and to be capable of assisting in his own defense. Dr. Bliss stepped down. Winder then told the court that there was also a motion pending to have a Dr. David Hubbard from Dallas, Texas, an expert on the mental makeup of hijackers, and Dr. Peter McDonald, a renowned psychiatrist from Denver, examine Richard.

"Why?" Ritter demanded, then read Winder a brief chastise-ment for being frivolous with the taxpayer's money, and ruled against him, detouring to laud Dr. Bliss. "The reputation of the University of Utah School of Medicine," Ritter said, "the Psychiatry Department, and its director, Dr. Bliss, extends far beyond the state of Utah. Dr. Bliss has told us that Richard McCoy has the mental horsepower to formulate intent, knew what he was doing, knows what he's charged with now, and can assist you, Mr. Winder, in his own defense. That's what this court is interested in, not whether he was picked too soon or wound too tight. Take his plea," Ritter said.

Richard entered a plea of not guilty, and his trial date was set for 26 June 1972.

Willis Ritter turned seventy-five that year. He stood five foot seven and weighed in at 240 pounds. He described himself as a Dem-ocrat, a Catholic, and a civil-rights advocate who had been graduated from the University of Chicago Law School in 1924 and from Har-vard in 1940 with a doctorate of jurisprudence. A law professor at the

University of Utah for nearly twenty-five years, he had a reputation for teaching more in the first two hours of class than others taught all year. Ritter had been appointed to the federal bench as Utah's chief judge in 1949 by President Harry S Truman over the protests of conservative Mormon leaders. From his earliest days, Ritter had never been shy about stepping over or on top of cultural lines in Utah, and age had only made him more splendidly cantankerous.

"Harry Truman," he would intone after a judicious pull on his whisky glass in chambers, "was one of the greatest statesmen the Western world has ever known. His philosophies, his decisiveness under fire, even his appointments, will go on to influence the entire world for the next five hundred years." Pausing just long enough to freshen his glass from a quart of twelve-year-old Wild Turkey bourbon, Ritter would continue, "Truman took office during some of this country's—the world's—most turbulent times. Truman had to decide alone whether or not to drop the atom bomb on Hiroshima and Nagasaki that brought the Japanese to the bargaining table. What a terrible decision for a man to have to make! He was responsible for the Berlin Airlift and George Marshall's European Recovery program after the war ended.

"And, by God," he would chortle, "not the least of Harry Truman's more controversial legacies was the appointment of yours truly to the federal bench. Those sniveling little Mormon sons-a-bitches wore a path between here and Washington, D.C., trying to hold up my appointment. Now they come parading into my courtroom as if nothing ever happened. Well, I know exactly who they are! I got myself a copy of the FBI investigation where they went into my background—who they talked to and who said what. And I got a copy of the Senate Judiciary Committee's hearing! And I remember word for word what was said."

Spittoons had long since been removed from Ritter's seventy-five-year-old courtroom, but an imaginative eye could still trace a circle of errant tobacco shots on Ritter's worn lime-green carpet where they had once sat. The two west windows behind the bench were framed by light-ash wooden pediments. A huge gold American eagle was set in creamy marble on the west wall between the windows. This would be where Ritter would hold the McCoy trial—but not always where court was held. The majesty and paralyzing power of the court was in His Honor's presence. A few years earlier, Ritter, in a clearing beside the San Juan River in southern Utah, had tried a suit between the Department of Interior and the Navajo Nation over a herd of wild mustangs. The saying went back then, if you were an Indian, a black, or just plain poor and happened to be right, you wanted Ritter to hear your case. If you were wealthy and wrong, you didn't. "Over the past thirty years," his bailiff Spence Van Noy used to say, "this old courtroom has heard more pleas, confessions, and prayers for forgiveness than the Cathedral of the Madeleine four blocks up the street, where even Ritter occasionally stops to remind himself he's only a federal judge."

Ritter, although married, had lived alone for the past twenty years at the old Newhouse Hotel, located on the southwest corner of Main Street and Fourth South directly across from the federal courthouse. Built in the early 1900s, its marquee bragged about the liquor lounge, advertised dancing, and was the antithesis of the Mormon-owned Hotel Utah located next to the Mormon Temple four blocks up Main Street. The Newhouse was where the Democrats had held their fund-raisers and political victory parties over the years, but now its dangerously decaying red brick exterior was a detailed reflection of Utah's Democratic political climate. The interior was also old, rococo but comfortable.

From Suite 1000, located in the far northeast corner of the tenth floor, Ritter could look down and across and keep an eye on those who worked for him in the federal court. "You gotta watch 'em like a hawk," he'd say, "watch 'em constantly, or nothing ever gets done." The afternoon sun had, over the years, cracked and peeled a lifetime of white paint from worn wooden windowsills, leaving them yellow and the windows hard to open. His combination bedroom, living room, and kitchen had the loud overhead scars to remind the parade of senators and governors who dropped in to pay their respects that it had once been two separate rooms. Furnished with antique Louis XIV chairs, couches from the Mediterranean, an Early American four-poster bed, and paintings and drapes purchased from the Franklin Delano Roosevelt estate, it was an eclectic old gathering place where people and ideas went to become legends.

I remember seeing Ritter's reflection once in the long mirror that stood in the entrance hall. The evidence of trauma, suddenly apparent in the reversed features, was startling: many small strokes had accumulated over the years to give the face in the mirror a twisted, gestalt configuration. Independent facial characteristics, pulling against each other, as if in pain, would as always, just in time to take the bench, again become coconspirators in reconstructing the image of Utah's seventy-five-year-old chief federal judge. It's reasonable to speculate that Charles Darwin could have singled Ritter out personally to prove his theory of natural selection. Given the same environment for the next hundred and fifty years, two additional arms may have unfolded . . . making it possible for His Honor to thumb his nose at the United States Supreme Court, the Tenth Circuit Court of Appeals, the GEEEEESUS-KURRRIIIIST of Latter-day Saints, and the Republicans—all at the same time.

I can also remember standing in mortal awe of Willis Ritter, convinced that, after a few strong bourbons, I would make an absolute fool of myself by blurting out something that didn't make a bit of sense. King Solomon, compared to Judge Ritter, I thought, ran nothing more than an ordinary court of domestic relations back then. Yet, somehow there was something strangely familiar in the way both men handled small courtroom disputes.

12

The First Two Days of the Trial
Monday–Tuesday, 26–27 June 1972

The line of witnesses, spectators, and reporters began on Main Street and gradually worked its way down to the federal courthouse, up two flights of stairs, through electronic metal detectors manned by U.S. marshals, and into Ritter's courtroom.

By the time Ritter's gavel came down for the first time, Richard had been the subject of a long article with photographs in *Time* and the hook for an exposé in the *Wall Street Journal* on how hijacking affects the airline industry. I heard a rumor that Myrtle and Karen had already sold book and movie rights to Der Stern, a West German publishing company.

Helped from the back seat of the government's old Plymouth that warm Monday morning by U.S. marshals, shackled hand and foot to six feet of belly chain, Richard looked straight into the barrel of NBC's live On-The-Spot television camera. Out-of-town newspeople had made hay with Brigham Young's Utah and Richard McCoy's Mormon connections. There were now, the press said, three kinds of Mormons—practicing Mormons, jack Mormons (nonpracticing), and skyjack Mormons.

Ritter had a·policy against chains and handcuffs, so the marshals stopped just outside the door and took them off. I was standing against the wall next to the north door when Richard and the marshal entered, then looked around, confused, I thought, about where to go. Richard stood dignified and erect, scanning the courtroom. His eyes found his mother about the time mine did.

Myrtle was seated on the front row, to the right of R. E. Holland, to whom she was engaged. She and Floyd McCoy had been divorced for a year or two, and Floyd had remarried. He and his new wife were sitting a little farther down the row with Russell, now using the surname Holland, sitting between his biological father and his stepfather. I wondered what Richard was thinking. After all the bloody knuckles he'd had as a boy, it must have been painful to see Myrtle with Holland. Karen and the two children were sitting at the far end. Everyone sat erect, carefully groomed and dressed in their best summer clothes.

Spence Van Noy, a heavy-set, lighthearted man of about fifty, who had been Ritter's bailiff for years, had seated the McCoy clan on the front row behind a long, green, braided rope that separated spectators from lawyers and other officers of the court. Now he beckoned Richard and the marshal forward, and Richard took his seat at counsel's table, next to his attorney, David Winder.

Richard and everyone else in the courtroom stood up as Ritter entered in his invariable dark blue suit and red tie. It was Spence's moment of glory. It wasn't necessary and Ritter didn't much like it, but Spence, a romantic, lived for it—his shining moment in days that involved a lot of being sent to, called from, and talked down to in public that had left him limping with gout and taken a lot of the fun out of his face. So Ritter let him do it once in a while. "Hear ye! Hear ye!" Spence would intone proudly. "This honorable court in and for the District of Utah is now in session! God save the United States of America and this honorable court!" Then he'd go back to sleep.

"If the Court please," Winder started things off, "before we begin to voir dire [examine] the jury, defense, Your Honor, has motions pending that haven't been ruled on, and we feel those ought to be argued first. Those motions will have an effect on how defense counsel goes about voir diring these jurors."

Winder had filed his motions four days earlier, but Ritter had not read them, saying he would rule after he had heard the case. Ritter nodded at the eighty-four potential jurors. They dutifully stood as if at a fire drill, followed the marshal out of the courtroom, and marched down a long, dim hall to the petit jury room.

Ritter got impatient easily, and watching eighty-four potential jurors leave the courtroom was not his idea of entertainment. When the door swung shut behind them, Winder was already on his feet, his rimless reading glasses leveled in Ritter's direction. "Your Honor, Mr. Hanni, my associate, and I have two motions to argue this morning, and promise to be brief. Our first motion is to eliminate any consideration of the death penalty. We feel that given the facts of this case, the death penalty is grossly and manifestly inappropriate."

Winder's next motion was to suppress evidence. He and his partner Glenn Hanni had been consumed for weeks by the McCoy case, had interviewed Richard McCoy time after time, had spent hours with his parents and Denise, and had pored over the prosecutor's file. There wasn't any possible way to defend McCoy successfully.

Yet, as Percy Foreman, an old Houston trial lawyer, once told me when I was a probation officer there, "Any lawyer worth his salt knows that if you have the law on your side, you try the law. If the facts are with you, you try the facts. If you have neither the law or the facts in your favor, you do like I do. You try the Houston City police department." In this case, it was the Federal Bureau of Investigation. With over one hundred FBI agents working around the clock between San Francisco and Salt Lake City some seventy-two hours, someone had to have made a mistake. Four days before the trial, Hanni, a dark, stocky man, who looked like Omar Sharif as Dr. Zhivago, shook the McCoy file again, and this time out fell the Fourth Amendment of the Constitution of the United States, prohibiting illegal search and seizure.

"Your Honor," Dave Winder continued, "the defendant this morning moves that any evidence found by the FBI on Sunday, April 9th, 1972, or subsequent thereto in the McCoy home be excluded from this trial. The defendant claims, first of all, that the affidavit that requires the government to show probable cause was based on hearsay, double hearsay and, in some instances, triple hearsay. Mr. William Geiermann, the FBI agent who prepared the affidavit for the search warrant, spoke on the phone—and only on the phone—to other FBI agents in Washington, D.C., San Francisco, and Provo, Utah, who had interviewed witnesses." By that he meant Coggin, Surdam, Van Ieperen, Denise, and Tunstall, the handwriting expert from Washington. "Based solely," Winder intoned, "on those second- and third-party interviews, the search warrants were issued. A second point, Your Honor, and even more important is this: Agent William Geiermann, the affiant who prepared the application for the search warrants and was later put under oath by the U.S. magistrate, is never mentioned in the application for the warrants."

"The application," Winder said, "for those warrants, your Honor, lists Agent Lote Kinney as the affiant. The Fourth Amendment of the Constitution of the United States, which the Court is well aware of, legislates 'the right of the people,' Your Honor, 'to be secure' "—Winder's hands came up in front of his face, as if he were about to catch a football—" 'in their persons, houses, papers,' and in their other personal effects, against unreasonable searches and seizures. And it goes on to say, Your Honor, that those rights 'shall not be violated.' Now this, Your Honor, is plural. 'No warrant(s) shall issue, but upon probable cause, supported by oath or affirmation' and with particularity, 'describing the place to be searched, and the person or things to be seized.' It shall," Winder pointed out, "also state the grounds or 'probable cause' for its issuance and the names of the persons whose affidavits have been taken. We claim this was never done.

"Your Honor, Geiermann went before the U.S. magistrate that morning purporting to be the affiant, taking the oath and swearing that it was he who accumulated the probable cause, however flimsy, when in fact the warrant application names another agent—Lote Kinney—not Geiermann at all. So Your Honor, we propose that anything—the gun, the grenade, and, most of all, the money found in McCoy's house as a result of that faulty search warrant be ruled inadmissible."

Ritter liked this argument. After having had his own personal life rummaged through by the FBI at various times, he held the Fourth Amendment sacrosanct. Had the McCoy case been a routine robbery or automobile theft, he would have thrown it out without ever listening to the government's side. Prosecutor James F. Housley had only the day before been apprised of the defense's motions and, since his superior, U.S. Attorney C. Nelson Day, had actually worked with Russ Calame and others in preparing the application for the search warrant and the actual search warrants themselves, Housley was at a loss to explain how the wrong agent's name had been typed into the papers. "All the agents were working on the case together, Your Honor," Housley said plaintively. "Sharing information. It's nothing more, Your Honor, than an oversight, a typographical error—and what's more, I submit, it is a harmless error."

Ritter, shaking his head in disgust, wasn't persuaded by Housley's limp side of the story. At the same time, he wanted McCoy tried. "I'm going to reserve my ruling on this motion," Ritter said, "until such time as the evidence found in the McCoy home is to be entered into evidence. Then you two fellows had better have some case law for me. But, frankly, Mr. Housley," Ritter added with relish, "I don't see how you can get around this problem."

Housley was a calm, well-seasoned trial lawyer in his mid-thirties with fiery red hair, who, in the three or four short years he'd been with the United States Attorney's office, probably hadn't lost more than a handful of criminal cases. He came to the prosecutor's office in 1968 as a Democratic appointee near the end of the Johnson administration. Then when the Salt Lake office, in early 1969, went Republican, Housley, because he was a good lawyer, was kept on. Ritter liked Housley and couldn't stand the Republicans. He despised Richard Nixon. Even worse was Nixon's attorney general, John Mitchell. "Put 'em both in a barrel," Ritter would say, "roll 'em down the White House lawn, and there'll be an asshole on top all the way down." Then he'd chuckle and throw his hands in the air.

Housley and Dave Winder had suggested to Judge Ritter that, with all the publicity the McCoy case had received and the death penalty at stake, it could take as long as two or three days to find twelve jurors and two alternates who had not already read about the case and made up their minds about McCoy's guilt. "Mr. Housley," Ritter said, "you and Mr. Winder listen closely. I am an old man. I don't have long to live. So I don't intend to spend the rest of my life listening to you fellows badger the jurors over what they've been up to the past fifty-five years. Be quick about it. Let's get me a jury picked and sworn in."

A brisk two hours later, the jury had been impaneled. There was an extra edge of excitement in the air as Judge Ritter peered down from the bench. "Are you ready to proceed, gentlemen?

Housley rose. "The government is ready, Your Honor."

"Defense is ready, Your Honor," came from Winder.

"Then," said Ritter impatiently, "proceed, gentlemen."

Borg Sveland, a ticket agent for United Airlines at Denver, Colorado, was the government's first witness. He testified that on the afternoon of 7 April 1972 he had sold a one-way ticket on United Flight 855 to a man identifying himself as James Johnson and assigned him seat 20D. He had later seen McCoy's picture on TV and was reasonably sure that McCoy and Johnson were the same man. FBI fingerprint expert Roy McDaniel of Washington, D.C., compared Richard's fingerprints against two latent prints found on a

Mainliner magazine in seat 20D. They possessed, he reiterated, the same physical characteristics.

By mid-afternoon the government's star witness was sworn in. Being the star witness in Ritter's court generally meant you were on the witness stand until the Novocain wore off, an experience no one looked forward to. Diane Surdam, almost from the beginning, was on the ropes. The gentle, low voice that had prevented chaos aboard Flight 855 now just seemed inaudible and confused. Housely actually only wanted Diane Surdam to put across three main points: the handwritten note, identifying the hijacker, and the hijacker's weapons. But it was tough work even getting through the preliminaries.

"Now, Miss Surdam," Housley tried again after a difficult fifteen minutes, "—and again I'll ask you to keep your voice up so His Honor can hear—do you see the person in the courtroom today that gave you a handwritten note just before you took off from San Francisco?"

"No sir, not the way he looked on the plane, no."

Together they did an adagio describing Richard in his glad rags, gradually sidling closer to the main point. To Housley the handwritten note was the government's strongest piece of physical evidence, and he intended to put it back into Richard McCoy's hand no matter how he'd looked on the plane.

Housley took Diane Surdam through the boarding and taxiing preliminaries. "Now after you were in the air, what, if anything, out of the ordinary happened?"

"I was first confronted by two men sitting next to the hijacker. I believe it was Mr. Lawless and Mike Andria. They both, at separate times, mentioned to me that there was something odd going on. Then, about Grand Junction, I believe it was Mike Andria that handed me a white envelope containing written instructions."

"And what, if anything, did you do with that first envelope?"

"I took it to the cockpit and gave it to Captain Hearn."

"And what was in that envelope, if you remember?"

"Hand-grenade pin and bullet, I believe."

"Were there any writings or other papers in that envelope?"

"Yes, there were typewritten notes. But I didn't read them."

"Okay, now after you delivered that first envelope to the captain and observed some of the contents, what, if anything, did you do?"

"I went back to the hijacker and told him his instructions would be followed, for him to please keep calm, that we were doing everything he wanted us to do."

"And did you see anything in that passenger's possession at that time?"

"Yes, he had a hand grenade in one hand and a gun in the other."

"Did that concern you, Miss Surdam?"

"Yes, it scared me half to death."

The adagio continued. Up the aisle to the cockpit. Back to the hijacker. The hijacker's gestures. The notes. It was now early evening and Housley's slow, methodical line of questioning and Miss Surdam's barely audible answers had teamed up to induce what looked like deep sleep or mild coma on the bench.

What was in the notes? Housley plodded forward. The crew said it was demands, the stewardess murmured—and suddenly Winder was on his feet, objecting to the hearsay evidence. Ritter's sagging blue eyes opened, and there was nothing unfocused about their gaze. He instantly sustained the objection, instructed the witness, and added smoothly, "Maybe this is a good place to let this child off the witness stand for a while. The six o'clock news is on so we'll recess now until ten A.M. tomorrow morning."

The next morning, Diane Surdam was back on the witness stand. "Miss Surdam," purred Jim Housley, laying a clear plastic evidence envelope in front of her, "will you please examine the contents of what's marked government's Exhibit Number One with particular reference to the pencil writing on the yellow paper inside this plastic container. Tell us, if you can this morning, if you've seen this before."

"Yes, I have."

"And what, Miss Surdam, did that piece of paper instruct you to do just before Flight 855 was permitted to leave San Francisco?"

"The note says: EVERYBODY OFF NOW EXCEPT STEWARDESS. THEY STAY PUT. GET THE HELL OFF THE GROUND. BE QUICK ABOUT IT. USE THIS RUNWAY." Miss Surdam read it loud enough this time for the jury to hear clearly.

"And at that time, Miss Surdam, while you were there in San Francisco, did you notice anything different about that note?" Housley asked, "different than the others he gave you?"

"Yes, of course. It was a handwritten note. The others had been typed."

"Now Miss Surdam," Housley said, "Let's take it from the beginning. Was anything said between you and the hijacker when he handed you this handwritten note in San Francisco?"

"First of all, Mr. Housley, he referred to me as Jane. He said something about, 'Take this note to the captain.' Then he said, 'Have all the people outside on the ground leave the area immediately.'"

"Do you recall, Miss Surdam, seeing any of the contents of any of those other messages?"

"Just the last one. The handwritten one. The one I just mentioned."

"And again, with reference to Exhibit Number One, if you remember, Miss Surdam, what did that note tell you to do?"

"It told me to get everyone off the plane and have the captain proceed to the active runway. Runway nineteen."

Miss Surdam's voice was fading again. Judge Ritter interrupted testily. "Have the captain do what? Mr. Housley, I can't make heads or tails out of what this young lady is saying. I can't hear your witness!"

"Your Honor," Miss Surdam said, turning and taking perfect aim at Ritter, "the note said, 'Proceed to runway nineteen.'"

Ritter again. "Where was this?"

"This was on the ground in San Francisco, Your Honor."

"And what did you do with that note, if anything, Miss Surdam?" Housley continued.

"We were in a hurry to get the passengers off so first I put the note down the front of my blouse. Then, later, I crumpled it up and put it in my purse."

"Think carefully while I show you again what's marked government's Exhibit Number One, Miss Surdam, and ask if you're positive you've seen this before."

"Yes, this is definitely the same note the hijacker handed me just before we departed San Francisco."

"Your Honor," Housley said, relieved, "the government offers Exhibit Number One at this time."

And that brought Dave Winder to his feet. "If the court please, defense objects to that note being admitted at this time. I don't think there's been adequate foundation laid by the government."

Judge Ritter dabbed at his broad pink forehead from an open box of tissue, looked at the jurors, then Housley, then back to Winder: "What foundation are you talking about?"

Winder, still on his feet—which was the way Ritter ran his courtroom—then said, "She said she left the note in or on her purse, Your Honor, so I don't think there's any chain established as to this being the same note or how it came to be in the government's possession."

Judge Ritter sighed. "You fellas have to understand we can't try this lawsuit in one gulp. We have to take it a little bit at a time." He squinted at Miss Surdam. "Now, have you looked at this exhibit?"

"Yes, I have, Your Honor."

"Hand it to her again, Mr. Housley," Ritter directed. "Now, is this the same note you put in your purse on the plane or isn't it?"

"Yes, Your Honor."

"Then what did you do with it?" Ritter was taking the witness away from Housley. He was good at that.

"When we landed in Salt Lake City, Your Honor," Miss Surdam said, "we had to evacuate the airplane immediately and leave all our belongings on board. When I returned on board, I started to go through my purse to get it out and the FBI showed me the note and said they had already looked in my purse and found it so I know it's the same note."

"Well, who got the note then, Mr. Housley?"

"Your Honor," Housley said, "I think she's identified that as the note she received from the hijacker and put in her purse. She's testified that she didn't deliver it to the FBI agent, that they got it out of her purse, but I don't think that alters her identification of it."

Ritter again asked Miss Surdam, "Are you absolutely sure this is the same note?"

"Yes, Your Honor," Miss Surdam answered softly.

"Speak up so the court can hear you!" Ritter was scowling.

"I'm speaking as loud as I can, Your Honor."

"I betcha you can talk louder than that if I ask you to."

"I can scream." Was this, I wondered, a side of Miss Surdam we hadn't seen before?

"Yes, that's all right," Ritter said. He was no longer scowling. "Scream if you have to. The jury can't hear you and I can't hear you. And talk slowly! There's no reason for you to be anxious or nervous in my court. Nothing is going to happen to you here. Just take your time and talk slowly and very distinctly."

And Miss Surdam answered yes, three times, in a voice His Honor could hear plainly and for good measure assured him once and for all, "that is definitely and positively the same handwritten note."

"That's more like it, child," breathed Ritter. "All right, Winder, you're overruled. Government's Exhibit Number One is admitted into evidence."

After that, things picked up. Frank Williams, custodian of army personnel records in St. Louis, Missouri, quickly confirmed that he had provided McCoy's military data to the FBI on Saturday, 8 April. Palmer Tunstall, the FBI handwriting expert, testified until well after seven o'clock in great detail that the army records and the note Diane Surdam hid had been written by the same person. On Wednesday, Perry Stevens testified that he packed and bugged four chutes Friday night in San Francisco. Thirteen-year-old Korey Allen testified that he found chute 171 in the culvert between Springville and Interstate 15 while his dad was changing a flat tire. Korey knew the minute he showed it to his father that he wasn't going to get to keep it.

Nancy Bowen, a waitress at Springville's Hi-Spot Drive-In, described how she sold a large Coke about midnight to a man who walked east from I-15. Eighteen-year-old Peter Zimmerman testified that he gave the man in the business suit and paratrooper boots a ride to Provo Friday night. The next Monday he looked at Richard McCoy's face on the six o'clock news and picked up the phone. When Jim Theisen answered the phone at FBI headquarters, he told him the whole story. During the ten-minute ride, he and the man had discussed the brilliantly burning magnesium flares. How, Zimmerman had wondered out loud, could they stay in the air so long? They were, his passenger had answered, attached to small parachutes.

D.B. Cooper
The Places and the Players

Artist's drawing of D. B. Cooper from witnesses' descriptions following 24 November 1971 skyjacking.

Photograph of Richard McCoy taken 9 April 1972 following his arrest. *Salt Lake Tribune* wire photo

McCoy as a Green Beret during his first tour of duty in Vietnam.

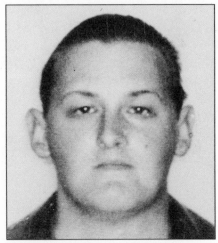

Skyjacker Michael Lynn Hansen photographed in 1975 in New York City on his return to the United States from Cuba. UPI/Bettmann photo.

Richard McCoy in U.S. Army para-trooper jump uniform.

Northwest 727-100 airplane at the Seattle-Tacoma airport awaiting delivery of $200,000 and parachutes to D. B. Cooper. Photograph courtesy of William E. Scott, pilot of the hijacked plane.

Crew of the hijacked Northwest plane at a news conference at the Reno International Airport. The plane had landed at the Reno airport for refueling after Cooper had parachuted from the rear of the plane. From left to right: Captain William Scott, First Officer Robert Rataczak, stewardess Tina Mucklow, and Second Officer Harold Anderson. AP/Wide World photo.

Artist's drawings of D. B. Cooper with and without sunglasses he wore during his hijacking of Northwest plane.

The Seattle Times

Largest daily and Sunday circulation in Washington

60 PAGES · FRIDAY, NOVEMBER 26, 1971 · 10¢

Closing markets

Dow Jones: Up 17.96

The Dow Jones average of 30 Industrials closed up 17.96 at 816.59 today for the biggest gain since August 16, apparently on the strength of favorable economic news. B 3.

Jet crew doesn't know where hijacker jumped

IN THE UNITED STATES DISTRICT COURT

FOR THE DISTRICT OF OREGON

UNITED STATES OF AMERICA,	)	
Plaintiff,	)	CR 76-**229**
v.	)	I N D I C T M E N T
JOHN DOE, also known as DAN COOPER, and more particularly described below,	)	(49 U.S.C. §1301(15) and (34), §1472(i) and 18 U.S.C. §1951)
Defendant.	)	

THE GRAND JURY CHARGES:

COUNT I

On or about the 24th day of November, 1971, in the District of Oregon, JOHN DOE, also known as DAN COOPER, a male Caucasian, age mid-Forties; height 5'10"-6'; weight 170-180 lbs.; physical build average to well built; complexion olive, medium smooth; hair dark brown or black, parted on left, combed back, of greasy appearance; sideburns at low ear level; eyes brown or dark; voice low without particular accent using an intelligent vocabulary; and a heavy smoker of cigarettes, defendant, did knowingly commit and attempt to commit aircraft piracy

DOJ

Form No. USA-40-65-1
(Rev. 7-74)

First page of the grand jury indictment of John Doe, aka Dan Cooper.

United 727-200 airplane at the San Francisco airport during the McCoy hijacking, with fuel truck moving into position according to McCoy's instructions. Photograph courtesy of Gerald Hearn, pilot of the hijacked plane.

Crew of the hijacked United plane meeting newsmen at the Salt Lake International Airport. McCoy had earlier parachuted from the rear of the plane west of Springville, Utah. Left to right: copilots Ken Owens and Ken Bradley, pilot Gerald Hearn, and stewardesses Margie Newby and Diane Surdam. AP/Wide World photo.

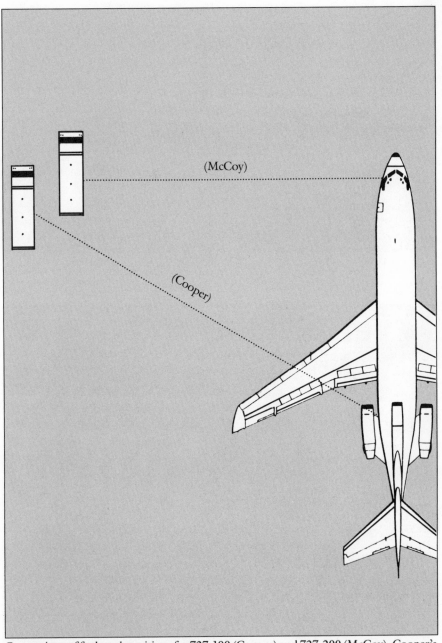

Comparison of fuel truck positions for 727-100 (Cooper) and 727-200 (McCoy). Cooper's instructions: fuel truck to be fifty yards away from plane at ten o'clock from Cooper's position in aft of plane. McCoy's instructions: fuel truck to be 100 feet away from nose of the aircraft on left side. Redrawn by Scott Engen from a scaled diagram by Russ Calame.

Mosaic of farmland at the site of McCoy's landing after parachuting from rear of plane.

Culvert where McCoy stashed the money and parachute after his landing. Russ Calame photo.

Two-lane road leading east from McCoy's landing site to Hi-Spot in Springville, Utah, where McCoy purchased a soft drink. Russ Calame photo.

Hi-Spot in Springville, Utah. Russ Calame photo.

House at 360 South 2d East, Provo, Utah, where Richard and Karen McCoy with their two children resided in 1971 and 1972. Russ Calame photo.

Richard McCoy in handcuffs and ankle shackles in custody of United States Marshall Royal Buttars en route to court. Photograph courtesy of *Salt Lake Tribune*.

NR 003 LV PLAIN

355 PM URGENT 4-18-‍ EB

TO DIRECTOR, FBI ‍-2111   FEDERAL BUREAU OF INVESTIGATION
                             COMMUNICATIONS SECTION
LOS ANGELES

SALT LAKE CITY   APR 18 1972

SAN FRANCISCO   TELETYPE

PORTLAND

SEATTLE   ALL OFFICES VIA WASHINGTON

FROM LAS VEGAS 164-68

NORJAK

RE RICHARD FLOYD MC COY, JR., AKA DAN COOPER, D. B. COOPER,

D. COOPER, J. JOHNSON - SUSPECT.   utah
                                     ore
                                     Nev

RE SALT LAKE CITY TEL APRIL SEVENTEEN LAST.

SALT LAKE CITY TELCALL APRIL SEVENTEEN LAST NOTES POSSIBILITY

MC COY DROVE FROM SALT LAKE CITY TO LAS VEGAS, FLEW TO PORTLAND

TO COMMIT HIJACKING, RETURNED TO LAS VEGAS, AND DROVE BACK TO

SALT LAKE CITY. INVESTIGATION INDICATES COLLECT CALL TO MC COY'S

RESIDENCE NOVEMBER TWENTY-FIVE LAST AT TEN FORTY-ONE PM FROM

LAS VEGAS AS WELL AS GAS PURCHASE IN LAS VEGAS SAME DATE USING

BANK AMERICARD.   ST-105

RECORDS, WESTWARD HO MOTEL, LAS VEGAS, CHECKED FOR ENTIRE

MONTH OF NOVEMBER, SEVENTY-ONE AND NO REGISTRATION LOCATED FOR

MC COY UNDER KNOWN NAMES AND ALIASES OTHER THAN RESERVATION ON

NOVEMBER TWO, PREVIOUSLY DESCRIBED. ALL AIRLINE MANIFESTS THAT

HAVE FLIGHTS TO PORTLAND FROM LAS VEGAS DESTROYED AFTER

END PAGE ONE

REC-59 164-2111-554

16 APR 19 1972

57 APR 25 1972

Copy of first page of FBI teletype dated 18 April 1972 from Las Vegas FBI office describing results of some of the investigation into McCoy's activities as a suspect in the D. B. Cooper skyjacking.

$499,970 extorted from United Airlines 7 April 1972 by Richard McCoy and recovered by the FBI from the McCoy home in Provo, Utah, on 9 April 1972 being viewed by Assistant Special Agent in Charge Vic Schaefer, FBI, Salt Lake City.

The Salt Lake Tribune

Vol. 204, No. 178   Salt Lake City, Utah — Monday Morning — April 10, 1972   Price Ten Cents

Deputy Marshal Jerry M. Smith, rear, escorts hijack suspect.

Richard McCoy, carrying Guard uniform McCoy wore at arrest.

—Tribune Staff Photos by Steve Wayda

FBI Captures Student, 'Evidence' in Skyjack

By Clark Lobb, Steve Wayda,
Craig Hansen, David L. Beck
and George A. Sorensen
Tribune Staff Writers

A 29-year-old Brigham Young University junior majoring in law enforcement was arrested early Sunday morning on two counts in connection with the Friday hijacking of a United Air Lines 727 jet from which the hijacker parachuted over the Provo area with $500,000 ransom.

FBI agents removed four large cardboard boxes and two black overnight bags from the suspect's Provo home about 5 p.m. Sunday and returned to Salt Lake City. The FBI refused to say whether the ransom was recovered.

No Incident in Arrest

Apprehended without incident at his residence as he was preparing to attend Utah Army National Guard drills was Richard Floyd McCoy Jr., Raleigh, N.C., a former Green Beret helicopter pilot in Vietnam and a skyjumper at the Alta Skydiving Center, 8700-17th East, Sandy.

He was wearing Guard fatigues, but changed into a gray business suit and vest after his arraignment at 8 a.m. before U.S. Magistrate A. M. Ferro in Salt Lake City. He is being held without bond

in Salt Lake City-County Jail pending a preliminary hearing April 19 at 2 p.m.

Has Wife, Two Children

McCoy resides at 360 S. 200 East, Provo, with his wife and two children. FBI agents spent the morning and most of the afternoon searching the McCoy house, yard, garage, a dog run, two automobiles, and surrounding areas, dusting for fingerprints, collecting material from the auto tires, etc.

Activity in the house increased about 4 p.m. when all nine agents involved were inside. They could be seen carrying boxes.

Suspect's Wife Leaves Home

The suspect's wife was driven to the home by an unidentified woman about 4:30 p.m. The blonde Mrs. McCoy was crying. She was in the house about 10 minutes, then left by car with the same woman.

The agents left the home shortly after 5 p.m. and placed the boxes and valises in trunks of FBI autos and returned to their headquarters.

The suitcases and boxes were removed from the house following a search which included digging in the yard. Each one of the boxes bore a sticker marked "evidence."

A short time after the evidence was

taken to Salt Lake City, an FBI agent indicated a news release was being prepared for clearance in Washington, D.C.

Later No Release Expected

However, at 8:40 p.m., an agent would say only that "we have no release at the present time and we are not anticipating one right now."

Russell P. Calame, Salt Lake City agent in charge, was reported not in his office. His wife said he was not home and that if he was not at the office she did not know where he was.

The FBI office in Washington said late Sunday night there would be no further release on any information regarding the hijacking until Monday.

Provo police said the hijacker landed at Provo Airport on the west end of town and got into a green Volkswagen bearing North Carolina license plates.

They said McCoy had not been at home for two days. The residence had been under FBI surveillance from early Saturday afternoon until the arrest, police said. Sunday a green Volkswagen with North Carolina license plates was parked at the rear of the McCoy residence.

Maj. Gen. Maurice L. Watts, Utah adjutant general, said McCoy is a warrant
See Page 7, Column 1

Russell P. Calame, 1991.

Bernie A. Rhodes, 1965. *Deseret News* photograph taken when he was appointed Chief
U.S. Probation and Parole Officer for Utah.

Chief Judge Willis W. Ritter, appointed to the federal bench by President Harry S. Truman, took the oath of office 1 August 1950. Photograph Courtesy of *Salt Lake Tribune*.

David K. Winder, defense counsel for Richard McCoy, shown here in 1979 at the time he was sworn in as Federal Judge, District of Utah. Photograph courtesy of David Winder.

FBI agent Nicholas O'Hara, 1979. O'Hara was one of the agents involved in the manhunt for Walker and McCoy. Photograph courtesy of Nicholas O'Hara.

Charlie Shepherd (left) and Jim Stewart at the FBI firearms session in 1971. Both men were agents who were involved with the McCoy skyjacking investigation. Photograph courtesy of Jim Stewart.

Melvin Walker, who escaped with Richard McCoy from the Lewisburg federal prison, at a photo session for prison volunteers in 1980 just prior to his release. Photograph courtesy of Melvin Walker.

U.S. Penitentiary at Lewisburg, Pennsylvania, where McCoy was to serve out his forty-five-year prison sentence. Federal Bureau of Prisons, U.S. Department of Justice photograph.

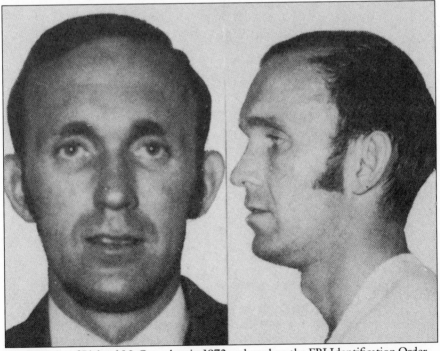

Photographs of Richard McCoy taken in 1973 and used on the FBI Identification Order.

Identification Orders issued by the FBI following the escape of Richard McCoy and Melvin Walker from Lewisburg federal penitentiary in August 1974.

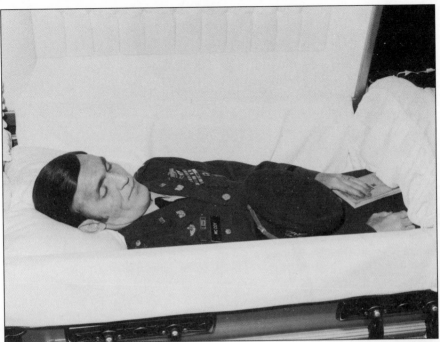

Richard Floyd McCoy, Jr. Funeral services were held 13 November 1974. He was buried in the family plot in Cove City, North Carolina. Photograph courtesy of Melvin Walker.

Today's Weather

Cloudy
High Today 70
Low Tonight 53
SE, 10-15 m.p.h.
For current report call 836-1212

The Virginian-Pilot

Today's Chuckle

Here's how to reduce the
number of mistakes you make
a t work—get there late and
leave early.

109th Year. No. 355   Norfolk, Portsmouth, Virginia Beach, Chesapeake, and Suffolk, Virginia, Monday, November 11, 1974   ★ ★   Price 15 Cents

FBI Kills Escaped Hijacker in Beach

FBI agents guard the house at 735 N. Great Neck Road.

Virginian-Pilot Photo by J. T. McClarty

Fired at Agent;
Fugitive Arrested

By BILL HOYLE
Virginian-Pilot Staff Writer

VIRGINIA BEACH—A prison escapee who two years ago hijacked an airliner for $500,000 was shot and killed in a Virginia Beach suburb by FBI agents late Saturday and his friend, a fellow escapee and one of the FBI's 10 most wanted fugitives, was arrested.

"Gerald Coakley, special agent in charge of the Norfolk office of the FBI, said Richard Floyd McCoy, 31, was killed by a shotgun blast in the chest after he fired an an FBI agent about 11:15 p.m. at the front door of a house he and the other fugitive rented in the quiet middle-class neighborhood of Wolfshare Plantation.

Melvin Dale Walker, 35, who escaped from the federal prison in Lewisburg, Pa., with McCoy last August, was arrested about a quarter mile from the house after a brief chase by federal agents.

Walker, one of the FBI's 10 most wanted fugitives, was arrested without incident, although a revolver and a shotgun were taken from the car by FBI agents after his arrest.

McCoy and Walker were described as "the best neighbors we've ever had" by residents on both sides of their rented house, at 735 N. Great Neck Road, which they had occupied since about Sept. 1.

The FBI had had the single-story brick house staked out for two days after a tip that McCoy and Walker were living there, according to an FBI spokesman.

McCoy and Walker arrived at the house about 11:15 p.m. Saturday. McCoy went to the front door and Walker drove away from the house to survey the neighborhood.

An FBI spokesman said the two "were very suspicious, professional types."

When McCoy reached the front door, an agent waiting for him there identified himself, and told McCoy he was under arrest.

RICHARD F. McCOY ...
... dead

MELVIN D. WALKER ...
... in custody

A recent photograph of Melvin Walker, who now resides with his wife in a Southwestern metropolitan area. Photograph courtesy of Melvin Walker.

Melvin Walker (left) and Bernie Rhodes at Alta ski resort in Utah in 1987. Photograph courtesy of Melvin Walker.

Russ Calame (left) and Bernie Rhodes at Alta ski resort in 1987. Photograph taken by Melvin Walker; courtesy of Melvin Walker.

Richard McCoy at the time of his trial, July 1972. *Salt Lake Tribune* photo.

A Dark, Narrow Tie and a Mother-of-Pearl Tie Clasp

In April 1972, Russ Calame made a decision. He knew that Hoover liked how he was handling matters in Salt Lake City. More important, Calame heard, he would soon be transferred and promoted to a larger office back east. It would have been a prestigious appointment, a reward, a promotion. But Russ didn't want another transfer. He was fifty years old, eligible for retirement. So he and Mary, as he put it, "talked it over and decided bilaterally to retire here in Salt Lake City." He sent in his request for retirement in the usual stately and regretful prose, and Hoover's acceptance, in equally stately and regretful prose, came back.

Calame was the last FBI division head to submit his resignation while Hoover was still director. Only a few days later, on 2 May 1972, twenty-four days before Richard McCoy's arraignment and about seven weeks before he came to trial, J. Edgar Hoover died. As far as most FBI employees knew, Hoover had not been sick, and so his death was sudden and unexpected. L. Patrick Gray, a former submarine captain, was appointed the new director. Problems with Gray would develop later. As one writer summed it up, Hoover wouldn't have been very effective at captaining a submarine and Gray didn't have the background to direct the FBI effectively. By accident, Calame's timing had been perfect.

He was only a month into his retirement when Richard's trial began on 26 June 1972. And here he was, spending almost a full week back in the federal courthouse. He hadn't actually been excluded from sitting in on the trial itself, but he recognized the possibility of testifying on Winder's motion to suppress and had spent Tuesday and Wednesday morning outside the courtroom with the other witnesses.

When Jim Theisen walked by and caught his eye, Calame got up and fell into step with him. "What'd she say, Jim?" Calame asked.

"She said, 'That's Richard's,'" Theisen responded matter-of-factly.

"Which one? The mother-in-law or Denise?"

"Both," Theisen smiled tightly. "They both did." Suddenly he was grinning. "I take them one at a time, okay," Theisen said, "into the U.S. Attorney's office and I show them that picture of Cooper's clip-on tie and his mother-of-pearl tie clasp. Separately, you see, so that one won't get to the other. The mother-in-law, Mildred Burns, right off the bat, identifies it as Richard's without even a second look. Then I bring Denise in and she studies it like she's fixing to buy it. Then she looks over at me and says, 'That's Richard's tie, and that's Richard McCoy's pearl tie clasp, so what are you guys doing with it?' I tell her—now listen to this—I tell her, 'Well, Denise, this photograph is of the tie and tie clasp D. B. Cooper left behind on the plane he hijacked up in Portland. I tell her how Cooper takes it off before he jumps and puts it in one of the seat pockets.'"

"What'd she say about that?"

"Breaks down and starts crying," Theisen, says, "'Well, wherever you got it from,' Denise says, 'that's Richard's! He always wore that tie clasp when he went somewhere.'"

"Well, Judas Priest!" said Calame reverently.

Theisen was forty, on the thin side, almost as tall as Calame. Fair-complected, with a heavy Minnesota accent and a big warm Scandinavian smile, he was an intent, driven investigator who chain-smoked filter tips and was true to the image of what we expect accountants to be like. Five months earlier, he had been assigned to handle the Cooper case in the Salt Lake City division. He was keenly aware of the similarities between the D. B. Cooper and the McCoy skyjackings and had been doing a point-by-point analysis ever since the McCoy arrest on the language of the notes, the skyjackers' physical characteristics, the method of operation. The further he went, the more convinced Theisen became that Cooper and McCoy were one and the same. "Portland and Seattle are both sending us more leads," he told Calame, "but I don't think the differences in these two men are nearly as significant as their similarities."

"That's about where I am, too, Jim," Calame answered. "I swear, I don't think there's been a day that I haven't talked to you or Portland or Seattle or Reno about these two guys. But I'm not nearly as convinced as you that Richard McCoy is D. B. Cooper. The crew aboard Cooper's plane said he was older, didn't they?"

"Depends on who you talk to, boss," Theisen half laughed. "We've got people on the McCoy plane who sat in the same row of seats with him and who still miss him by a mile. Henry Dale Rodenbeck described McCoy as five foot six and about forty-five. Josephine McLennan sat across the aisle in twenty-A. Says he was in his late thirties or early forties. An air force captain, Wallace Rogers, sat one row up in nineteen-F. He described McCoy as twenty-five years old and five foot nine or ten. And the Surdam girl yesterday in the courtroom," Theisen eyed Calame, "said she couldn't identify Richard, and she sat next to McCoy for most of the trip. The point is, boss, Cooper and McCoy were both wearing dark, heavy makeup, wigs, and disguises. Nobody but Coggin really got a halfway decent look at McCoy before he came out of that bathroom."

"But what about the ears, Jim?" Calame asked. "How do you get around the ears?"

"Have you seen the composite drawing of D. B. Cooper that we got from Seattle? Here, look close at it." Theisen slipped Calame his copy of an FBI artist's drawing of D. B. Cooper based on descriptions from passengers and crew aboard Northwest Orient Flight 305. "The people on Cooper's plane, Mr. Calame, remembered huge ears. They all agreed on that. When Judge Ritter breaks for lunch, take a good, long look at our friend McCoy. His close friends down at BYU call him 'Dumbo.'"

Calame grinned from ear to ear. "Before we get too far ahead of ourselves, Jim, why don't we grab Palmer Tunstall and Roy McDaniel before they fly back to Washington and see if they found anything on the Cooper plane we could use—handwriting or fingerprints. Reno have anything like that in the Cooper case, Jim?"

"There could have been," Theisen said mournfully. "One of the stewardesses on the Cooper plane said she saw Cooper thumb through airline magazines from his seat pocket. Just like our man McCoy. But you know what, Mr. Calame?" Calame looked at him in disbelief, a horrid surmise dawning in his eyes. Theisen nodded. "That's right," Theisen said. "No one bothered to send any of those magazines back to the crime lab."

Calame pursed his lips judiciously. "Of course, it's the first extortion case we've had like that, from the air. So you make mistakes."

"For all they knew," Theisen chimed in, "Cooper was still on the plane. When Captain Scott, the pilot, tells Cooper they'd have to refuel twice to get to Mexico City, Cooper tells them to make their first refuel stop in Reno."

"So they didn't, at that point," Calame was putting it like a question, "know for sure if Reno was their final destination, or merely their first stop for petrol."

"Exactly," Theisen said. "That 727 comes banging into Reno about eleven o'clock that night with that rear door slamming open and shut, the back stairs scraping the runway at over a hundred miles an hour, sparks flying in all directions. Jack Ricks, one of the Reno agents, said someone thought they saw a man in a black raincoat running from the rear stairs just before the Cooper plane came to a stop. They're only guessing, even now," Theisen says, "but, Seattle thinks Cooper jumped sometime between eight-eleven and eight-thirteen P.M."

"Is that based on what the captain says?" Calame asked.

"Scott, the pilot," Theisen says "wasn't much help because he never saw Cooper. As a matter of fact, none of the crew was, except for the flight engineer and the Mucklow girl. The flight engineer said that sometime between eight-eleven and eight-thirteen the plane oscillated. What he didn't do is plot exactly where they were when he felt the oscillation. So," Theisen shot an empty cigarette wrapper at a huge silver ashtray hooked to the courthouse wall, "when we talk about where Cooper jumped, we're only guessing."

When, on 21 January 1986, I filed a suit in Utah's U.S. District Court, asking it to force Edwin Meese, U.S. Department of Justice, and William H. Webster, director of the Federal Bureau of Investigation, to release certain documents in the Cooper and McCoy cases, I had already seen some of them back in 1972 and knew they would help link Richard McCoy to D. B. Cooper. Eventually the Department of Justice and I settled out of court, and the action was dismissed with prejudice on 3 March 1987 by the Honorable J. Thomas

Greene. Much of what I asked for I got. Some I didn't. Among the items not released were Jim Theisen's interviews with Mildred and Denise Burns that day in the U.S. Attorney's office.

In a letter dated 3 October 1986, Assistant U.S. Attorney Kathleen Barrett, in re *Rhodes v Dept. of Justice*, Civil No. 86C-0056G, advised me:

Dear Mr. Rhodes:
The FBI has approved our proposed settlement of the above matter, but has asked me to clarify and emphasize to you that a waiver must be obtained from McCoy's mother-in-law before that "302" [FBI Report of Interview] can be released. She is a living person they are primarily concerned about.

Through no small effort, I located Mildred Burns in Canton, Ohio. But she has refused to discuss the matter with me in person, on the telephone, or by letter. As recently as June 1989, Jim Theisen, now retired and living in the Southwest, reconfirmed to me, both on the telephone and in writing, those interviews with Mildred and Denise Burns about that narrow, dark clip-on tie and the milky mother-of-pearl tie clasp about the size of a dime that links Richard McCoy to D. B. Cooper.

Until now the FBI has released nothing to the public about either. For twenty years, the tie and clasp proved effective in screening out the kooks and crazies claiming to be D. B. Cooper. Many men, drunk or sober, have called the FBI claiming to be Cooper. Others claim to be Cooper in an effort to bargain away other pending criminal charges. Many, as you might expect, are men serving long prison sentences, bored and lonesome with nothing to lose. "Tell us, if you will," the FBI agent handling the "confession" asks in impeccably polite tones, "what it was that you left behind on seat eighteen-E of the 727 you jumped from that night?" So far, no one has known.

Calame, with what I call the secret handshake, requested the FBI photographs of the tie and tie clasp. In a letter dated 22 June 1989, Emil P. Moschella, chief of the Freedom of Information-Privacy Acts Section in the United States Justice Department, Washington, D.C., did what I considered to be a neat little double shuffle, stating, "We have not located a photo; however, the original evidence is maintained by the Seattle Field Office, which is office of origin in this investigation. Through discussions with the case agent it has been determined that should the photo exist, it would not be releasable pursuant to b7A of the FOIA.''

So they haven't located a photograph? I felt a twinge, just a touch, of skepticism. I'd seen a Polaroid with my own eyes during the McCoy trial in late June 1972. But Calame and I also knew that the necktie and clasp still existed, which was more than the Reno agents could remember. We never could retrack the photograph further than this, but we found out where the necktie and clasp had been kept all these years. The FBI Freedom of Information Act section told Calame in a telephone conversation in July 1989 that they had pinpointed the location of the tie and clasp. They were located in the evidence room at the FBI division office in Seattle, Washington. That conversation also confirmed that the tie and clasp were, without any question, found in seat 18E on 24 November 1971 by Reno FBI agents during their search of Flight 305. The FBI FOIA officer further reported that personnel in the Seattle office had checked and confirmed that the objects were in fact there.

Now it's true that an official FBI form FD302, dated 24 November 1971, reports the search of the plane by four agents in Reno; it's also true that it does not contain any mention of the tie and tie clasp. However, a few days later, Reno sent the actual tie and clasp to the office of jurisdiction at Seattle. They're listed on the letter of transmittal that the FOIA officer checked for us.

And furthermore, one of the interview transcripts released to us under the Freedom of Information suit had a nifty paragraph from Jim Theisen's interview with Robert Van Ieperen:

On April 18, 1972, Special Agent . . . Deletion . . . interviewed ROBERT VAN IEPEREN, 880 Sherwood, Salt Lake City, Utah, who advised that RICHARD FLOYD MC COY, JR., likes to wear conservative solid-colored clip-on ties similar to the tie recovered after the hijacking of a Northwest plane on November 24, 1971. VAN IEPEREN stated he had been out socially with MC COY and recalled that at a movie one night MC COY wore a clip-on tie and removed the tie when he sat down to watch the movie. VAN IEPEREN was shown a photograph of the tie clasp recovered in the above described investigation and he stated the clasp looks similar, but he could not say for sure if

MC COY had one exactly like it. He said it is the type of tie clasp that MC COY would wear.

VAN IEPEREN's wife, MARY ANN, was interviewed separately and had similar comments to her husband's concerning the tie and tie clasp.

VAN IEPEREN stated MC COY made his first free-fall parachute jump in October, 1971, while on a flight with VAN IEPEREN. He stated MC COY has made numerous military-type jumps and immediately following his first free-fall jump he began practicing jumps with the Alta Parachute Club in Salt Lake City, Utah.

I underlined the part about the photograph, then my eyes lingered on the last paragraph. So, I thought, McCoy made his first free-fall jump in October 1971, exactly one month before D. B. Cooper's free-fall on 24 November 1971. That's interesting. Very interesting.

What we know now—but did not know about the Reno investigation back in 1972—was this: Harold E. (Red) Campbell, the SAC at Las Vegas, Nevada, received a phone call late Wednesday evening, 24 November 1971, that a skyjacked Boeing 727 was heading for Reno. Campbell grabbed agents Warren Salisbury and Harry Hinderliter and rushed aboard an air force plane at Nellis Air Base, landing in Reno just before skyjacked Northwest Orient Flight 305 hit the runway. Supervising Agent John Norris and other agents assigned at Reno had already cordoned off the area Flight 305 would use. Campbell took charge and immediately issued instructions for all agents and roughly two hundred other law enforcement personnel to stay the hell out of sight and off the tarmac, until after Flight 305 had landed. The thermometer read 30 degrees. It was cold, wet, and windy.

At 11:02 P.M. Captain William Scott eased down on runway 1, wincing at the flying sparks spraying up from the banging back departure stairs. Flight 305 came to a stop at the end of runway 1 and parked in front of the old terminal building. Red Campbell, weapon drawn, said he moved forward, waving his men off, and entered Flight 305 alone by the damaged rear stairs. Quickly, he worked his way from back to front, searching the toilets and between the seats.

He found no one. The door to the pilot's compartment was locked. "It took some doing to get the crew to open up," he says laconically. Inside were Captain Scott, his copilot, the flight engineer, and Stewardess Tina Mucklow.

Campbell said he then brought Agents John Norris, Jack Ricks, and Alf Stousland aboard to search the plane and dust for prints. Warren Salisbury was assigned to the control tower where he said he handled communications until the wee hours of the morning. Northwest Orient Airlines was still small then and had no operational space at the Reno Airport, so United Airlines loaned them facilities. The airport had only six telephone lines. Salisbury kept one of them open to FBI headquarters at Washington, D.C.

The other five lines jammed with press calls. During the fourteen hours that Flight 305 sat there, some of the agents had to queue up at the pay telephones in the lobby. While Agents Tom Dempsey and Doug Bureau led a ground search, Jack Ricks and Alf Stousland found out from Tina Mucklow where Cooper had sat. "Alf started dusting the hot spots for fingerprints," recalled Ricks, "while I began gathering up cigarette butts and paper cups from around where Cooper sat." John Norris recalls it a little differently. According to his version, he was the first to speak to the crew as they deplaned through the rear stairway. And it was not the FBI but the Reno crime lab ("if that's what you want to call them," said Norris dubiously) that dusted for prints. And there was no chance for the FBI to do it over again, either. By 9:00 A.M. Thanksgiving morning, Flight 305 was released back to the airline and flew out.

Eleven prints, either partials or smudged, were sent that night back to the FBI Fingerprint Division. "We photographed and lifted anything we could find," Ricks said. "We knew Flight 305 was going to get a lot of attention. At the same time we knew it was useless." Two days later, 26 November 1971, Red Campbell received a teletype from FBI headquarters, confirming their educated appraisal about the smudges: "Finger prints found on Flight 305 of no value."

Inside the terminal, Red Campbell, John Norris, Harry Hinderliter, and Marvin Bell debriefed the flight crew until nearly 3:00 A.M. Captain Scott and the copilot had very little pertinent information. The flight engineer had at least noticed the air pressure change in the cabin sometime between 8:11 and 8:13 P.M., but a two-minute variance with Flight 305 traveling at roughly 190 miles per hour left Cooper's landing point pretty vague—somewhere, the FBI speculated, around Woodland or LaCenter, Washington, less than twenty-five miles north of Portland.

But they weren't sure. And they became less sure as time went on. The FBI and two hundred army troops conducted a detailed search of the twenty-eight-square-mile area in the spring of 1972. Later searchers scoured lakes and dragged the Columbia River. Nothing. They circulated the serial numbers of the bills. Nothing. And gradually, the suspicion solidified: they were searching the wrong area.

The first hard evidence came in February 1980 when a family was digging a firepit on the banks of the Columbia River nine miles downstream from Vancouver, Washington. They discovered a packet of water-soaked and badly damaged twenty-dollar bills. They dug deeper and found two more. About all that remained were their centers containing the picture of Andrew Jackson and the serial numbers. But it was enough. The numbers matched the list of Cooper bills. The FBI carefully dug and sifted the sandbar where the family had found the money. They found fragments of bills as deep as three feet.

How did the money get there? A Portland State University geologist and a U.S. Corps of Engineers hydrologist "felt the money had been in the sand for many years, and each believe it had been deposited there by natural means."[1] Even more telling, the stream that the hydrologist felt was the only Columbia tributary that might have deposited the money in the sandbank did not rise in the area that the FBI had been searching.

It reinforced the strong suspicion that Ralph P. Himmelsbach, the Portland FBI agent assigned to the case, had developed after a meeting with Continental Airlines Captain Tom Bohan, a pilot who landed only minutes after Cooper's Northwest Orient Flight 305. He was flying four minutes behind and four thousand feet above Flight 305. "That was one of the worst storm fronts I've encountered in twenty-four years of flying," Captain Bohan related. "I had eighty knots of wind from one-sixty-six degrees right on my nose." The FBI had calculated Cooper's probable landing place with a wind coming from 245 degrees—or out of the southwest. Bohan clearly remembered landing "east, in a strong crosswind that was near my fudge factor." By "fudge factor," he meant the design tolerances for his aircraft. "It meant he had close to a full crosswind on the ground at Portland International Airport," wrote Himmelsbach in his 1986 reconstruction of the Cooper investigation. "And, landing to the east at Portland meant runway ten, which is oriented at one hundred degrees. . . . What all this meant in plain, simple English, was that the wind component cranked into the computer to figure the drop zone where Cooper *should* have landed had been wrong, possibly by as much as eighty degrees. . . . We'd probably spent a hell of a lot of bucks and manhours searching the wrong area."[2]

But of course Ralph Himmelsbach didn't know all this in the fall of 1971. Calame and Theisen didn't know it either as they spliced together their case linking McCoy and Cooper. And by the time we put all of this together in 1986, it was too late to get the hard evidence that would make it more than a plausible theory. Bad timing again, and bad luck.

One piece of luck during the Cooper investigations was Tina Mucklow, the newest member of the crew. She sat next to Cooper most of the trip to Reno, lighting one Raleigh cigarette after another for him while he held the bomb that could at any minute have blown her and everyone else to smithereens. "Tina Mucklow," according to one of the interviewers, "was the person who had the brains." Holding a worn copy of the New Testament, she was calm and methodical as she gave the FBI artist a slow, blow-by-blow description of what their passenger looked like, his speech, how he was dressed, and how he occupied his time during the flight. It was Tina Mucklow who told the agents how she had watched Cooper unbutton his shirt collar and remove his dark, narrow, clip-on tie with the accompanying mother-of-pearl tie clasp which they later located in seat 18E.

What seems strange, even mysterious now in 1990, is that not one agent from the Reno office can remember anything about the tie and clasp. "Something is wrong here," Norm Stone put it. "Surely one of us involved in the Cooper case that night would remember something about that necktie." Stone, now retired from the FBI, told Calame in a telephone conversation on 3 July 1989, "I handled some of the communications that night in the United Airlines facilities, and never even went near the Cooper plane."

All of the Reno agents vividly remember that it was cold and windy that Thanksgiving eve of 1971. They hadn't quite sat down to supper that night when the phone rang. Now after almost twenty years, they remain close and see each other regularly. Most have retired and still live in the Reno area. But as if victims of some strange posthypnotic suggestion, no one, from SAC Red Campbell to Senior Resident Agent John Norris, to Stone, to Dempsey, to Stousland, to Ricks, can remember anything about a clip-on tie or a mother-of-pearl tie clasp.

One agent who requested anonymity said he believes his assignment that night was to take the role of an innocent passenger boarding the plane in Reno—as if either Northwest Orient Airlines, the FAA, or the skyjacker would consider for a minute accepting brand-new passengers on a plane that was not only hijacked but also had damaged rear stairs. This agent retired shortly after the Cooper case and does not recall what he actually did that night at the Reno airport. He believes he had a casual conversation with Tina Mucklow but claims no recollection of the tie or tie clasp. "The whole office would have been talking about it," he said. "This is the kind of thing agents drink their coffee over." I agreed.

Former Agent Tom Dempsey also didn't remember the details of his assignment that night in Reno. Vaguely it came back to him that he sat with the stewardess and the copilot for a short time in a waiting room while they were waiting to be debriefed. "Did you debrief them yourself?" Calame asked him on 28 June 1989. "Not that I remember," he answered. He eventually described himself as "holding their hands" while they waited to be interviewed by someone else.

Agent Alf Stousland, also retired, remembers finding nothing of consequence while he and Jack Ricks searched, dusted, and photographed Flight 305. He spent, ironically, almost the whole night working in the area of seat 18E. Did Tina Mucklow say anything about a tie and clasp? Not that he remembered. Nor did he recall anything "of significance about paper cups or soft drink cans, and especially nothing about airline magazines."

But agent John Norris does. He remembers, "We were criticized by the bureau for not picking up all the magazines, newspapers, and food containers from the cabin," he wrote to Calame on 17 November 1989. "But I do not recall, nor does Ricks, Stousland, or Lieutenant Wise of the Reno Police Department recall, seeing or hearing about a necktie being found on board the aircraft."

Among the many things nobody in the Reno office remembers, as Theisen found out, "is Tina Mucklow telling them that Cooper, at least part of the four hours they circled Seattle, sat thumbing through airline magazines." While trying a second and third time to refresh at least one of the Reno agents' memories in 1989, I remembered something someone said way back in 1972: "No matter how you cut it," one of the Salt Lake agents said, "from here on out that bunch in Reno will either have to hang together and stonewall it—or come up with some pretty sophisticated explanations why they let the Reno City police dust that plane for prints and why those damn magazines never got sent back to the FBI Fingerprint Division."

Tina Mucklow renounced the world after Flight 305 and withdrew to a convent as Sister Mary Alice. Her voice was crystal clear when she came to the phone, and her grammar was immaculate. She giggled at herself a couple of times about the spelling of her address. "Is Green Hill," she asked, "one word or two? I write so infrequently anymore I can't seem to remember." She tried to cooperate but could remember very little about the skyjacking of Flight 305 back in 1971. And nothing at all about the tie and clasp she had told FBI agents about in Reno. She agreed to look through photographs and composites of Cooper and McCoy if it became absolutely necessary. I knew as we talked that it wouldn't be necessary.

[1] Ralph P. Himmelsbach and Thomas K. Worcester, *Norjak: The Investigation of D. B. Cooper* (West Linn, Oregon: Norjak Project, 1986), 109–10.
[2] Ibid., 111–13.

14

Third Day of the Trial
Wednesday, 28 June 1972

Not permitted to photograph in the courtroom, the news media, looking at a twelve o'clock deadline, were lying in wait on the second floor to interview anyone remotely connected with the McCoy trial. Housley, to avoid being caught, took the back stairs up one flight to my office carrying a long yellow witness list and a brown bag lunch. Things, you could tell from his face, had gone well that morning. "Well, Cumshaw," he began—*cumshaw* was a street term meaning someone with power that Housley had picked up from a snitch in a cocaine trial. My cumshaw came primarily from Willis Ritter. Nothing illegal. Ritter wasn't crooked: simply a matter of cutting through miles of government red tape if a thing fit Ritter's philosophy or politics. So people came to me to get to the judge. "The only bumpy part, Cumshaw," said Housley, opening his lunch sack and pulling out a sandwich, "is Winder's motion to suppress." Housley chewed while he made check marks on a long yellow tablet and watched character sketches of himself on the noon news. I listened. My office, on the northwest side of the federal court building, had once served as chambers for a former federal judge and had all the old elegant judicial comforts of a full bath, soft pile carpeting, soft leather couches, television, and the light cedar conference table Housley was sitting at.

"It's either Hearn or Coggin, Cumshaw," Housley says. "One of the two I'll lead off with this afternoon."

Mrs. Starbuck, my secretary, then buzzed on a local line and asked if I could see a parolee for one of the other agents who was out

125

to lunch. I said I could, and in she came, carrying a thick, dog-eared supervision file followed by a John Madden-looking parolee. He told me his name as he sat down. I asked how long he'd been out. "A little over a month," he said. "I'm over at the halfway house, Mr. Rhodes, until I get me a job. But I might just as well go back to the joint," he was stammering a little, " 'cause I can't find one. Nobody wants an ex-con working for them here in Salt Lake."

"Of course they do," I started sympathetically and then broke off as I saw his teeth clench and the veins in his huge, red neck stand out. I looked at Housley. He raised his eyebrows at me.

"The minute they find out I've been in the joint," this guy said, "they seem to give up on me," looking down at a long crumpled job application in his lap, "shake hands with me, and say they'll think about it." I looked through his file quickly. He had spent several years at the United States Medical Center for Federal Prisoners at Springfield, Missouri. He had a long history of depression, alcohol abuse, and forging government checks, plus an old assault charge for throwing a bartender through a plate glass window.

"Lessee that application, podnuh," I told him, in my heaviest Texas accent. "Lessee what we can do with that thang."

"It's part seven," he said, handing it over, "prior employment, Mr. Rhodes, about where I've been and what have I done the past ten years of my life that's giving me all the trouble."

"Well," I couldn't resist saying, "that's not surprising, but in spite of your record let's try to give them what they want. Okay? If the sons-a-bitches want a clean one-owner, we'll just give them a clean one-owner," and the big-handed guy grinned back at me like we'd just opened a barber shop together. "Give me the full and correct name of that place in Missouri where you served your time," I said.

"United States Medical Center." He rolled the syllables off with a certain modest grandeur.

"That's way too long," I said, studying him and his thick file, "to get it all in section seven. Let's shorten it a little," I mused, "try putting just the initials in and let's see how that looks. Do it in big letters. Okay?" I looked hard at Housley. "USMC."

Housley got up, turned off the television, and the man said, "Okay by me, but how's that gonna help?"

"We ain't through yet," I told him. "Just hold on here. So

what's the first thing you did in the joint, when you got up every morning?"

"Clean my cell," he said, trying as hard as he could to help, "clean the commode," he said, "sweep and mop my cell floor. And last I make my bed."

"You, my friend, are what we call an orderly," I told him. "You've been doing orderly work all those years you were in the joint. Ever' day of your life," I said. He gave me a gigantic grin and started to giggle. "Now who'd you do this for? Who made you do all this mopping and cleaning and orderly work every morning?"

"One of the correctional officers," he said.

"And the initials for a correctional officer," I said dreamily, "are what, please?"

"C.O.," he said, trying to figure out what we had. "C.O., Mr. Rhodes, why?"

I told him to give me a minute while I looked up the area code in my manual and telephone number of the warden's office in Springfield and then I listed it in big bold letters and numbers across section seven: "USMC—TEN YEARS EXPERIENCE AS AN ORDERLY TO THE COMPANY C.O."

"Now, friend," I said, as Housley snorted something about cumshaw, "When you hand this application to the man, keep your eyes straight ahead, everything, remember, is yessir, nosir, stand, don't sit—and one more thing," I said, "just for luck, while he's looking over your application and you're standing there as stiff as starch in front of him, hum, very softly, an old favorite of mine: 'From the halls of Montezuma to the shores of Tripoli.' Just for luck," I told him. "Ten to one, you'll get the job."

Housley was still laughing as he dragged us back to the witness list. "Who"—Housley was one of those attorneys who took his time to find exactly the right word—"do I lead off with"—and then he measured and weighed them before he turned them loose—"this afternoon, Cumshaw?" He thought back over what he'd said, then added, "Coggin or Captain Gerald Hearn?"

"Whoever your best hitter is," I told him, "get him to the plate first. The jury has had a two-hour lunch and is probably half-asleep, so send someone up there that can knock the son of a bitch out of the ballpark."

It was 2:15 P.M. Ritter took the bench and asked Housley if the government was ready. "Government's ready, Your Honor," Housley answered and called as his first witness William Richard Coggin. Calame, in an effort to disguise Coggin's Harry Houdini escape history, had his hair cut short and his prison clothes switched to something the jury might believe. Someone in the FBI, although Calame denied it, promised Coggin that if he did right by the prosecution, they'd call the California Parole Authority and put in a good word for him. Although Coggin hadn't heard Surdam's testimony, the word about Ritter's hearing problem had obviously percolated back to the corridor and Coggin could have taken first place in the Loud Witness Contest. "Yes," he told the court, "he's sitting at counsel's table! On the left! Next to his lawyer!"

"Are you positive about this, Mr. Coggin?" Housley asked, stretching his arm in Richard's direction. "Is this the man you saw enter the rear bathroom on Flight 855 before he put his disguise on?"

"It is," Coggin assured the court and reeled, loudly and clearly through everything else that he'd been in a position to observe. Winder, on cross-examination, tried to rattle Coggin's confidence about what he had actually seen, and Winder was no slouch. I had always marveled at the talent he had for cracking witnesses like dried walnuts, but it backfired in this case. In fact, what I felt for Winder was something like sympathy. It was an embarrassment, I thought, for Winder to be defense attorney in this trial. Ritter had ranted and raved about the cost of out-of-state psychiatric evaluations. And it hadn't been easy trying to impanel a jury of twelve Utahns who hadn't already formed an opinion about Richard's guilt. Given all the television, radio, and newspaper coverage, Winder, to get a fair trial, needed jurors who had no eyes, who were totally deaf, or who suffered from the same sickness Rip Van Winkle had.

Captain Hearn was next. Housley needed Hearn to pin down two things: where the hijack took place and why Hearn went to San Francisco rather than Los Angeles. These, in a nutshell, were the requirements for the federal indictment of hijacking. And Hearn was obviously going to be a prime witness. His natty blue pilot's uniform set off his broad shoulders. He spoke up clearly, so that everyone in the room could hear his deep husky voice. And Captain Hearn was careful not to make any mistakes when he answered Housley, establishing his assignment on 7 April, about the sequence of events after they left Denver.

"And what was your original destination, Captain Hearn?"

"My original destination was Los Angeles."

"And did you in fact fly that Boeing 727, Flight 855, to Los Angeles?"

"No," Hearn said, "I did not."

"Where, in fact, did you go from Denver?"

"San Francisco."

"What occurred, Captain Hearn, that made you change your arrival flight plans?"

"One of the passengers hijacked the airplane and instructed us to go to San Francisco."

"Did you make a decision, Captain Hearn, to change your plans and fly to San Francisco?"

"I made the decision because this man in the back threatened to blow up the airplane and the people in it if we didn't go to San Francisco."

No reporters went running for the phones over this labored recital, but Hearn had just established that McCoy had committed an act of aircraft piracy within the jurisdictional limits of the United States by seizing and exercising control by force and violence while Flight 855 was in the air, forcing the captain to alter his destination. Everything after that was showmanship, more or less, to entertain the jurors—trying to determine how many hijackers were involved, identifying the note, pointing out the technically correct terminology in the flight plans that set up the zigzag route to Utah, and the change in pressure when Richard had Diane Surdam open the door to the area leading to the aft staircase.

"When the rear door opens, or any door for that matter," Hearn told the jury, "a warning light comes on in the cockpit."

"Which door was open the night of April seventh?" Housley asked. "The aft door to get into the stairs or the stairs themselves?"

"Both," Hearn said. "When I passed over Provo, the aft entrance door was open, and inside that door there's a handle. When you press the handle, the rear stairs are released. They are hinged, so the steps open down and out."

By early evening Housley had milked Captain Hearn dry. Trying to muddy up Hearn's testimony about where Richard jumped, Winder asked, "Now, you said that you were sure at some point that the person had left the airplane. What occurred to give you that impression?"

"The airplane," Hearn said in majestic detail, "was unpressurized, and when an airplane is unpressurized, there's an awful lot of noise. The noise level is very noticeable, especially in contrast to a pressurized airplane because of the soundproofing of the airplane. So when the aft air stairs opened and the aft entrance door opened, there was a noticeable noise level. Even up in the cockpit, it was quite noisy, but this noise level was a constant noise level. Sometime during the trip, about Provo, this noise level changed very abruptly for a moment—like it went from a noise that was level and then all of a sudden got louder and then back to another noise level. Upon thinking about it now, I assume that, with the air stairs extended and the airplane flying through the air, the stairs could not extend fully. In other words, they were trailing against the wind's pressure and as the hijacker climbed out upon the stairs, with his weight, the stairs must have dropped a tiny bit. Then as he threw himself off the stairs into the airstream, the absence of his weight from the stairs caused the stairs to close up again momentarily. Now, this is the only place where the airplane is unpressurized from, so momentarily the opening is closed. Because of this, I believe the change in the level of the noise occurred."

"But the door was opened," Winder said, "and the aircraft was unpressurized for a substantial time before Provo, isn't that true?"

"Yes," Captain Hearn agreed.

"And, in fact, Captain Hearn, you did fly on nearly to Price, Utah, before you turned around, did you not?"

"About five minutes before Price, Mr. Winder, yes, we did."

"So you were, in fact," Winder said, "indefinite to some extent about when he jumped, isn't that true?"

"I was almost ninety-nine percent sure he jumped over Provo, Utah, but I had no visual proof."

"Now, taking Exhibits Two and Three for a minute, if you will," Winder says, handing the two flight plans to Captain Hearn, "where were you again, when you first saw them?"

"Mr. Winder," Captain Hearn said, "if I could just back up for a minute?"

"Of course you may," Winder said, shimmying his shoulders as if, for the first time in the trial, he'd found someone other than himself going backwards. "You have Richard McCoy's okay, Captain Hearn, to go back as far as you need to."

"Well, I'd like to explain," Hearn says, "some of the misconceptions you have about these flight plans, if I may."

"I'm sure I have a lot of misconceptions," Winder said almost angrily, "about this type of thing on an aircraft. See, I don't fly airplanes, Captain Hearn. But I will, sir, continue now, with your permission, to ask you exactly where you were, and exactly who it was that gave you Exhibits Two and Three."

"There were so many notes and flight plans brought to the cockpit," Hearn finally admitted, "that I can't be absolutely sure when or where we were when I got them."

"Your Honor," Winder said, relieved it seemed, "we have nothing further of Captain Hearn."

At the very moment Captain Hearn walked out of the courtroom, Marshal Buttars was ushering Denise Burns in. Denise had been in protective custody since Richard's preliminary hearing back in May and had grown very fond of her guards, the San Francisco agents who had been required to stay in Salt Lake City to testify and help with security during the trial. Being held at the downtown Travelodge Motel under twenty-four-hour FBI protection was something of an ultimate fantasy for her, as Karen put it. Denise saw herself starring in this gigantic play.

"Richard," Denise confided breathlessly to their courteous ears, "said he'd kill me, if I said one more word to you guys."

Almost as fast as Denise could straighten her yellow double-knit slacks, blow her blonde bangs from her moist forehead, and croon that she most certainly would tell the truth, Ritter had the marshal take the jury out.

"Mr. Housley," Ritter said, eyeing Denise suspiciously, "this girl is under such obvious stress, upset as she seems, I'm afraid she might just blurt something out about that money down there. Then we've got a mess on our hands with the jury. Unless there's something you people haven't told the court, this might be a good time to take some testimony on Winder's motion to suppress. Then we can finish this thing up."

A. M. Ferro, the U.S. magistrate who had issued the faulty search warrant, had been vacationing near Mexico City and was still kicking and screaming because Ritter ordered him back a week early. A. M. or, as he was known around the courthouse, O. R. (because he released everyone on their own recognizance), took the witness stand angrily, with his mind about half made up to crucify Ritter. Instead, he melted as Ritter graciously thanked him for hurrying back from his well-deserved trip to Mexico and told everyone in open court how fortunate we all were to have Ferro as our magistrate. Cordial or not, however, he was unable to explain how Lote Kinney's name had appeared on the warrant application where Bill Geiermann's should have been.

C. Nelson Day, Jim Housley's boss, wasn't any more help. Neither, as Wednesday evening darkened outside the courtroom windows, were Agents Kinney and Geiermann themselves. Housley would grudgingly concede that the warrant wasn't right, but he wouldn't agree that it was hopelessly wrong either and pleaded with Ritter to let him amend it *nunc pro tunc* (now for then).

Ritter, who was tired and fed up, turned snarling on Housley. Even from the back of the courtroom, I could see a light shade of pink creep up the back of Housley's shirt collar. Winder triumphantly rose and cited several circuit and Supreme Court cases, then blinked when Ritter wouldn't budge, one way or the other, and sat down speechless. The judicial machinery had become high centered.

FBI clerk-stenographers Mary Edmondson and Louise Praught, who in all their years with the FBI had never had to testify, took the stand. "I was called to the office," Miss Edmondson told the court, "around midnight, Saturday, April eighth, 1972, and worked, Louise Praught and I, until around nine the next morning. That would have been Sunday morning," she said, "April ninth. Mr. Day, the U.S. Attorney, was there with Mr. Calame most of the night, dictating to me and Louise, and we, of course, took those notes and, from them, we typed the warrant application. I don't remember where," shrugging her shoulders apologetically, "where Mr. Kinney's name should have gone or how Mr. Geiermann got in there. And as a matter of FBI policy," she added very quietly, "our shorthand notes," Ritter could see it coming and looked off in disgust, "have to be shredded after thirty days, you see."

Ritter said he wasn't sure whether it was typographical, harmless error, or just plain stupidity, but what the U.S. attorney was asking him to do went against his "sacred oath of office and a half-century of protecting the Constitution, but, . . . " he sighed, and went on to admit that airplane hijacking was happening all too frequently. "So we'll just have to let the Tenth Circuit Court of Appeals wrestle with Winder's Fourth Amendment problem." He denied Winder's motion, told both sides he wanted to see them in his chambers, and sent the jury home until ten o'clock Thursday morning. It was 9:00 P.M. Wednesday.

15 Russ Calame's Retirement Party

I was very pleased to receive an invitation to Russ Calame's retirement party and polished my shoes to a high, maybe even an FBI, gloss before I drove up to the Fort Douglas Country Club. It was the latter part of June, cool with the canyon breeze and high enough on the east bench to make Salt Lake City a glittering jewel box to the west. The colossal old ivy-covered stone fortress built, someone said, by the army in the mid-1930s, was an impressive setting for the party, entirely befitting a high-ranking FBI personage like Russ Calame.

Charlie Shepherd, who was familiar with most of Calame's guests, was posted just inside the entrance of the main ballroom with a white leather guest book inscribed in gold relief: "S.A.C. Russell P. Calame, Retired, Federal Bureau of Investigation—June 1972."

It was still early when I got there, yet a hundred or even two hundred people had already formed a line to pay their respects to two extraordinary citizens who had quietly made a contribution to the Salt Lake community, Russ and Mary Calame. Next to Russ in the receiving line was a dignitary from Washington, D.C., and next to him was a very dapper, smallish man (by FBI standards), five foot eight, 190 pounds, balding slightly, who looked on, nodded nervously, licked his lips, and tugged at the knot in his tie.

After two or three quick trips to the bar I found myself one of the last to reach Calame. The press arrived a few minutes later for the closing conference, and I stayed on to enjoy it. Calame knew how to do press conferences. He knew people by name. He expressed his appreciation for their cooperation and did it sincerely.

"What I had hoped to do during my administration," I remember Calame saying, "was to give the people of Utah a chance to get to know their FBI—feel they could trust its agents, and know how to get in touch with us when they needed help. They watch the perpetrator on television and hear his side of the story, so I felt it was important that someone heard ours. One of the last bits of advice Mr. Hoover had for me before he sent me out here was, 'Get to know the people of Utah and let them get to know you!' To some people, I'm sure," Calame said—he half-paused with what looked to be a tear in his eye—"what Mr. Hoover asked me to do could be considered little more than public relations work. But the term P.R., to me, doesn't only mean public relations, it also means performance and reporting. If the FBI builds a strong record of performance, that speaks for itself. If I, as the SAC, supplement that with reporting—such as newspaper articles or public appearances, as we're doing now—then we build an image of the bureau, which forms a more solid foundation than any paid public-relations firm could possibly provide. That, ladies and gentlemen," he said, "is all I intended to do. Get the most out of my agents, arrest your troublemakers, and report back to you, the taxpayer.

"Of course," he continued, and the ladies and gentlemen of the press melted sweetly into smiles, "I'd like to have had all good news to report every day, but my job as agent-in-charge here in Salt Lake City wasn't the same as that of the man who manages K-Mart. When he makes a mistake by overpricing a product, his customer simply walks over to Walmart to shop. But when the FBI makes a mistake in a robbery or aircraft piracy case, someone often gets hurt." Then he went on to thank everyone, gracefully mention how pleasant it would be to encounter them during his retirement years, and say a few kind words about Maurice Slocum.

As much as anything else, the news conference, I'm sure, was to get his successor off on the right foot. And maybe part of Russ's speech about getting to know the people of Salt Lake had been delivered for Slocum's benefit. But Slocum failed to take the hint. Without making any effort to get acquainted with the press or even smiling, Calame's handsome little replacement officiously went back to pulling at his clothes, shuffling his feet, and straightening a lace monogrammed handkerchief in his left jacket pocket. It could have been a tremendous advantage, I remember thinking, meeting Salt Lake's political force and all the right people in the criminal justice field. Was Slocum jealous? Intimidated?

I said good-bye to Russ and Mary Calame and drove away that night with a bad taste in my mouth about Maurice Slocum. You could see a mile away that Slocum was a lemon. The nightstick, so to speak, that should have been passed from one old FBI agent to another was dropped on the sidewalk and no one picked it up.

It wasn't just the Cooper-McCoy connection that was lost on Slocum. He showed no interest in the other cases the office had under investigation. Hoover's death a month earlier could have had something to do with a general sag in morale. But it was probably vanity more than anything, a desire to create his own dynasty. Jim Theisen was transferred back to Washington the first week in July and Slocum, as far as we know, never reassigned the Cooper-McCoy case to anyone else.

16 Last Day of the Trial
Thursday, 29 June 1972

Denise Burns, perspiring nervously, fixed her big innocent blue eyes on George Sangas, her court-appointed attorney, who was there to see that she said nothing self-incriminating. Adamantly denying any attempt on her part to claim the fifty-thousand-dollar reward offered by United Airlines, she admitted that she had told Robert Van Ieperen on the telephone the night of the hijacking that she was sure Richard had done it.

Most of the testimony was simple and circumstantial—the dirty paratrooper's boots, the Coke in a Hi-Spot cup, the story Richard told her. Probably the most damaging part was her description of watching the news with Richard and Karen. When the camera focused on a dark, pretty stewardess, Richard had said, "That's the girl I gave the hijack notes to and stuck for the money. Just before Frisco, I made her get me a can of ginger ale."

Ritter's denial of Winder's motion to suppress had blown open the McCoys' walk-in closet. Carroll H. George, vice president of Wells Fargo Bank in San Francisco, provided a long list of serial numbers and denominations of the half-million dollars, and Housley introduced pictures of the money into evidence.

Then FBI agent Lote Kinney, team leader in Provo that Sunday morning, testified about the search. Along with a .45-caliber handgun, a parachute, and an inert green pineapple grenade, he said, they also found $499,970 in United States currency. Winder stipulated that the money found in the McCoy home was the same money drawn from the Wells Fargo Bank in California. There was hardly any point in demanding a bill-by-bill match of serial numbers. Winder's cooperativeness was also a strategy: He could not, by any conceivable stretch of the imagination, get McCoy acquitted. But the death penalty was still staring Richard in the face. One or two of the jurors might show compassion—enough to stave off the death sentence. This was not the time or place, Winder knew, to make enemies of either judge or jury.

After the money was accepted into evidence, Housley rested his case, nodded at Winder, then to the jury, and took his seat at the counsel table next to Charlie Shephard.

For the defense, Winder called a few of McCoy's army friends with whom he had served overseas. Some had come long distances at their own expense. They all did what they could, talked about his religious and peaceful nature and how he especially loved his children.

Winder had, after all, managed to convince Judge Ritter just before the trial to have Dr. David Hubbard and Dr. John McDonald, well-known psychiatrists from Dallas and Denver, examine Richard. They had both spent hours with him, and, like most high-priced auto mechanics, had a dozen hypotheses about why Richard wasn't running right. But nobody could make Ritter or the jury understand how a man of Richard's intelligence and loyalty to country, God, and family could hijack an airplane. The defense rested. Winder could hardly put Richard on the witness stand. He was guilty. He would at best perjure himself and possibly bring on himself the death penalty.

If probation officers afforded themselves the luxury of sitting through every extortion or murder case that came along, they'd have time for very little else. So they stay very close to the prosecutor, learn which witnesses to watch for, and slip in to cover the final arguments. They need at least some understanding of who the good guys are and how bad the bad guys are.

Ritter gave Housley and Winder forty minutes for final arguments, and Housley was still tying up loose ends when Ritter cut him off. Winder took less than thirty minutes. It could anger the jury if he were to play fast and loose with the facts or try to blame someone else. So instead, Winder spoke of Richard's honorable war record, of his two small children, of his dedication to the Mormon church, and of his clean record.

After a short recess, Ritter returned to the bench looking pleased, even refreshed, as he leaned forward and looked at the jury.

"I have a little announcement to make, ladies and gentlemen of the jury. Something," Ritter said, "that pleases this court and I'm sure has been weighing heavily on you people's minds. Whether or not you'd eventually have to give this fellow the death penalty. Well, the court's gonna help you solve that little problem right now. You can, as of now, dismiss that dilemma from your minds. While we were in recess, I had a caller from Washington about this very issue. I know Mr. Winder's pleased about it so I'll ask him if he'd like to explain to you people what the Supreme Court of the United States did a little earlier today."

Winder said no, thank you, even though he'd been in chambers with Ritter when the phone call came. "I'd prefer Your Honor did that. If it's all the same to the court, I think, I too would enjoy having the court tell us what they did."

The U.S. Supreme Court only that morning, 29 June 1972, in *Furman v Georgia* had just ruled the death penalty "cruel and unusual punishment" in violation of the Eighth and Fourteenth Amendments and accordingly unconstitutional. With that out of the way, by 5:40 P.M. Ritter had instructed the jury on the finding of facts and on points of law. Ritter especially belabored Richard's right under the Fifth Amendment "to choose, without any presumption of guilt from you people, not to take the witness stand and testify against himself. It's the government's duty to prove beyond a reasonable doubt. And that means without any help from the defendant."

Ritter's instructions, as always, were strictly off the top of his head, to the point, and, as most trial lawyers would agree, brilliant. It was nearly six o'clock when he dismissed the jury to have dinner, pick a foreman, and begin deliberations.

No one actually gets shot out of a cannon or falls off a high wire; but with these minor limitations, courthouse halls turn into a two-ring circus while a jury is deliberating. Nearly everyone who has sat through the trial has formed an opinion about who won and who lost, so you have the laughter of a wedding celebration at one end of the hall and the sadness of a funeral taking place at the other. This night was no exception. Within a few minutes, cigarette smoke had formed blue-gray clouds in the long, dingy hallways. A runty pimp from another trial, wearing a white silk, one-bottom-roll suit, black and white spectator shoes, and a diamond the size of a walnut roamed the halls looking for change for more cigarettes. One of the deputy U.S. marshals sat with his chair cocked back against the petit-jury door, reading the sports page, while two more were shadow-boxing just outside lockup. Newspaper and television people huddled at one end like refugees. Periodically they strolled slowly past the jury room with serious Walter Cronkite expressions on their faces, listening for sounds—laughter, a raised voice, or a toilet flushing. "Vital signs," one whispered to another, "to a good news person on which way the jury seems to be leaning and how soon they'll finish up." Calame and his men worked in the law library of the U.S. attorney's office, away from the defendant and his supporters, where they wouldn't be cursed at or spit on.

At a little after six o'clock that Thursday evening, I walked through the law library to get to Jim Housley's office, and there were Jim Theisen and Russ Calame. Russ Calame, his men said, avoided small talk and cigarette smoke with equal dislike, and pushed everybody around him as hard as he pushed himself. While I couldn't say they were exactly waiting for me, they certainly didn't try to hustle me on through.

"We can't talk to McCoy," Theisen said, "but you will, Rhodes, won't you? Even after we convict him, he'll appeal it, so it could be years before we ever get to question him about the Cooper case."

And then he told me about that dark, narrow, clip-on necktie and the mother-of-pearl clasp. I was fascinated.

"So that," I stated, "is a photograph of the actual tie and tie clasp left on the plane by D. B. Cooper, and Richard McCoy's family identifies it as his. What the hell more do you guys want? Something signed in blood from him?"

"It's his mother-in-law," Calame said, pursing his lips, "and sister-in-law."

"What about his wife or his mother?" I asked. "Have you talked to them?"

Theisen lit up a Winston and shuffled his feet in and out of a pair of penny loafers. I took a chair at the end of the table and lit up a Marlboro. Calame pulled a three-cornered handkerchief with "RPC" monogrammed on it from his breast pocket and wiped his forehead. I like Jim Theisen, I thought. Anyone in the FBI human enough to be a tobacco addict would forever be a friend of mine.

"Can't talk to his wife." Theisen answered me almost absently. "Or his mother. They won't talk to us."

"We couldn't," Calame corrected, "even if they would. It wouldn't be proper to do that now, especially during the trial."

Richard had refused all along to discuss anything with the bureau about United Flight 855, with or without the presence of counsel, so a brand-new line of questions regarding D. B. Cooper certainly would not induce loquacity either. Theisen asked if I could get family albums and old photographs which might show Richard or someone else in the family wearing that mother-of-pearl clasp. I told him as long as we didn't get crossways with Judge Ritter, I'd see what I could do.

And then suddenly both of them were laying out for me the entire scenario that linked Richard McCoy with D. B. Cooper.

Richard's records at Brigham Young University confirmed that he finished his last class before the Thanksgiving break at 9:30 A.M. Tuesday, 23 November. The next day, the day of the hijacking, he was supposed to be on National Guard duty, but he wasn't. The duty roster showed that Richard attended four drills the week before 20 November and five drills three weeks later, 12–16 December 1971. He wasn't assigned to attend particular drills—just so many within a given time period—and could work the details out for himself. So he had. And he'd worked completely around the week of the D. B. Cooper hijacking.

According to Calame and Theisen that's because Richard wasn't even in Utah on 24 November 1971. Their scenario had him getting in his Volkswagen bug early on the morning of Wednesday, 24 November, and driving to Las Vegas, arriving in the late morning. He put his car in overnight parking at McCarran International Airport and flew to Portland, presenting himself at the Northwest Orient ticket counter at about 2:00 P.M. Using the name Dan Cooper he purchased a one-way ticket to Seattle and, soon after takeoff, showed Tina Mucklow eight sticks of dynamite. Calame was more inclined to think that they were railroad or highway flares. Cooper had instructed the Northwest Orient pilot to follow airway Victor-23, along I-5 out of Seattle, just as Richard McCoy had used I-15 as a landmark. At about 8:12, Cooper jumped. "That area isn't as rough or forestlike," Calame explained, "as some people think, so he should have been just fine. He walks or hooks a ride into Portland, stays all night, and the next day catches a plane, or bus or whatever, back to Vegas." By that time, he'd removed his dark makeup, ditched his wig, and changed clothes.

Richard McCoy had done exactly the same things. I nodded with real interest. Calame and Theisen had more than hot air to stiffen their hypothesis. They had Richard's signature on a credit-card slip showing that on 25 November he had purchased 5.6 gallons of gasoline at the Power Thrust Service Station, 6176 Las Vegas Boulevard, using BankAmericard 4763-160-217-773. The FBI crime lab in Washington, D.C., confirmed that the signature was McCoy's. That sales slip also recorded the license plate number of the McCoy vehicle as "SA 1334 NO CAROL." Richard still had North Carolina plates on his car, and SA 1334 was, indubitably, his license number.

Furthermore, Richard's telephone bill pitilessly recorded that someone had placed a collect call to the McCoy residence, (801) 375-2930, at 10:41 P.M., on 25 November from (702) 731-9820, a pay phone in the lobby of the Tropicana Hotel, less than half a mile from McCarran International Airport.

If Richard McCoy was, for the sake of argument, I put it to Calame and Theisen, D. B. Cooper and if he had jumped out of the 727 that night in a rainstorm, and had walked away scot-free with $200,000 in November 1971, why in the world would he go back five months later and hijack Flight 855?

"He lost it," Theisen said. "He lost the damn money! All but eight or ten thousand dollars." When Cooper offered the stewardesses $2,000 each as a tip, he had removed several packets of money from the bank bag. They had refused the tips, and they remembered seeing Cooper stuff the packets, each containing $2,000, either into his pants pocket or coat pocket before he jumped.

"So what happened to the hundred and ninety thousand?" I asked.

"Got away from him," Calame shook his head.

"He had the money in a Seattle First National Bank money bag." Theisen said. "He'd insisted the money be brought aboard the airplane first, before the parachutes. Tina Mucklow described to the Reno agents how she'd left the plane by the front exit, walked halfway down the front air stairs and was handed the money bag by an FBI agent. She noticed the bag had no zipper or latches to keep the packets of money from falling out. Then, when the two front chutes and two back chutes—exactly like the ones McCoy ordered—were brought aboard, Tina watched Cooper cannibalize one of the chest chutes by cutting several nylon shrouds just below the canopy into six- or eight-foot lengths. He used a couple of the shrouds to wrap up and tie the money bag into a tight little package about two feet square. He then threaded a couple of the nylon cords through his belt loops and tied them to the money bag. She remembered the cords were cut plenty long, allowing the bag to drag six or more feet behind him when he walked. This way, the bag, which must have weighed more than twenty pounds, would reach the ground before he did. We believe that sometime during his jump that night, the knot gave or the nylon popped and the bag got away from him.''

"All but eight or ten thousand," Calame agreed. "The Portland office says it was below zero that night at ten thousand feet. Ralph Himmelsbach, an agent in Portland, says Cooper's hands would have frozen before he could pull the ripcord."

"Calame and I believe," Theisen said, "or, at least I believe, when Cooper sent Tina Mucklow to the front, he changed to warmer clothes he'd brought aboard in a small carry-on bag. No one remembers seeing a bag, but that doesn't mean he didn't have one, does it?"

"No," I agreed. "The plane was less than half full. He was one of the first to board. He could have very easily stored it in the over-head luggage before he became the center of attention."

"So he lost the money," concluded Theisen, "except for what was in his pockets."

"That's not exactly small change," I said, "so why is Richard McCoy dead broke five months later?"

"Oh, he *had* money," Theisen said, rummaging through his briefcase. "I'm in the process now," he said, pulling a handwritten FBI standard interview form 302 from a thick government file, "of writing up an interview with BankAmericard."

"The first week of January 1972," Theisen said, "which was between the Cooper and McCoy hijackings, McCoy purchased air-line tickets for himself, his wife, two children, and, believe it or not, Denise Burns to travel from Salt Lake City to Raleigh, North Carolina. The tickets, amounting to nearly twelve hundred dollars, were originally charged to his BankAmericard. He paid that off in cash within thirty days so they never showed up on his billing. We know he and Karen were struggling financially, so where did the twelve hundred come from?"

"These things are more than just coincidental," Calame told me slowly and convincingly, as if reciting a laundry list of things he'd been sitting there memorizing under his breath. "There are dozens of similarities. McCoy sat in the last row of seats on the right, facing forward, on both his practice run and during the actual hijack. Cooper, five months earlier, sat in exactly the same row on exactly the same side. The only dissimilarity," Calame conceded without sounding a bit apologetic, "is that the stewardess said she thought Cooper had brown eyes and of course we know McCoy's eyes are blue."

"How do you get around brown and blue eyes?" I asked. "You can dye your hair and put on heavy makeup, but you sure as heck can't change the color of your eyes, can you?"

"Yes, of course, you can change the color of your eyes," Calame said, without even implying that it was a dumb question. "If you want to bad enough. First of all, we're not sure they *were* brown. The stewardess could have been mistaken. Passengers guessed his age at somewhere between thirty and fifty-five. Now that's quite a spread, isn't it? What's more, Cooper wore wraparound mirrored glasses at least part of the time. Eyewitnesses are only human and trying to remember things that happened when they were under tremendous pressure. They weren't sure about the color of Cooper's eyes. Even Coggin, the only one to identify McCoy from a photograph, couldn't tell us the color of his eyes. The general lighting on an airplane," Calame said, "is pretty low intensity. The reading lights are high intensity, of course, but they shine down."

Theisen lit another filter tip and cleared his throat. "Cooper chain-smoked Raleigh filter tips. Tina Mucklow lit most of them while Cooper kept his hand on those dynamite wires. Mucklow noticed the first two fingers on his bare right hand. Said they had dark yellow stains. I've been a heavy cigarette smoker for twenty years," Theisen explained, "and so have you, Rhodes. We don't have stains on our fingers, do we? And neither did D. B. Cooper."

"That was the yellowish stain left when he wiped his hands after putting on that makeup," Calame said, "on the two fingers he used to apply the makeup, I'll betcha. And let's take this thing one step further. If McCoy, a Mormon, smoked as part of his disguise, he would have needed to buy a pack of cigarettes in the Portland airport. What brand would he choose? Well, it's naturally going to be Raleigh, his hometown, his home brand, isn't it?"

Theisen was nodding. I realized that my own head was nodding, too. Here's Richard McCoy, a boy from Raleigh, North Carolina. And Calame had more. The investigation showed twenty different brands of cigarettes are manufactured by only seven companies. Raleigh cigarettes were the least popular of the three brands sold by Brown and Williamson Tobacco Company product, barely 1.5 percent of all cigarettes sold. So the statistical odds were slim against someone choosing Raleighs at random. I nodded, impressed. Defense attorneys sometimes call a case built solely on circumstantial evidence "loading the wagon." That's what I thought Calame was doing, but I had to admire how skillfully he was doing it.

"He laundered the eight or ten thousand dollars that didn't get away from him during the jump. He commingled," as Theisen put it, "the marked money with Tropicana chips and casino money and drove back to Provo with clean unmarked bills."

I kept listening. Russ and Jim kept talking. The Power Thrust Service Station is located on a street that borders the west side of the airport. The Tropicana Hotel is less than a mile north of the service station.

Furthermore, that same credit card was used the morning of the 24th to buy gas in Cedar City, Utah. Cedar City is 182 miles northeast of Las Vegas, and a Volkswagen bug averages thirty-two or thirty-three miles per gallon. The drive from Cedar City to Las Vegas, Theisen said, with mathematical significance, would therefore require approximately 5.6 gallons of gasoline, the exact amount he bought at the Power Thrust station.

"But wait," I asked, leaning forward, looking for a hole. "Let's assume Denise was telling the truth. Richard was home from two to six P.M. Thanksgiving night. Is it possible that he drove to Las Vegas and *then* called home as soon as he got in town?"

Calame and Theisen shook their heads simultaneously. In November 1971, the road between Provo and Las Vegas was Highway 91 plus the partially finished I-15. It was exactly 410 miles. Las Vegas, it's true, was located in the Pacific Standard time zone, which would have given Richard an extra hour. So he could have had a maximum possible total of five hours, forty-one minutes to reach the Tropicana, the farthest hotel driving south on the Las Vegas strip, park his car, and make the call. He would have had to average eighty miles an hour to do it. But I-15 was rough and unfinished, with half a dozen major detours. And Richard was driving a 1969 Volkswagen. I tried to visualize it and then, like Calame and Theisen, shook my head, too. Richard had been leaving Las Vegas, I was convinced, and was calling Karen to tell her so.

"So okay," I said, "it's an eight-hundred-mile round-trip. Richard McCoy isn't a crap shooter. And he isn't the kind to leave his family on a holiday to go take in a nightclub show. Why," I asked, "is Vegas so important? I mean, why not Phoenix or Albuquerque? What's more, has anyone been able to pin down the manner of transportation, McCoy or Cooper, whichever, took to Portland?"

"We have not," Calame said, and you knew unequivocally you could trust him. "An effort, of course, has been made, Mr. Rhodes, by checking with United, Western, and Air West, the three airlines that service the Las Vegas–Portland route, but it looks as if we're about four months late. Airlines destroy old passenger lists after thirty days. Very unfortunate."

I agreed.

"And another reason for Vegas," Theisen added, "well, actually a couple. Las Vegas offers excellent air connections to cities all over the world. Furthermore, it's a city with a great number of transients, conventioneers, and visitors coming and going all hours of the day and night. And it's a spree city. What we know of criminals who score big on money crimes is that they frequently go to a resort town like Vegas to relax, maybe gamble a little, and launder the money."

Calame nodded soberly. "It therefore raises serious questions as to the truthfulness of Denise Burns about Richard's whereabouts that Thanksgiving evening. Everything we know now," he said, "would indicate Denise is supplying Richard and—who knows? maybe even herself—with an alibi."

Herself? I raised my eyebrows. The San Francisco agents had slipped the word to Calame and Theisen during the trial that Denise was saying Richard had talked to her months earlier about helping him extort money from an airline. The gist of Denise's comments was this: "Richard had a plan once where he wanted me to call the airlines and—this was several months ago—tell them there was a package of instructions in a locker and a bomb on one of their planes." Another time, she said, Richard wanted her to pick him up out in the Nevada desert. "I said, 'No sir, Richard. I'm not going to set out there in the middle of no place by myself and then have the police come pick me up.' " This was way before the one they caught him on."

Calame rubbed his eyes. "It is not known for sure how many months before the Cooper case Richard was formulating these plans; but we believe it to be during the summer of 1971." Even tired, Calame sounded as if he was giving a news bulletin.

"And look at these," Theisen gloated. He set down the service records for Richard's Volkswagen from Peterson Motors in Provo from 25 November 1970 through 5 April 1972. "Each time the vehicle was repaired or serviced, some conscientious mechanic recorded the mileage. The average number of miles per day was very consistent—right at thirty-three and a half miles per day. We left out of those calculations the period we were most interested in—October thirtieth through November thirtieth." He looked at me. I was giving him my undivided attention. "Then the average jumped to fifty-six per day."

"How much more is that than you'd expect?" I said. I couldn't do math this late at night.

"Eight hundred sixty," said Theisen. "And that's allowing for the fact that McCoy wasn't using his Volkswagen between the second and sixth of November because he was with the National Guard in Arizona and Nevada."

"And the trip to Vegas would take how many?"

"About eight-twenty," said Calame. "And that means he didn't drive to Portland to hijack Northwest Orient Flight 305. No, he drove to Las Vegas. We were trying to determine McCoy's whereabouts during the entire month of November 1971, but especially for the Wednesday, Thursday, and Friday—the twenty-fourth through the twenty-sixth. We found something interesting, too—or Jim did," Calame said, and I felt like a tennis ball at Wimbledon, "didn't we, Jim?"

Theisen, in going through McCoy's National Guard records, found he'd been assigned to go to Davis Monthan Air Force Base just outside Tucson and fly a helicopter back to Salt Lake City. McCoy's orders gave him five days, 2–6 November 1971, to get down there and back, but they didn't specify a mode of transportation. Theisen learned from other National Guard pilots that Richard could have simply shown his military identification and hooked a ride on a plane out of Hill Field at Ogden or asked a guard friend to fly him down to Nellis AFB at Las Vegas.

"We were never able to establish how he got down there," Theisen said, "but that's really not important. Whether it was a military plane or a Greyhound bus. What is important," Theisen said, raising his heavy blonde eyebrows and tapping a Winston cigarette on the face of his wristwatch, "is that we can definitely put him in Vegas on Tuesday night, November second, registered at the Westward Ho Motel on Las Vegas Boulevard. It was a perfect opportunity to dry-run his Portland-to-Seattle hijacking, checking on the timing, number of passengers, number of crew members, and any peculiarities in the flight. Two days later, on Thursday, November fourth, he flew a Utah helicopter from Tucson back to Salt Lake City.

"So you think he went to Vegas a day early, flew to Portland Wednesday, took a Northwest Orient flight to Seattle to see what it was like, and then flew back to Las Vegas—either that day or the next and then took the guard helicopter from Tucson home on Thursday?" I asked.

They nodded. Theisen added one last detail. "The guard helicopter could average seventy knots—about eighty miles an hour. He could fly home in ten hours."

We were still at it a little after eight when an impassioned woman clerk's voice sent everyone, janitors included, scampering for Ritter's courtroom. A few minutes over two hours, which included dinner, and the jury was back with a verdict! Everyone stood up while Ritter took the bench and formally inquired if the jury had reached a decision.

"We have," the foreman said, handing a folded piece of lined yellow paper to Hanna Shirata, the court clerk.

"Read the verdict, Hanna," Ritter said. Dave Winder and Richard McCoy came to their feet simultaneously and turned, facing the jury.

"We the jury," Hanna read loudly, yet sympathetically, "in the duly described case, find the defendant, Richard Floyd McCoy, Jr., guilty as charged."

"Is your verdict unanimous, Mr. Foreman?" Ritter asked.

The foreman nodded and said yes, it was.

Ritter, I could tell, was pleased. He closed court with a generous round of congratulations to a "sage and wise jury for reaching the right decision" and to "learned," I think was the word he used, "defense counsel" Dave Winder, "for a most stellar performance." Looking over his calendar for a sentencing date, he spotted me standing against the wall next to Marshal Buttars and, in a voice suggesting a party in chambers had already started without me, announced: "Mr. Rhodes, my chief probation officer, I see, is still in the courtroom, so I'll ask him to personally conduct this presentence investigation. So's," he explained, "so's we can sentence this bird right."

Two things about Richard had caught my eye every afternoon I slipped in the east door to check on the progress of the trial. One was his spontaneous and easy affection for his two children. Chanti had turned four just before the trial but could already wink back at her father without using her hands. It was a game they played often. The second was the cold poker face Richard gave cocksure witnesses like Coggin when they stood there flatfooted in the courtroom pointing a finger at him. A third thing also impressed me. Surrounded by lawyers, marshals, and a full battalion of newspaper people, he recognized me from Ritter's public introduction as I moved through the crowd and reached through the wall of noisy legal cacophony to shake hands. I found myself easily liking this man.

Earlier that day, I'd been having a cigarette in the hall with a tall, blonde newswoman who looked, I remember thinking, like Lee Remick when two U.S. marshals escorted Richard from a detention cell back to Ritter's courtroom. Richard must have recognized her as someone he'd seen before—either that or as a woman you know you want to know more about—because when he passed, he nodded, then suddenly swung around and said in a low voice, "Wish me luck, ma'am." She smiled back, not at all surprised, and nodded "Yes."

Then when Richard had passed out of hearing range, she said something, turning toward me but talking, I think, more to herself, "Was it Hemingway, damn it," she said out of either anger or putting on airs, "or Steinbeck?! Or who in the hell was it?!" Crushing the fire out of a half-smoked Benson and Hedges with the toe of a red high-heeled shoe, she said, "Well, whoever it was that had the good sense to come up with it must have been thinking about our boy McCoy when they came up with the line: 'You show me a hero and I'll show you a tragedy.' " Meaning, I remember thinking, that in order for someone like Richard McCoy to become a hero, we needed first to come up with a tragedy, such as the war in Vietnam.

I spent what was left of Thursday night reviewing grand jury transcripts and the U.S. attorney's file in addition to going over things with Jim Housley. Early Friday morning, I drove in to the office, mulling over Richard McCoy's motives. Why would the father of two young children drive 410 miles to Las Vegas over the Thanksgiving holiday unless he had something extremely important to do? He was, as Karen had said, an all-American hero and, until fairly recently, an active Mormon. He had at various times served as a Sunday-school teacher; both he and Karen had drifted into inactivity during the fall of 1971.

Based on what the FBI found out from friends and neighbors, Richard was having a difficult time in his marriage and was in terrible financial shape. He was a father and a college student desperately trying to get along on his G.I. Bill, his meager National Guard pay, and Karen's equally meager salary from the Department of Social Services as a caseworker. They said he was faithful to Karen, cared deeply about his children, and had decent habits generally. He didn't smoke or drink that they knew about. His language was respectable, too, with only occasional "hells and damns." And no one, not one person, had any information that Richard had ever gambled so much as a nickel.

But then he came up against something that courage and discipline alone couldn't handle. His body, always the instrument of his will, served notice that it was going to fail him. Oh, not the faint rumors of future dissolution and ultimate disintegration that begin to whisper to everybody in the forties and talk a little louder in the fifties, but clear and present danger. As Richard himself put it, with admirable restraint, clarity, and lack of bathos in a later motion to reduce his sentence:

> During the fall semester of my senior year in 1971, I discovered that I had a medical problem which seemed, at the time, to shatter my plans for law enforcement. After several days in the hospital and extensive tests, the problem was diagnosed as severe migraine headaches or a possible brain tumor. This meant that I was no longer employable in the field I felt qualified for. I could withhold this information from employers, but I realized that it

would be only a matter of time before I would have a blackout spell while on the job and be discharged. With a background in aviation and a degree in law enforcement, I had hoped to go into the aviation side of law enforcement. Both of these fields require high medical standards with physicals on an annual basis. I was going on twenty-nine years of age with less than a year till graduation. The cutoff age for entering these fields is thirty. Under the circumstances, I felt I had no choice but to continue along my present course, due to the time element and the monetary considerations. I tried to keep so busy, but grew despondent much of the time. My personal life then took a turn for the worse. Something that had been building up for several years. My wife's sister Denise was living with us and contributing to the problem by siding with my wife in family matters. It was not a very happy situation and a divorce seemed inevitable. The only thing that meant anything to me was my children. I even considered suicide, but there was something undignified about taking my own life. I had faced death on many occasions and had never gone out of my way to avoid it, but killing myself seemed a cowardly act. That leads up to my state of mind in March and April of 1972.

Early as I was, Theisen and Calame met me at my office on the third floor of the courthouse. No one in the FBI had interviewed McCoy after Dave Winder was appointed—and couldn't until after all of the appeals. The Federal Rules of Criminal Procedure, however, require the probation officer conducting the presentence investigation to interview the convicted person as well as others important in his life; consequently, I would be spending the next several days conducting interviews with Richard and his family.

If I had learned only one thing during those fifteen years in what I often referred to as the Department of Pest Control, it was that a good interview was the foundation for understanding a defendant. Next, with an understanding of a person's past, it's possible to predict to some extent how he may behave in the future. Not unlike a medical examiner searching through the blood, urine, and offal of a dead body for signs of disease or for more traumatic phenomena which may have been the cause of death, a probation officer as a social scientist attempts to understand the individual's personality by examining the interplay of his inherited traits, his environment, any unique tendencies of thought and behavior, and influences from disease or injury. The big difference, I think, between a dead body and the man waiting to be sentenced is that the dead body doesn't lie. With the man trying to avoid a prison sentence, often all you get for your long list of "how comes?" is an even bigger bunch of "lookie heres."

One of the first things Calame and Theisen stuck under my nose that morning was FBI memorandum "NORJAK," the code for the D. B. Cooper case, derived from abbreviating "Northwest" and "hijack."

Salt Lake City, Utah
December 23, 1971
MEMORANDUM TO ALL AGENTS:
Re: "NORJAK"

Captioned matter concerns the hijacking of Northwest Airlines Flight 305, 11/24/71, at Seattle, Washington, office of origin Seattle.

Unknown Subject boarded captioned flight at Portland, Oregon, using the name DAN COOPER. As the plane was taxiing toward the runway, Stewardess FLORENCE SCHAFFNER occupied the seat reserved for the stewardesses on the right side of the plane and behind the last row of passenger seats. Unknown Subject, who occupied the center seat in the left [last] row of three seats, turned and handed her an envelope, which she did not open for a few minutes until he glanced at her several times. She then opened the envelope and read the enclosed note, which said:

"Miss—I have a bomb here and I would like you to sit by me."

At this point Stewardess TINA MUCKLOW came toward the rear of the plane and SCHAFFNER handed TINA the note. TINA then called the pilot on the intercom.

Stewardess SCHAFFNER then sat next to the hijacker who opened a black attache case and showed her what he said was a bomb. She described the contents of the attache case as a bundle of red sticks, which she believed was dynamite. The bundle consisted of six or eight red-colored sticks approximately six to eight inches long with no writing on the outside. The hijacker was holding in his hand a wire which lead [*sic*] to the bundle of sticks and indicated that he could detonate the bomb by touching the wire to a contact. Also in the attache case was a cylindrical shaped battery about eight inches long.

At first the hijacker asked for $200,000 and two parachutes.

After SCHAFFNER left her stewardess seat and gave the note to TINA, SCHAFFNER sat beside the hijacker who, after showing the contents of the attache case, told her to, "Take this down." From her purse she obtained a pen and notepad and he dictated the following message:

"I want $200,000 by 5:00 P.M. in cash. Put it in a knapsack. I want two back parachutes and two front parachutes. When we land, I want a fuel truck ready to refuel. No funny stuff, or I'll do the job."

The crew of Richard McCoy's hijacking had hastily scribbled down phrases from his instructions to them, returning the originals to him—those originals Karen had burned. The FBI had only crude copies. Richard McCoy's instructions about landing in San Francisco, or possibly one of the flight plans, had ended: "No funny stuff. Return note to me."[1]

Both Cooper and McCoy had used small-aircraft FAA flight-plan forms to send instructions to the pilot's cabin designating flight path, altitude, flap settings, and speed. But McCoy couldn't have known that Cooper used FAA forms, Theisen pointed out, since that information was never released to the news media.

And although the news media and FBI received crank letters from dozens of people purporting to be D. B. Cooper, Theisen found one of them particularly interesting. A "patched" letter, using words and sentences clipped from magazines, was sent to the *Los Angeles Times* in December 1971. As Theisen described it, read in effect: "I got away with it, as I knew I would, and will never be caught by the FBI—signed, D. B. Cooper." The day that the letter was postmarked, said Theisen, eyeing me with great earnestness, Richard McCoy flew to Los Angeles with his Utah Air National Guard unit.

Russ Calame was a fixed-wing pilot with a college degree in engineering. So the next straw bending the camel's back was a lot clearer to him than to either Jim Theisen or me. On the ground in Seattle, Cooper had required the fuel truck to park fifty yards from the left side of the plane in, according to Cooper, "the ten o'clock position." McCoy's instructions were that the fuel truck should be a hundred feet to the left of the plane's nose. Calame drew a sketch of the two planes, taking into account that the 727-200 Boeing hijacked by McCoy is twenty feet longer than the 727-100 Boeing hijacked by Cooper. The result of overlapping the sketches was that the fuel truck in each instance was in the same relative position and about the same distance from the hijacker inside the plane. The instructions in each instance provided the hijacker with the view of activities outside the plane that he desired.

Both the Cooper and McCoy hijacks occurred close to holidays. In Cooper's hijack, it was the eve of Thanksgiving, 1971. In McCoy's hijack, it was the Friday after Easter, 1972. Both hijackings were committed, in other words, when BYU students were on vacation.

The hijacker in each instance wore a dark-brown business suit, white shirt, and tie. Cooper was believed to have worn heavy clothing like thermal underwear under his suit, while McCoy took extra clothing and ordered it brought aboard at San Francisco.

The hijacker in each case sat in the same relative position aboard the aircraft, namely the last row of seats in the coach section on the right side of the aisle. Due to the differences in the size of the two Boeing 727s, the seats occupied did not have the same seat number.

Both Cooper and McCoy wore large, wraparound, mirrored sunglasses at least a part of the time during the hijackings.

Witnesses described D. B. Cooper as olive-complected, possibly Spanish. They said he was in his late twenties to mid-forties, approximately five feet ten inches tall, weighing 160 to 170 pounds. He had short black shiny hair, probably a wig, with sideburns below his earlobes, large protruding ears, and dark eyes.

Richard McCoy, as Theisen put it, was also dolled up. Witnesses pegged him at five foot ten, 170 pounds, and in his late twenties to mid-forties. "Just look at the two of them," Theisen said, "and you'd authorize prosecution!" Richard wore a dark wig which covered his ears, heavy, dark makeup, and dark mascara on his long sideburns and mustache. Several witnesses thought him Spanish. Stewardesses aboard the Cooper plane, when shown photographs of Richard McCoy, agreed that he appeared very similar to the FBI artist's conception of D. B. Cooper. More than one witness, however, noted that Cooper's ears were much bigger than McCoy's. McCoy later admitted he used a headband under his wig to keep his ears from sticking out. Both men parted their hair on the left and wore dark reflector or wraparound sunglasses. Witnesses said Cooper's eyes were dark—possibly brown, they thought. McCoy's eyes were blue. Calame, of course, had already satisfied my curiosity about eye color.

On Saturday, 8 April 1972, when the FBI in Salt Lake City interviewed Richard, he was limping badly. "He claimed to have done it skiing," Calame said, "right in front of a BYU skiing instructor" in the middle of March. A doctor at the BYU health clinic put a cast on his ankle. On Wednesday, 5 April 1972, two days before he hijacked United Flight 855, Richard cut the cast off. "I tell you what I think," Calame said, "if it was, in fact, injured, I think he just might have injured that ankle up in Oregon under the name D. B. Cooper. Then he faked that skiing accident in front of his teacher."

In both instances, the hijacker sent the initial message advising the crew of the hijacking forward to the pilot's cabin rather than taking it forward. Cooper ordered a stewardess to take it forward; McCoy showed passenger Mike Andria an envelope with "Hijack" on it and told him to have the stewardess come back. In both hijackings, the hijacker was thoroughly acquainted with pilot terminology. Some of the terms used were "interphone," "air stairs," and "azimuth."

Both hijackers ordered four parachutes. Cooper ordered two backpack chutes and two front or chest-pack chutes (normally considered to be reserve chutes) without specifying the name or where the chutes were to come from. McCoy also asked for four chutes, Commander make, but specified that the backpack include a stopwatch and wrist altimeter to be obtained from Perry Stevens at Oakland, along with two chest packs. In both cases it was obvious that the hijacker was familiar with military chutes and also the packing of the chutes. McCoy was familiar with both military and nonmilitary parachutes. Cooper jumped with an NB-8 military chute which had a twenty-eight-foot canopy. McCoy intended to jump with a sport chute he borrowed from Larry Patterson, but that chute released in the plane prior to jumping, so he used a Commander backpack chute.

Both hijackers tried to secure the money bag to their bodies. When the parachutes were brought aboard in the Cooper hijack, Cooper asked where the D rings were and commented, "You should have known I would need D rings," then cannibalized a parachute for its nylon shrouds, which he used to secure the money around his waist and which he fashioned into a six-foot lead rope. McCoy did basically the same but was better prepared. Among the equipment he ordered aboard at San Francisco was an H harness with D rings to fasten a duffel bag he brought with him to hold the money. McCoy also gave himself a ten-foot lead rope which would allow the bag to hit the ground before he did.

Cooper insisted that Northwest Flight 305 be flown at 10,000 feet with the landing gear down and flaps lowered to 15 degrees—instructions which would obviously slow the Boeing 727-100 and facilitate his jump. Based on these instructions, Northwest personnel calculated that Cooper knew the plane could barely stay in the air at 170 knots without stalling. McCoy ordered United's Boeing 727-200, which was twenty feet longer, to fly at 16,000 feet at 175 knots per hour, indicating that he was also familiar with the slowest possible speed the 727-200 could fly without stalling. The higher altitude, Theisen said he thought, was designated because McCoy knew his flight path would take him over 10,000-foot mountains.

In the Cooper case, there was some discussion between Cooper and the flight crew about the flight path and the distance the 727 could fly on its load of fuel. McCoy, however, gave detailed, typed-out flight instructions, thus avoiding time-consuming conversations and confusion. This, Calame said, was a definite improvement by McCoy, who needed considerably more time to prepare for the jump.

Nor were these all of the parallels. Both Cooper and McCoy instructed that all written materials be returned. Both Cooper and McCoy had passengers deplane using the frontmost door of the plane. Both Cooper and McCoy allowed at least one stewardess to deplane. In each case, they had at least one stewardess stay in the tourist section while they were preparing for the jump. Just prior to jumping, Cooper ordered Tina Mucklow into the pilot's cabin. On her way up, she closed the first-class curtain as instructed and turned out all cabin lights. After McCoy put on his jumpsuit and shaved his mustache, like Cooper, he ordered Diane Surdam to turn off all cabin lights in the tourist section and go forward to the pilot's cabin.

"One thing we haven't listed," Calame said as if he himself wasn't sure, "is which one needed help getting the aft cabin door open and the rear stairs down, and which one didn't. Cooper,"

Calame said, "needed help, I think they said, and McCoy didn't. That's right, isn't it, Jim?"

"If McCoy needed help," Theisen said, "he never let any of the crew know about it."

"Could I do it, Jim?" I asked. "I mean if I'd never been shown or had any prior interest in it, could I just walk to the back of a Boeing 727, open the necessary doors, and bail the hell out while the plane was in flight?"

"Well, I know I couldn't," Theisen said. "Not without being shown. First you have to open the rear door between the two bathrooms. Then there's a small narrow hallway that leads to another door where the stairs are released from. There's a plaque next to the door with a bunch of instructions; but unless someone helps you, you're probably not going to make it alone."

"So," I said, "if McCoy did the Cooper plane first and had help like the stewardess said, then he wouldn't need any help on the one you all caught him on, would he?"

"Exactly," Theisen smiled, "exactly. And you remember how Tina Mucklow said Cooper lit one Raleigh cigarette after . . . "

"Yes," I interrupted, "and McCoy's from Raleigh, North Carolina, so you don't need to get into that again."

"Many of these small bits and pieces may seem insignificant to you, Rhodes," Calame said disapprovingly, as if I were intentionally playing the devil's advocate, "but when we lay them all out end-to-end, they stretch all the way from Provo to Las Vegas to Portland, Seattle, and back, full circle, to Provo, Utah."

There was a problem with timing for both Cooper and McCoy. Calame pressed on to the next point. During the Northwest hijacking, the flight from Portland to Seattle was so short it didn't provide the necessary time to obtain the money and parachutes without the plane's circling the airport three and a half hours before landing. The total time in flight, circling, and time on the ground was a little over four hours—obviously a long time for one hijacker to maintain absolute control over a planeful of people, especially when it's on the ground with FBI swarming around. McCoy solved this problem the next time by picking a longer flight.

"Prior to the hijacking of United Flight 855," Calame said in his most ordinary lecture voice, "McCoy told his wife she should pick him up at Spanish Fork between eight-thirty and nine-thirty P.M., but not to wait past ten P.M. This," Calame said, "I believe, is a valid explanation for how McCoy arrived at the hour Karen was to pick him up. United Flight 855 was scheduled to depart Denver for Los Angeles at two-thirty P.M. Mountain Time, but was late and actually departed closer to three P.M. McCoy let his hijack intentions be known at about three-fifteen to three-twenty P.M. Assuming he knew from the hijacking of the D. B. Cooper plane that it would require approximately four hours and twenty minutes to get the money and be back in the air, he could plan on flying from Denver to San Francisco in that length of time, obtain the money and parachutes, and leave San Francisco by six or six-thirty P.M., Pacific Coast time. Computing the actual flight time from San Francisco at a hundred-seventy-five knots per hour, he would be jumping south of Provo, Utah, between eight-thirty and nine-thirty P.M. Mountain time. However, Gebhardt's stalling in San Francisco wrecked his timetable, and when he touched ground about eleven-fifteen P.M., Karen was in the wrong place to pick him up."

"What else?" I said.

They hadn't run out of parallels. Both Cooper and McCoy inspected the money before letting the plane leave the runway. Both Cooper and McCoy insisted that a stewardess sit near to act as a messenger. Cooper had Tina Mucklow sit beside him; McCoy had Diane Surdam sit beside him at first and later sit in front of him. Having the stewardess in front was a definite refinement; the hijacker could see everything she did but she couldn't study his characteristics.

In both hijacks, the flight path paralleled a major north-south interstate freeway. In Cooper's case, he had Interstate 5 and the lights of Vancouver, Washington, and Portland, Oregon, to orient himself as he crouched out on the extended aft staircase. McCoy had Interstate 15, Provo's lights, and Utah Lake for bearings.

"And that's not all," said Theisen. I'd heard that before, but he still had my undivided attention. "Following McCoy's arrest, we found newspaper articles about Cooper in McCoy's Volkswagen with a file of Cooper clippings at the house."

"If all it took," Calame said, his voice hoarsening slightly from the long, dry conversation, "was a preponderance of evidence, as it is in a civil case, we'd convict McCoy of the Cooper hijack in a two-day trial or I'd buy you lunch."

Yes, I thought, if all you needed was to show x number of similarities, there were certainly enough of them. That tie and tie clasp were dynamite. Handled right, that alone was enough to convict, with his family saying, "That's Richard's. Where'd you guys get it?" Then watch the jury when Agent Theisen testifies in his unemotional Minnesota accent: "The tie and the clasp, Your Honor, were located during a routine FBI search of the D. B. Cooper plane." The fact that McCoy just happened to be in Las Vegas during the Cooper hijack was damn good, too, I thought.

"But," Russ Calame said, shrugging his shoulders, "a preponderance of evidence isn't good enough. In a criminal case, the jury must be convinced of guilt beyond a reasonable doubt. So what we needed," Calame said, holding his first finger straight up at Jim Theisen, "was one good, clear fingerprint from one of those airline magazines on the Cooper plane. The ones Reno forgot to send back to the Identification Division. Either that," and now he was looking at me, "or hope Rhodes can squeeze something worthwhile out of McCoy tomorrow."

Judge Ritter had given me from Thursday evening, 29 June until the following Tuesday, 4 July, to find out what made Richard McCoy tick. Four days, including the weekend. Then I had to submit a report along with my recommendation.

---

[1] The NORJAK memo containing the Cooper hijack note was interesting, but, frankly, the threat, "no funny stuff," had absolutely no significance for me. Years later it would come back to haunt me. In 1982, just before leaving office, I decided to resurrect the old 1972 Cooper-McCoy hypothesis. Ten years had passed, McCoy was dead, and the case was closed—so agent friends began to loosen up a little. Half a dozen, probably, in both the Salt Lake City and Washington, D.C., offices, would return my calls, laugh about the Ritter era, and read me what they could find out of the McCoy file. Later, in 1985, when this book was started, my old notes from those telephone conversations had McCoy in his instructions to the crew using "no monkey business," "no tricks," and the same banal little threat Cooper had used, "no funny stuff." Suddenly, written documentation from both the Cooper and the McCoy files, where the exact same threat had been used, became vital. In 1986, material, as provided for under the Freedom of Information Act, was released by the bureau. We received a copy of the 23 December 1971 D. B. Cooper memo which had ended with "no funny stuff," but the FBI either couldn't find or wouldn't release the note from the McCoy case where the same threat was made. We had only my notes to go by.

Our final effort, in October 1990, was to have the U.S. Clerk of the Utah District Court, Marcus Zimmer, order the court's file returned from the archives at Denver, Colorado. Not all of the crew's notes on Richard's instructions had been entered into evidence—but we were hoping. Those hopes were dashed. Only a skeleton file of the McCoy trial remained. It had, as is traditional, customary, and legal, been purged of nonessential materials after a legally specified interval—and that interval had passed. What the file did contain, however, was an empty, clear plastic evidence envelope labeled "Exhibit: Note." We found that disappointing. It's possible that the court officially transferred the evidence back to the arresting agency—the Salt Lake FBI office—after the trial. That's fairly routine procedure. In fact, the federal court docket on the case shows Ritter's order to return all "exhibits" to "contributors" dated in February 1973. But in that case, the court should have sent it back in the plastic evidence envelope. Even more interesting is the fact that the FBI *also* has an empty envelope. Responding to a request that Russ Calame made, the Salt Lake City FBI office checked its file for him and specified that the numbered evidence envelope containing that particular note had been sent to the court 26 June 1972. The empty evidence envelope remained in the file. Interviews with case agents, court reporters, and others who heard the testimony, interviewed McCoy, read the notes, or saw them got the same response: "It sounds familiar, but that was almost twenty years ago."

Interview with a Hijacker
Saturday, 1 July 1972

Early July mornings in Salt Lake City generally arrive bright and cool, masquerading as spring if it's early enough, and arid, too, with the crystalline snowfields looming brilliantly on the surrounding Wasatch Mountains. The jail, by contrast, was overcrowded and sweltering hot. It smelled of cigarette butts and stale brown tobacco water. I remembered having a thousand bits of information swirling around in my head from the conversation with Theisen and Calame. But the pattern was becoming clearer.

It was after three o'clock Saturday afternoon when I finally got around to Calame's and Theisen's list of what I had labeled "Cooper questions." By that time of day, the monotonous morning smells of french toast and Folger's coffee had been chased away by the smell of hot Crisco and chicken frying down on the first floor. Neither Richard nor I had eaten all day and it was beginning to tell on both of us. But Richard looked drawn, much older than his twenty-nine years.

"Physical and emotional ups and downs," one of the women jailers told me on the elevator, "have taken their toll on Richard. Four months in jail, the trial, reporters, and the guilt he carries around over what he's done to his children. It must be a lot the same," she said, "as when we're told we're dying; denial at first, then self-pity followed by fits of anger, eventually the final and weakening stages of acceptance." Watching for signs of what she had said, Richard's mood, I thought, seemed to straddle the latter two: anger over his sister-in-law Denise's betrayal and acceptance of the inevitable—spending the rest of his life in prison. I left Theisen's copy of the composite drawing of Cooper in plain view between Richard and me on the interview table.

I started off more or less in the middle of what I'd been asked to do. Starting in the middle gave me the option of working both forward and backward in questioning. Shifting the subject around keeps a suspect off balance and keeps him from anticipating questions before they're asked.

"Do you smoke?" I asked. "Cigarettes. Do you smoke cigarettes?"

I knew he didn't. But D. B. Cooper had. It may have been reaching somewhat, I thought, on Calame and Theisen's part, but you couldn't rule out the possibility that Cooper's smoking was just something he did to throw people off.

"Nope," Richard answered. "I don't use tobacco, Mr. Rhodes, but it doesn't bother me when you do."

"Never?" I asked. "And you born and raised around Raleigh, North Carolina, the tobacco capital of the world?" I lit up a Marlboro and told him I thought everyone smoked or chewed tobacco in Raleigh.

"I have uncles and aunts who smoke, close friends that smoke, and of course I've tried it too, if that's what you want to hear," he says, as if he'd just been appointed Surgeon General, "but no, I can't say I enjoy smoking."

Calame had explained that tying the two cases together had been a tough job. The memories of witnesses having to do with the everyday movements of someone like McCoy, who was not under suspicion in November 1971, were hazy at best. Many of the records seven months later were unavailable.

"Do you gamble, Richard?" I asked. "Shoot dice? This sort of thing?"

"No. I don't gamble. Don't have the money to shoot dice," he said. "Don't know how. Probably wouldn't if I did. I have a wife and two children, you know."

The next question was whether he drank.

"Do I drink?" he repeated.

"Yes," I said. "Do you drink alcohol?"

"Nope, don't drink or gamble. I've had liquor a few times in my life, Mr. Rhodes, but when you're ready to jot these things down for Judge Ritter, give him the truth: Richard Floyd McCoy, Jr., doesn't drink, smoke, or gamble. Because he doesn't."

From where I sat that morning, the face across from me seemed identical to the composite drawing of D. B. Cooper that lay between us. Except for the color of the eyes, of course. Richard's eyes were light blue, close together. Something about his nose and scarred cheekbones gave him the look of a lanky prizefighter. Richard's eyes rested often on the Cooper drawing. He was clearly curious, but he never touched it with his hands. To me that seemed unnatural.

"If you can," I began softly with what Calame and Theisen felt to be their second strongest piece of evidence, "and I know this was a while back, Richard, but try to remember where you were last Thanksgiving. November 25th," I said, "and the day before—Wednesday, November 24th, 1971."

His complexion turned the color of potted ham and his head turned toward the drawing of Cooper—but his small blue eyes stayed on me.

"Thanksgiving? Well, let's see, Mr. Rhodes. Thanksgiving is still a holiday, isn't it, so naturally I would have been around the house. I didn't have school and I didn't have guard, so"—he's onto me, I thought, and then he said—"I was home. Why?"

"Careful now," I tell him, "about how you answer these next few questions. Any one of them could cause you a whole lot of trouble."

My next few questions would come very slowly, in deliberate whispers. This was a questioning technique I used to control the rhythm, the opposite of a rapid-fire, staccato approach used generally by two or more interrogators capable of keeping track of the answers. Mine was a simple litany of short questions that shifted the suspect's attention to hearing what was said—followed back and forth by a series of nervous rejoinders.

"Cook or clean," I asked, "or help Karen with anything she might remember, Richard?"

"Yes," his voice was low like mine; he cleared his throat. "I cooked, yes, and helped Karen with Thanksgiving dinner."

"What time of day was this you helped Karen and Denise around the house?"

"Most of the day I'd say, Mr. Rhodes. I'm sure I was home until after six o'clock."

"What time did you eat?" I asked.

"Two o'clock?" he answered, with a rising inflection, as though he were asking a question, "two or two-thirty?"

"Are you absolutely sure about the time, Richard?" I asked him. "Are you positive?"

"You have my permission to ask Karen or Denise, either one," Richard said.

"And you were home," I asked, "with Karen, Denise, and the kids all day, November 25th, 1971, Thanksgiving Day. No question in your mind about that, is there? Were you there all evening too?"

"If you don't believe me," he said, with some heat, "ask Karen then, and Denise, for God's sake. They'll tell you where I was."

The FBI still had Denise in protective custody. And they couldn't talk to Karen—a wife can't be forced to give evidence against a husband. "The FBI's already talked with Denise, and you're dead right, Richard," I told him, "Denise has an alibi for you. Spits it out," I tell him, "like she'd been rehearsed."

"So then what's the big deal?" Richard snapped back in a voice not nearly as upset as he'd have me believe.

I looked at Richard. And I hadn't even mentioned yet the dark, narrow, clip-on necktie and mother-of-pearl tie clasp that Denise and Mildred Burns had positively identified as Richard's.

I was saving the tie and the clasp for the next day, Sunday, when I would have more time. "What I'd like you to tell me," I continued, "so I can tell Theisen, is how you can be in Provo until after six in the evening, cooking Thanksgiving dinner, Richard, and still make a collect call from the Tropicana Hotel-Casino in Las Vegas, Nevada, at ten forty-one that same night. Someone, Karen or Denise, accepted the charges. Now tell me, Richard, how do you go about that?"

"And how do you know it was me who made the call, Mr. Rhodes? Could have been anybody."

"And what these agents also want to know," I continued, "is why Denise would find it necessary to alibi for you when all she had to say was, 'I don't remember where Richard was. I simply don't remember.' But she's sticking her neck out a mile about you being home that day. But for the sake of argument, let's assume for a minute that you're right. You didn't make that call—someone else made it, okay? Well, I've got an even better one for you. Explain, if you can, how someone driving your green Volkswagen bug, with North Carolina license-plate number SA 1334, purchased 5.6 gallons of gas just after eleven P.M. Thanksgiving night at the Power Thrust Service Station in Las Vegas, using your credit card? Someone using

BankAmericard #4763 160 217 773—which is yours, isn't it?—signed your name, Richard Floyd McCoy, Jr., to that credit charge slip. How about it?"

"Well, how about it?" Richard said. "You seem to have all the answers. You tell me."

"One more thing Calame tells me. Calame said the Vegas office sent a copy of that charge slip from Power Thrust back to the FBI lab in Washington with some of your military handwriting for comparison. The writing on the gasoline charge slip was definitely yours. Calame said his lab men say there's no question about it: you bought the gas, you signed the ticket, and you, he said, were in Las Vegas Thanksgiving night. They say there are three flights a day from Vegas to Portland and return. He and Theisen have it in their heads you might have purchased that one-way ticket at the airport in Portland under the name Dan Cooper."

Richard admitted nothing, nor did he jump up and frantically deny anything either. We sat looking at each other. I wasn't sure how much further I should go, so I just sat studying his face, ears, and the rest of him, trying to fit Calame's and Theisen's narratives and Richard's answers into some sort of mosaic. For the moment, at least, Calame's hypothesis had more substance than Richard had sound explanations.

"What Calame can't get through his head," I mused, as much to myself as him, because I really didn't want to believe Richard did it, "is what a Brigham Young University student, with two small children, who neither drinks, smokes, shoots dice, nor chases around on his wife would be doing in Las Vegas on Thanksgiving Day. Someone who has no money. Calame said three weeks earlier, November 2d, 1971, this same destitute Mormon boy finds his way to Las Vegas, registers under the name Richard McCoy at the Westward Ho Motel on Las Vegas Boulevard, pays the bill himself, and spends the night. Why would he be there," I said, "why, unless it were a Tuesday, which it was, and this same young man, using the name McCoy, intended to catch a plane the next morning from Las Vegas to Portland—then on to Seattle—to get the feel of the Wednesday flight. A dry run, a carbon copy of the rehearsal flight you made, Richard, from Salt Lake to Denver the Friday before you actually hijacked Flight 855."

Richard said nothing.

It was now five o'clock. Karen and Myrtle had been waiting for

Richard since about three o'clock, so he and I hauled off and kicked the cell door a couple of good ones. I left, planning to come back on Sunday morning.

Although Richard and I hadn't put anything on paper Saturday, I'd hit him pretty good with what he and I eventually ended up referring to as the other thing. "Where were you last Thanksgiving, Richard?" I'd pushed. "Home," he'd say. "I've got witnesses. Denise and Karen." Then I'd hit him with how his ankle felt, how he had injured it, and had he seen a doctor. Then we'd jump back to why he was in Vegas during the Cooper thing. "How many times do I have to tell you," he'd swear, holding his right hand in the air, "I helped Karen cook turkey dinner," and he'd frown and shake his head as if in disgust. His story was full of holes, and no matter how hard he tried or how innocent he looked, he knew I knew.

Good investigators and interrogators put together a series of questions with which they control the interview. That gives them a chance to concentrate on not only what was said but also how easily the suspect answered it. When you hit a nerve, you make a mark by that question, continue forward a few more, and then, bam! without warning, you jump back to that question, watching for the same body English given you on the first go-round. When a person is sitting comfortably, he nearly always has his hands behind his head, folded chest-high in front, or in his lap. Then watch him. When he's lying, or about to lie, his dominant hand is compulsively drawn to his mouth, his nose, or his eyes. They're among the body's most sensitive areas. You feel stress there first.

A little like the lie detector machine, a seasoned old investigator isn't going to be the easiest person in town to bullshit. That Saturday in jail, Richard had fidgeted, sweat, stretched the bottom of his T-shirt over both knees, and, just before I'd called it a day, picked his teeth with an open paper clip until blood ran out both corners of his mouth. That was when I gave him my handkerchief and told him, "Tomorrow, Richard, I'll be back! After you're out of church. Around nine," I said, "and I want answers," furrowing my forehead, squinting my eyes and looking as much like a son of a bitch as I could. "Calame wants answers. So does Jim Theisen. And you, my man, have what they want. Think about it," I said. "Sleep on it, if you need to."

Actually, I didn't sleep too well myself that Saturday night. But what kept me awake wasn't Richard McCoy at all. It was Willis W. Ritter. Ritter trusted my opinion, and I knew that. But he'd liked other chiefs just as well before I came, and he'd gotten rid of them. He'd embarrassed a couple of them in public—brought one chief to tears in open court, the marshal told me. "Ritter," as Dave Winder used to say when he was the federal prosecutor, "knows, more than any other man alive, how to use power."

Judge Ritter wasn't mentally ill in the classic textbook sense. But as we got closer to the end, you'd hear the word *paranoid* more often than adjectives like "arbitrary," or "capricious." Judicial intemperance and a secretary who both looked and typed like the Mona Lisa had once brought Mike Wallace and his *Sixty Minutes* crew to Salt Lake City. Both Utah senators were mustering national support to have Ritter impeached. The Republican U. S. attorney assigned his best deputies the single task of researching ways of either neutralizing Ritter's powers as chief judge or somehow getting rid of him altogether. So, in fairness to Judge Ritter, I have to say that most of his suspicions about people being out to get him were not imagined. And the last thing I wanted to do during those last difficult days was add to his problems. Because if he needed someone to turn on, Rhodes was never far away.

Rule 32(c) of the Federal Rules of Criminal Procedure mandates that the probation office prior to sentencing on any person found guilty of a crime against the U.S. government "shall make a presentence investigation and report to the court . . . any prior criminal record, information about his characteristics, his financial condition, and the circumstances affecting his behavior as may be helpful in imposing sentence." Ritter, like most federal judges, insisted that the report include a "Statement of the Offense" from the defendant. It not only helped the judge better understand what the offender did and how he went about it but also, in mitigation of punishment, how the defendant felt about the damage he'd done. Remorse, hostility, or whatever. Once the person had either pleaded or been found guilty of the offense, he was no longer in danger of self-incrimination. In other words, nothing he told a probation officer about the crime subsequent to his finding of guilt could be construed as a violation of his Fifth Amendment rights. Even when he appealed his conviction, the appellate court never asked for nor received a copy of the presentence report—which very often included an admission of guilt. But I was never sure Judge Ritter understood the way it worked or agreed that it didn't violate the defendant's Fifth Amendment rights.

I knew Richard was on the verge of saying something significant about the Cooper case. David Winder had specifically told Richard Thursday night after the trial to "cooperate with Rhodes. Give him everything he asks for," he said. "Ritter listens to Rhodes." And I had no objection to doing the FBI the favor of asking their questions. Besides that, I was downright curious myself. But balanced against those forces was my uneasiness about Ritter who, with all the news media around, was wrought up to an even higher pitch of paranoia than usual. The upshot of my uneasy night was a firm decision not to get any deeper into the Cooper thing with Richard. At least, not that Sunday. I'd wait until after he was sentenced on the United Airlines case. He wasn't going anyplace for awhile. What I'd do, I thought, was wait until after Ritter sentenced him. Ritter would then lose all interest in the case, forget who McCoy was. Then, just before the marshal moved Richard to a federal penitentiary, I'd slip over after work quietly and "do the people of Utah," in Russ Calame and Jim Theisen's words, "a public service."

18 Second Interview with a Hijacker
Sunday, 2 July 1972

Richard was housed in maximum security on the third floor with half a dozen guys in for murder and other serious crimes against the person, separated from the general population. The social structure in a prison is pretty much the same as it is on the outside. A prisoner gains status according to his accomplishments. A bank robber commands more respect than a liquor-store bandit, a burglar more than a bad-check writer, and so on. The number of arrests a man has isn't important. Some small-time convicts have criminal records as long as the Dead Sea Scrolls and can't find out when they're supposed to be in court. A federal prisoner however, suggests class and commands the respect of guards and inmates alike. Richard was not only a daring criminal but also a well-publicized one. He'd made *Time* magazine and was being treated as a celebrity.

It was a little after nine o'clock that Sunday morning when Mormon services let out in the jail chapel and Richard was led into the interview cell. Without so much as a good morning he dropped a very official-looking 5 x 7 envelope in front of me and flopped down in one of the two steel-latticed chairs. I opened the envelope and read a letter that managed to make itself perfectly clear:

THE CHURCH OF JESUS CHRIST OF
LATTER-DAY SAINTS
THE OFFICE OF THE STAKE PRESIDENT
June 8, 1972

Richard F. McCoy:

This letter is to notify you that on June 6, 1972, the Provo Stake High Council Court, in accordance with the law of the Church of Jesus Christ of Latter-day Saints, excommunicated you from the Church on the grounds of skyjacking and extortion.

Excommunication from the Church means that the rights and privileges of Church membership have been withdrawn, and that you no longer possess the priesthood of God. You may attend sacrament and auxiliary meetings and general conference sessions. Tithing and other contributions may not be paid, but you should be encouraged to deposit such funds until the time of your possible baptism.

It is sincerely hoped that the day will come when through your genuine repentance you may once again be associated with the Church of Jesus Christ of Latter-day Saints. Repentance is not only to desist from a sin but also to keep the commandments of the Lord.

> Provo Stake Presidency
> Roy W. Doxey
> Bliss H. Crandall
> Dean E. Terry

I looked up at Richard. He was wearing baggy, faded blue jeans, the kind the Navy used to issue, anchored to his lean hips with a piece of black shoestring. A white T-shirt, almost too small for his broad shoulders, labeled him PRISONER SALT LAKE COUNTY JAIL. He'd lost twenty pounds, he told me. I remember thinking that he'd also lost something else. It was his will to live, I could see, that had taken the beating. Sunday looked to be a long day for both of us. The day before, I had intentionally come into the interview without pencil or pad. I wasn't going to push him too hard the first day. Loosen him up a little, I had thought, plant a few of Theisen's and Calame's D. B. Cooper seeds and see what sprouted Sunday. This morning, I pulled out a pocket-sized dictaphone and set it on the table between us.

Richard and I had no more than given it a couple of good one-two-threes when one of the jailers swung open the heavy steel door and set a cup of coffee in front of me. "Would you like a cup, Richard?" asked this young, easygoing guard wearing a new stiff brown sheriff's uniform, as if to say, since you've been excommunicated. . . .

"I'd better not," Richard answered, as if he wasn't completely sure himself what his status was. "Still against the Word of Wisdom, you know," studying me from his side of the long, green metal table. I lit up a Marlboro to go with my coffee, took a couple of deep drags, and asked him if he still felt himself to be a Mormon.

"Yes," he answered, "I guess I do. And you, Mr. Rhodes," he asked, "what are you?"

"Catholic," I said, at least I guessed I still was, and suddenly the guard was standing next to us again pouring more ninety-octane coffee. It wasn't me he was buttering up. It was Richard. Probation officers are generally looked upon by jail guards as would-be priests who at the swearing-in ceremony got cold feet and now wander around aimlessly under the Father Flanagan Doctrine: there is no such thing as a bad boy.

We talked about Richard's sentence. He sounded desperate but beaten. He could receive a forty-five-year sentence, and not less than twenty, and there was no reason to hope Judge Ritter would give him anything less than the maximum. As if turning through the pages of his life one at a time, he said, "I can't even comprehend forty-five years. I'm only twenty-nine now, and I feel like an old man. Even if I got out in say thirty years," he said, "Chanti . . . " Tears came to his eyes. I looked away. He stopped talking for a minute and then went on. "Chanti would be thirty-five years old; Rich, thirty-two." There was a long pause. I looked at him again. This time, his eyes were steely. "I don't think I'll put them through that," he said, "or me either."

Karen, two days before, on Friday, had confessed: "Richard McCoy is hell-bent, Mr. Rhodes, on taking his life, and he's asked me to bring something to him at the jail to do it with. I haven't made up my mind yet," I can still hear her saying thoughtfully, "but this whole thing, you understand, is as much my fault as it is his."

Richard and I that Sunday morning thumbed through a standard probation worksheet and recorded his family and marital history, military service, financial situation, and health (physical and emotional), then took a statement in his own handwriting of how he went about taking over United Flight 855. Richard added at the bottom, for Ritter's benefit, that he wasn't surprised by the jury's verdict. "They had no other choice, Your Honor," he wrote. Then he gave Judge Ritter and Dave Winder both a bunch of nice adjectives. I believe he meant them.

In his statement of offense, which we wrote and rewrote to protect Karen, I painstakingly avoided any mention, matchup, or comparison of the McCoy and the Cooper cases. This statement, I emphasized to Richard, at least for today, will deal only with what you are convicted of. Okay? Not what Calame and Theisen or anybody else might speculate you did, and he nodded that he understood. But he didn't. His mind was on something else. Because when I started gathering things up to leave, I noticed he was holding the FBI's composite drawing of D. B. Cooper.

"Aren't you forgetting something?" Richard said.

"I don't know," I told him. "Am I?"

"That's up to you," he said. "You wanted to talk bad enough yesterday about—you know, that other thing."

I tried my damnedest to keep a straight face and not say, "What other thing?" but I couldn't.

"This thing," he said, slowly and carefully, as if he were just entering a dark room and having trouble finding the light switch, "this guy here," thumping Cooper's wanted poster with his thumb and second finger.

We'd been locked up together already six or seven hours that Sunday. We hadn't eaten anything. I'd played it right down the middle that Sunday with Richard. Hadn't used the tough-guy approach like I had the day before. Nor had I tried to con him with the soft, sweet phony stuff defense lawyers and tape recorders can see right through. Honesty and straightforwardness was what I wanted. Integrity, I thought. Something I could stand up with in front of Ritter, if I had to, and shake my head "no." McCoy, I'd say to a packed courtroom, just blurted out the thing about D. B. Cooper. Until then, Your Honor, I'd swear under oath, nothing until he unexpectedly blurted it out. The entire conversation, I'd tell Ritter like one of his children, was recorded on tape that Sunday.

"Shall we have the clerk," Ritter probably would say in this deep judicial voice he used to get the answers he wanted, "play this tape of Rhodes's back?" Jim Housley and Dave Winder, not wanting to irritate Ritter, would both stipulate that "any conversation or connection between McCoy and Cooper found on that tape was not, we feel sure, provoked by the probation officer."

A suspect would sometimes blurt something out intentionally about a second crime, and it wouldn't be your fault at all. The Supreme Court said you could use it, too, as long as you didn't know it was coming. I reached over and punched the record button on the Sony dictaphone between us and told Richard I was sorry, I wasn't following him. What was it again? This thing you want to talk to me about?

After all the time I'd spent listening to Theisen and Calame talk Cooper-McCoy comparisons, I was dying that Sunday to see how the name D. B. Cooper fit in Richard's mouth. What it sounded like when the man who actually thought it up used it. Would he trip himself up and somehow refer to Cooper as I? Would he know enough to use Dan Cooper, laugh about how the press mistakenly printed D. B. in the paper, and how that caught on? Or would he blurt out something that Calame and Theisen either forgot to tell me or intentionally withheld to see what I came up with? With Ritter's stand on a person's constitutional rights, anything I asked about Cooper, I knew, could get me fired. But Richard hadn't said "no." In fact, it was he who seemed to be pushing the subject. "Do you, or don't you, Mr. Rhodes," with a take it or leave it expression on his face, "want to talk about this thing or not?"

"What other thing?" I say, trying to cover my ass with Ritter later on. "Be more specific."

"*This* other thing," he said, flapping the wanted poster of Cooper back and forth as if it were a wet photograph.

"Are you absolutely sure you know what you've got there?" I asked him.

"Yes," he answered. "I know what it is, but I'm beginning to wonder if you do."

I said, "You tell me, then. What is it?"

"Let's just forget it," Richard said, standing and sailing the poster of Cooper across the table and raising his eyebrows like I'd lost my mind. "You know what I think," he said, just above a whisper, "I think you're having a harder time, for some reason, than I am."

"The trouble I'm having," I said, and I could hear myself catch my breath, "is it's late." Then I tell him, "Maybe we ought to give it up for today. We'll get into this thing much deeper later on, okay?"

Richard nodded, and I remember thinking that he may have been every bit as anxious to clear up this Cooper thing as Theisen and Calame.

I grabbed the jail elevator down to the first floor just as the loudspeaker announced that Richard had family waiting in the visitor's room.

I never went back. Now, twenty years later, it's pretty easy to see what we should have done. Back in 1972, pieces of information were available but didn't seem to be pertinent; consequently, no follow-up was conducted or detailed records ever kept. Now that same information has become pertinent, but Karen McCoy still refuses to talk, or to sign authorization forms under the Freedom of Information Act giving me access to obtain many of the files. I can't say that I blame her. Even though her children are now grown, she feels she has to protect them and has struggled for twenty years to keep some semblance of family pride and privacy.

The direction of most investigations changes as the pieces of the puzzle are located and put into place. A suspect in a particular crime may emerge in the early stages of the investigation and be eliminated quickly by subsequent developments, only to be resurrected again later in the investigation. That's what's happened in this case. In the Cooper-McCoy hijacking cases, no one from the FBI ever interviewed Richard McCoy, a prime suspect. No one, to my knowledge, ever asked Karen McCoy those same questions, either.

And I didn't either. But one person did: McCoy's court-appointed attorney David K. Winder, now an active United States District Judge in Utah. Judge Winder told me that he asked McCoy if he had pulled the D. B. Cooper hijacking. McCoy simply answered, "I don't want to talk to you about it."

19 Ritter on a Monday Morning
Monday, 3 July 1972

Just before noon on Monday, 3 July, a call came into my office on a private line labeled "Judge Ritter" in a discreet but definite red.

"Rhoooowdes," I answered in a long, deep voice.

"Riiiiiitter," Ritter answered back, and we both had a belly laugh.

"Where are you, Judge?" I asked. "Hotel?"

"Hotel," Ritter said, "but I'm on my way over."

"How about a few oysters on the half shell?" I said.

"Blue point?" Ritter asked.

"Fresh, plump blue point," I told him. "At the Hilton."

"No, no," Ritter said, "I've just eaten an orange." Then he laughed again and added, "and two apples. Clothes won't fit me, but I need to see you in chambers. A little before one," he said. "I need to go over a few things with you."

Ritter's necktie, when I got there, was already thrown to one side, his shirtsleeves pushed up rather than rolled. He was writing as if his life depended on it. His desk was about as old as he was. It was made of heavy dark walnut, too big for most judges even back then, when being a federal judge really meant something. A waist-high pedestal on his left held a leatherbound dictionary about the size of an apartment house. On his right stood a brown-shaded world globe the size of a Volkswagen. Pushing himself far enough away from his desk to be comfortable, he said, "It wouldn't surprise me to find out I've spent as much time answering complaints instigated by these sons-a-bitchin' Mormons the past quarter of a century as I have out front trying lawsuits. Put an eye on this thing," Ritter said, handing me a dozen or so yellow handwritten pages addressed to the United States Congress. "Tell me what you think of it."

The Honorable Peter Rodino
Chairman, House Judiciary Committee

Dear Congressman:
This morning the *Salt Lake Tribune* arrived with my breakfast with an article about the House Judiciary Committee meeting the day before. That meeting and a previous *secret* meeting of the Sub-Committee concerned me very much.

I have been a United States District Judge for nearly thirty years. Because I am a working Judge I have long recognized the obligation to keep my own counsel and not speak out for publication. I have something of a reputation for refusing to talk to the press. I told N.B.C. this week that: "I am an old hand at telling the press where to go."

However, the so-called "judicial controversy" about me has gone too far so I enter the lists in defense of my own good name. I protest against any more "secret" meetings with my detractors. I want to meet with them face-to-face. I want the opportunity to present my side of the matter—the truth. Before the prestigious Committee on the Judiciary of the House of Representatives recommends another Judge for Utah, I most respectfully request an opportunity to be heard. This is of the utmost importance to me. This incessant drumfire of malicious and scurrilous character assassination must be laid to rest once and for all. The *Tribune* article reported that: "During the debate Representative Ramano L. Maxxoli, D., Kentucky, wanted to know if there is also a 'religious overtone' in the Utah judicial controversy. 'That's preposterous—that's malicious and can't stand the light of day,' replied Representative Santini, whose father-in-law is a Mormon L.D.S. Stake Patriarch in Nevada.

"Again Representative Santini emphasized he was offering his amendments in behalf of Representative Gunn McKay, D., Utah, and in the interest of dealing with 'the judicial nightmare' in the Utah Federal District Court.

"Representative Santini again mentioned the Writ of Mandamus before the U.S. Tenth Circuit Court of Appeals in Denver to bar Judge Ritter from hearing any cases involving the Federal

178

Government. Another member of the Committee stated, however, that there had been no action taken on the Writ."

Members of the Judiciary Committee, I say to you that Representative Santini is wrong on both scores: One, there is no "judicial nightmare in my Court" and, two, it is damned right, there are religious overtones in this judicial controversy—and worse. That is what it is all about.

Malicious Mormonism, McCarthy-Nixon "dirty tricks" and conspiracy to bring down a Federal Judge are written all over it by the extreme right elements in the Republican Party.

Two of the Mormon Church's principal character assassins and muck rakers are its TV station, K.S.L., and its daily scandal sheet, the *Deseret News*, known widely as the Deserted News. The Mormon Church has taken over practically every other public office in the State of Utah. They have been trying for a long time to take over the Federal Court for the District of Utah. The extreme Rightist Republicans, the John Birch Society, Nixon "dirty tricks" element has been fighting me for thirty years. They fought my appointment by President Harry S Truman in 1949. In 1950 they fought and defeated Senator Elbert D. Thomas, who recommended me to President Truman for appointment to the Federal Bench.

Having failed in his vicious efforts to defeat me, Mormon Stake President Arthur V. Watkins (a Stake President is an administrator governing several bishops), seeking to fence me in, succeeded in obtaining a second Federal Judgeship in Utah, and appointed a Mormon of his choice to that Judgeship. Not only that, Watkins also succeeded in appointing a man of his choice to a vacancy in the Tenth U.S. Circuit Court of Appeals, Judge David T. Lewis. Former Republican Governor J. Bracken Lee had earlier given Lewis a State District Judgeship to fill a vacancy there.

Shortly after the second Federal Judge took office—very shortly thereafter—he petitioned the Tenth Circuit to adopt a rule for the assignment of cases between the two of us. This the Circuit did. As a result of this Order, I, as Chief Judge, have had nothing whatever to do with the assignment of cases in our Court. The Circuit Court Order set up sort of a lottery. One of the falsehoods widely circulated is that as Chief Judge I abuse the power of assignment. I had nothing whatever to do with the enactment or the provisions of the law which said I can hold the office of Chief Judge until I die or retire. Congress enacted that law, and at that time several judges were affected by it. As a matter of fact, I found out about it while sitting in San Francisco in the U.S. District Court for the Northern District of California. U.S. District Court Judge Chase Clark, of Idaho, was also there. The San Francisco Judges were kidding him about it. The important point about this Chief Judge furor is that it is a very small matter except for one thing—the Constitution of the United States is involved. The Constitution forbids Bills of Attainder. Article I, paragraph 9, provides as follows: "No Bill of Attainder . . . shall be passed."

It would be unconstitutional to enact a repealer of the so-called "Grandfather Clause." The "Grandfather Clause," as it is called, will be inoperative if our Court ceases to be a two-judge Court, i.e., becomes a three-judge Court and this is the reason these character assassins want Congress to create a third judgeship for Utah—they can't wait for me to die, and they don't give a damn that a third Federal Judgeship, where it is not needed, is a very costly matter.

I guess Federal Judges have constitutional rights, [but] after living in Utah most of a lifetime, it makes one wonder. I have confidence that your Committee will let this legislation take its usual and ordinary course through sub-committee, and full-committee, with opportunity for hearings. So many Representatives and Senators have judgeships in the Omnibus Bill it has a lot of pressure for passage.

The pressure for passage of the Omnibus Judgeship Bill does not appertain to whether a repeal of the "Grandfather Clause," or a bill creating a third Federal Judgeship for Utah. Time can and should be taken for hearings on these matters. It has been part of the tactics of the sponsors of these two proposals to rush them to passage.

Most respectfully submitted,

WILLIS W. RITTER, Chief Judge
United States District Judge
District of Utah

"Whaddya think?" Ritter asked, after I'd had a chance to read through most of it a couple of times. "It's like you insist everyone else write," I told him, "brief and straight to the point." The line where he called the *Deseret News* the Deserted News, I remember thinking, was beneath him but nothing to spend a half day rewriting, so I said it was good. How do you tell a man like Ritter, who had corresponded as friends with Learned Hand, the legendary justice of the Second Circuit, that he ought to rewrite something, let alone rethink it?

"And another thing," Ritter said, "while you're here. I didn't give you enough time the other day on that McCoy kid. Take as long as you need," Ritter said, in an agreeable, friendly manner, most people, I thought, ought to see. "We need to be extra, extra careful around here for awhile," jiggling his jowls a little like Richard Nixon.

I said yes, I agreed completely. But I was up with him on McCoy, I assured him, ready when he was.

"Have you met with his people yet?" Ritter asked, his mind, it seemed, still on his letter to Congress. No one, I thought at the time, not even his children, understands Judge Ritter better than you, Rhodes. Something I'd realized from the beginning that couldn't be done very long on a trial-and-error basis.

"Met with his parents Friday," I couldn't wait to tell him, "then with Richard over the weekend. Got a damn good confession from him too," I said, while Ritter swung his huge red neck around agreeingly. "Statement," I said, "on the United Airlines case he refused to take your witness stand on." As if for some strange reason I alone had been granted sacerdotal powers to mediate omissions, disputes, and other minor misunderstandings between God and his long line of imperfect images.

Suddenly, like a grizzly powering his way out of hibernation, Ritter's eyes squinted and his mouth flew open like he was trying to catch something in it. I could feel the room temperature drop, just before I heard this clap of something emanating from every corner of the room: "YOU DONE WHAT?!" Cold, undiluted terror almost knocked me to the floor. All the years of horror stories I'd heard but never seen in Judge Ritter passed through me, and I remember thinking, Oh! Oh, my God! Somehow I've got to get the subject changed before I'm bludgeoned to death. "Now, wait just a minute," I heard myself say, trying my best to turn a possible massacre back into our friendly little powwow.

"Gaawd," Ritter bellowed in the same bottomless voice I'd always liked "Old Man River" sung in. "You may have blown"—

trembling, frothing from both corners of his mouth—"this whole Gaa . . . awd daaa . . . mmm . . . case! Don't anybody around here, understand," his words coming out in sobs, "that this McCoy thing is going to end up back there before the United States Supreme Court on some dinky-assed technicality? Winder," he said, "that Gaawd . . . damn motion to suppress Winder filed, and here they go," his whole body bobbing up and down in his huge bouncing overstuffed chair, "thumbing through McCoy's file—another Judge Ritter case they'll say—and what do you think they find? McCoy's confessed to the probation officer. Full confession. Tells everything he knows."

I tried to ignore him and concentrated on a sign outside the west window, a 20-by-40-foot billboard with a woman who looked like Carmen Miranda pouring Bacardi Rum into two tall frosted glasses of ice cubes. The terror eventually subsided into a glittering, gilt-edged rage. I remember thinking, Now it's me. It's you, too, Rhodes, even you. Another thing I thought I'd tell him and didn't was, You old fat son of a bitch, you're going to kill every greedy little bastard in this court if you don't hurry up and friggin' die.

"Now," he was still going on, "what'll they do? Now you've made the United States Supreme Court a party to our little conspiracy. Even," he said, "if they rule with Winder, they can't just turn this bird loose. You know why?" I did, but I wasn't going to give him the satisfaction of thinking I was even listening. "Because he has, over the weekend, admitted everything he's ever done in his entire life to some insignificant little probation officer way out here in Salt Lake City, Utah, in Judge Ritter's court." He didn't stop there either. He went on. And on. While I sat wishing one of those tall frosted rum glasses out on that 20 by 40 billboard was in my hand and imagining tomorrow's newspaper headlines: *AIRPLANE HIJACKER RICHARD McCOY RELEASED ON TECHNICAL-ITY—RITTER GIVES RHODES PRISON TERM.*

By Wednesday Ritter had slowly calmed down enough to realize that the world hadn't ended. After a couple of almost friendly little powwows, we took my dictaphone tape of Richard's interview, his handwritten confession, and most of my notes, put them in a lock-seal evidence envelope, licked it, sealed it, scribbled our names across the front, and, together, put it in the clerk's evidence vault.

Years later, after Richard and Ritter were both dead, I was in the vault on other matters and discovered that the envelope was gone.

There was, of course, nothing in either the written confession or on the tape that could incriminate Richard in the D. B. Cooper hijack. There could have been, I feel sure. But thanks to Ritter's fit, I didn't dare go back to the jail to talk about the "other thing" like I'd said I would. With Ritter it was too risky. So Richard and I never picked up where we left off that hot July Sunday afternoon on the third floor of the Salt Lake County Jail.

On Monday, 10 July, exactly one week after Ritter's display of judicial paranoia and temperament, Richard McCoy was sentenced in a brief, anticlimactic hearing before the court. Dave Winder and Richard stood facing the bench, their backs to the spectators. Winder briefly reminded Judge Ritter in a shuffling, apologetic way, as if he were pleading for his own life, that prior to 7 April 1972, Richard McCoy had led an exemplary life, that he was the father of two small children, that he and Karen were closer now than ever before, and that something less than the maximum sentence of forty-five years would not be inconsistent with society's needs.

Ritter waited when Winder paused to see if there was something else he wanted to say. When there wasn't, he turned to Richard. "I don't know that there's much you can tell me that either wasn't brought out in the trial or in Mr. Rhodes's probation report," he said almost forgivingly, "but I'm prepared to listen. I've just about been covered alive with letters the mailman brings us every morning. Some of the people write in your behalf. Some don't. Some I haven't read. But I'm dismissing all of those from my thoughts this morning. I'm prepared to go forward. Now do you, young man, have anything to say before I pronounce sentence?"

Richard had prepared a statement to read. He took it out of his pocket now. He had been in jail for three months and looked years older. His hair had thinned, his eyes had dark circles under them, and his hips couldn't quite hold up his suit pants. He took a long, deep breath, as if he were preparing to go under water, then he began reading:

First, I would like to thank the court for appointing Mr. Winder as my attorney. He's done all he can do.

Next I will attempt to give you some insight into my personality and, in part, answer the questions that may have come to your mind as to why someone with my background, reputation, and apparent good future would risk everything to involve himself in such an ill-fated, destructive venture.

It was a dignified, even moving statement. And while I didn't think it would work, I found myself hoping to some extent that he wouldn't get the maximum.

Richard continued:

My current problem began innocently. The original idea was to write a research paper for one of my university law enforcement classes on how to prevent skyjackings. I felt my background and life experiences had given me an advantage over others in solving the problem. After working on this project in a haphazard fashion for a couple of months, it became apparent that I wouldn't be able to prove my original theory. After carefully analyzing the steps a well-equipped skyjacker would employ and the countermeasures the FBI would take, I concluded that there was no effective deterrent once an airplane had been taken over. Although I fantasized on what the experience would be like, as people do in reading an adventure story, or watching an exciting movie, it was later, when my problems seemed insurmountable, that I seriously considered undertaking such a project. In working on the project, it was necessary to play the roles of the people involved. The person I identified with most was the skyjacker. Playing his role and figuring how he would handle different situations seemed, at the time, to be a harmless escape from reality.

I searched the courtroom for the tall, blonde reporter with the green eyes who resembled Lee Remick, but saw only local reporters.

Somewhere along the line, it occurred to me that this was the solution to all my personal problems, one way or the other. If I was successful I would not have to worry about physical handicaps, taking care of my children after the divorce, or supporting a second family if I decided to remarry. If I wasn't successful, according to my thinking, I would be dead. Those were the only two alternatives I ever considered. As far as the occupants of the airplane were concerned, I intentionally made my plans so they would be exposed to a minimum of danger. I

184

would never under any circumstances have harmed anyone even if it came to a showdown. The only real danger was from outside interference, and I had made it clear that no one from the outside would be allowed on the plane. There were no explosives involved. The hand grenade, as was demonstrated in court, was inert. I gambled that no one would call my bluff. They knew from the notes I sent to the pilot that I knew what I was talking about. Other than the crew, only a few were aware that anything was amiss. The passengers were not informed of the situation until just before they disembarked in San Francisco, as I did not want to frighten anyone unnecessarily.

I am now going to mention one last reason that I hope Your Honor will consider in making your decision. This involves my immediate family. As I have mentioned, my wife and I were having serious marital problems prior to my arrest. These problems have not been resolved completely, but considering my present circumstances, they are insignificant by comparison. Karen said she is sticking by me. How long she will continue to do this is impossible to predict. According to her, in all probability, she will wait fifteen or twenty years. I doubt that personally, Your Honor, but it may turn out that she won't have any option. There aren't many men that will take on the responsibility of a woman with two small children. At present Karen is supporting herself and our children working as a caseworker for the County Welfare Department. How long this will continue is a matter for speculation. As you may be aware, Karen is afflicted with a deteriorating bone condition, a rather distressful form of arthritis. While I was awaiting trial, she underwent a bone transplant in her right wrist. The doctors are now recommending another operation to remove two inches of the ulna. Even this is only a stopgap measure. She has been told that she will eventually altogether lose the use of her right arm. Her situation would be bad even under normal conditions but worse now, due to my inability to help. In spite of Karen's and my problems, I care for her very much and would provide for her if circumstances were different. Even more, I am concerned for the welfare and future of my children. I love them more than life itself. They have done nothing wrong and are completely innocent.

He didn't need to spell out the horrors of trying to raise a family decently on state disability, if and when Karen became unable to work. Or how tidy, even noble, it would be for Richard to be eligible for parole then, to step forward and pick up the family burden again.

In conclusion, Judge Ritter, let me say that I am not attempting to excuse what I did. I have made a big mistake and I am willing to pay for it. All I can do is ask you, one man to another, to give me a sentence I can serve. Forty-five years is not realistic. I wouldn't even attempt it. My children by that time would be thirty years of age before I was released on parole. I have been a good citizen and I hope you will consider this in passing judgment.

Most of the press, I had noticed earlier, had gone on to other things, leaving only the two local papers and local television stations behind to take note of the number of years a man gets in Utah for a half-million-dollar crime. Ritter, that day, like any other, "was not," he said, "concerned with what newspaper people thought." Without lecturing or trying his hand at rehabilitation, he quickly sentenced Richard to the maximum. "Forty-five years," he announced, "in a federal penitentiary."

20 To Prison
Lewisburg, Pennsylvania,
July 1972

Richard was returned to the Salt Lake County Jail and, because of his long prison sentence, was assigned to a maximum-security prison in Pennsylvania. Prison designations then were made in Washington, D.C., and teletyped to the marshal's office in Salt Lake City. For security reasons, no one—not the judge, the prisoner, nor his family—was told when or where the transfer would be made. Hijacking a marshal's car hadn't happened for awhile, but such stories still circulated in the marshal's service. Organized-crime figures and "high risk" prisoners got special attention. So did Richard.

Two deputy marshals left the Salt Lake County Jail before daylight Thursday, 20 July, heading east, with Richard in the back seat. Six feet of belly chain had been threaded through his belt loops, fastened to handcuffs in the front, and locked to leg irons at his ankles. Highway 80 east through Parley's Canyon was a steady twelve-mile winding climb to a 7,000-foot summit. For the marshals, it would be one of the most dangerous pieces of highway between Salt Lake City and Denver, their next stop. Traffic, as they had planned, was light and their unmarked, brown 1969 Plymouth, rigged with a powerful 450-cubic-inch interceptor engine, seemed half-asleep, even at seventy miles an hour. Richard, with help from the deputy marshal seated on the front passenger side, knelt in the back seat looking through the rear window. He watched as Kennecott Copper Corporation's huge smokestacks blew sleep from the eyes of its morning shift. Sunshine forced its way through thick mountain pines and perched atop the Mormon temple. Karen would already be up, getting ready for work. The kids would still be asleep.

At Parley's Summit was another inconspicuous brown 1969 Plymouth parked facing west. A U.S. deputy marshal leaned against the front fender holding binoculars in one hand and a 30.06 in the other. The marshal driving Richard's car only nodded as he passed.

In Brighton, Colorado, that evening, Richard was logged into the Adams County Jail as a federal prisoner in transit and housed in the drunk tank. When the marshal arrived the next morning to check out his prisoner, Richard was gone. Deputy Sheriff Robert Hodge's routine morning duties included transporting drunks, vagrants, and misdemeanors jailed during the night to city court for arraignment. During the night, Richard had switched wristbands with a drunk driver. The next morning when Benjamin Namepee's name was called, Richard answered, "Here," stepped forward, and joined the group bound for Judge Hallick's court to be arraigned. "He told me he was sick," Hodge told the judge, "so I took his handcuffs off and walked him down the hall to the restroom. The minute I turned my back, Judge Hallick, he bolted." Captured late that same afternoon several blocks from the courthouse, Richard was wrestled back before Judge Hallick, still insisting he was Benjamin Namepee.

With no one the wiser, Richard entered a plea of not guilty and asked to be released on his own recognizance. "Deputy Hodge," he told Judge Hallick, "hit me, kicked me in the groin, and called me dirty names."

Judge Hallick accepted his not-guilty plea, looked down from the bench, and said, "Mr. Namepee, I know Deputy Hodge. He's a good man and if he did what you say he did, I can tell you right now you had it coming." Benjamin Namepee was still snoring when Richard was returned to the jail, where the U.S. marshals finally untangled the mystery.

Late Monday evening on 24 July, the day Mormons in Utah were celebrating the arrival of Brigham Young in 1847, that same marshal's car turned off Interstate 80 in north-central Pennsylvania and headed south on U.S. 15. One mile north of the small farm community of Lewisburg stood eight tall gray guard towers. Behind them lay twenty-six acres of concrete, steel, and razor wire and eleven hundred federal prisoners. Built during the Great Depression to hide America's mean and unpredictable, it loomed against the Appalachian foothills as deadly and incongruously as a nuclear power plant. A mausoleum for misfits, local people called it.

When the gates closed behind prisoner number 38478-133, Richard McCoy, he became a resident of Dog Block where, four cells down the long catwalk lived a veteran of penal institutions, Melvin Dale Walker, age thirty-two, male Caucasian, five foot ten and 180 pounds. A thousand miles of bad judgment had brought him to Lewisburg Federal Prison. He would be Richard's partner in his second prison break.

21

The Partner: Melvin Dale Walker

Melvin Dale Walker was a powerful man with big hands and a slick black Fu Manchu mustache serving fifty-five years for bank robbery, escape, and kidnapping. Out of prison since 1981, Walker was my houseguest for a weekend in February 1987. He and Calame sat at my dining-room table making homemade handcuff keys, while the three of us foraged back through Richard McCoy's life. Calame and I listened enthralled to Walker's—and through him, to Richard's—account of the escape from Lewisburg and four blazing months of freedom between August and November 1974.

"Growing up as a child," Melvin Walker told Russ Calame and me, "I always needed plenty of freedom. My father left home when I was about twelve and my mother, bless her soul, was not very strict. So I went where I wanted to. Mostly on the Ohio River. My favorite place was Duck Island. My brother Gary, a boy named John, and I would take wieners and buns there. Apple cider, too, when we could get it.

"When I was young I did what I wanted to do. And that was mostly mischief. But the one talent I had, even then, was creating things with my hands. Which has got me in as many jails as it got me out of. John, Gary and me at thirteen, were the first juveniles ever to hit the headlines of the Evansville, Indiana, newspaper.

"An older brother, Glen, was the first in the family to go to prison. There were six of us kids—four boys and two girls, so our mother needed to work. By the time I was sixteen I had burglarized and shot my way across most of the United States. When I reached eighteen, John and me got our first adult sentence in the state of Illinois."

Walker took us on a guided tour of his thirty-five-year run-in with the law. He reached J. Edgar Hoover's Top Ten Wanted List with a special notation, "quick to kill," nicknamed "The Flying Bank Robber." "My brother Glen and I started off robbing motels and supermarkets across the country," he explained, "but by 1967 had switched to banks."

He told how he and Glen, after hitting a bank in Norfolk, Virginia, flew up to Montreal and then to West Berlin for the night. "Then we went to Frankfurt, where I blew seven hundred dollars in one night on champagne and a big-busted German girl."

By early 1968, Melvin and Glen had robbed more than a dozen banks across Missouri, Indiana, California, and—Melvin's favorite—Norfolk, Virginia. But it was Norfolk where their luck ran out. As they both stood in the lobby of a Norfolk bank they'd robbed before, a security guard recognized Glen. Just as they turned to leave, the FBI "pulled up out front and drew down on us." Melvin only had a little .22 Derringer and Glen a .25 Baretta, so they just dropped the guns and stood there with their hands on top of their heads. That was Melvin's first encounter with FBI agent Nicholas V. O'Hara.

Melvin Walker, after pleading guilty to eleven of the known bank robberies, was sentenced to fifty-five years and was transported to the maximum-security prison at Atlanta, Georgia, while Glen was given thirty-five years at the federal prison in Terre Haute, Indiana.

After less than five months at Atlanta, Walker was scheduled to be moved to the even more secure prison at Marion, Illinois, a three-day trip by car. Unfortunately, no one bothered to brief the two deputy U.S. marshals about Walker's long assault record, nor did Walker volunteer the information that he had hidden in the mouth of his toothpaste tube a homemade handcuff key made from the refill cartridge of a ballpoint pen. Although he was double-handcuffed with both Smith & Wesson and Peerless cuffs, the key would fit both.

On the first day of the trip, Walker had noticed two things. James Parham, about thirty years old, did a thorough strip and cavity search in the morning, but did not require him to remove his socks. The other deputy, Arthur Worthy, about forty, was asthmatic and terribly nearsighted without his glasses. On the second morning when Parham and Worthy showed up at the jail for their prisoner, the two-inch metal handcuff key lay flat against the sole of Walker's right foot.

As their blue Pontiac Tempest pulled out of the jail parking lot that morning, downtown traffic was still heavy. Worthy was helping Parham locate the fastest route out of town and paid no attention at all to Walker in the back seat removing his shoes.

The conversation was casual, even friendly. Both deputies, as if they were restaurant critics, described in great detail where and what they'd eaten for supper the night before. "How 'bout you Walker? Get enough of that sorry county-jail food last night?" drawled Parham.

"The food was okay," Walker said, as he slid both sets of hand-cuffs over the knuckles of his powerful right hand.

"You'll be in Marion prison tomorrow night, Walker," Worthy said, laying his prescription sunglasses on the dash of the Tempest and yawning. "Ever been there?"

"No, sir," Melvin replied, as he unfastened the cuffs of his freed right hand from six feet of belly chain, "I've only heard stories about Marion."

"Princeton, Kentucky," Worthy suddenly announced. "Sign says four miles to the next exit. Coffee break, Jim! How about you, Walker, you go for a cup of hot Kentucky coffee this morning?"

The deputy's shit-fire sudden invitation could screw the whole thing up. There wasn't time, for God's sakes, to get back inside the leg irons, lock both handcuffs to the belly chain and be ready to crawl out of the backseat for coffee in less than four minutes. It's either now, or it's big trouble.

Just as Worthy on the passenger side leaned forward to pick up his sunglasses, Walker's cuffed left wrist snapped hard against Parham's Adam's apple while his freed right hand went straight for the snub-nosed .38 on the driver's right hip. Worthy barely had time to set his eyes before he heard the hammer lock and felt the short, fat, oily barrel rub against his nose.

Walker ushered them into a thick wooded area about three hundred yards off the main highway, took their shoes, and handcuffed them together, their backs against the same old hard maple tree. Then he relieved both of their weapons, cash, credit cards, and U.S. marshal's credentials, and delivered his farewell address.

"I don't intend to shoot either one of you. I have nothing

against either of you personally. You've both been decent to me. I'll stop before dark, call a local sheriff, and let him know where he can find you." A little north of Springfield, Tennessee, he did.

When the feds found Walker four months later in mid-July 1969, he got to see the maximum-security prison at Marion, Illinois, for the first time.

"Something happens when they lock me up, Mr. Rhodes," Walker said without changing expressions or taking his cold blue eyes off me for a second. "I can't breathe. I sweat. I become desperate. I have something I wrote," he said just above a whisper while unfolding a scrap of faded tablet paper, "that is, if you're interested."

"Yes," I said. "I'm interested."

He read:

If I'm destined to be in your prison,
Then bury me deep under ground
Just the sight of a light, for a man like me
And I know I am freedom bound
For my soul and my strength were born to be free
And free is the way I must stay
Until my enemy the guard, and his high powered gun
Have taken my life away.

When Melvin talked, even at close range, you had to strain to hear. His English, for a man who had spent, by then, nearly twenty-six years in prison, was better than most people's. "Even in prison," he told Calame, "I never cursed, and I never lowered myself to use prison slang." He spoke without moving his lips and his eyes seemed to follow every word until he was sure it could stand on its own. "Something," he said, "you learn to do in prison."

Features of this overpowering menace that even newspaper photographs couldn't hide had disappeared. The red, white, and blue American eagle tattooed across his big left hand seemed to be the most menacing thing about him now. His calmness could have been the serenity of faith—he had become a born-again Christian—or perhaps it was the absence of the burning will for freedom that had consumed him back in 1974.

Calame was only a few pounds heavier in 1987 than he had been in 1972 and had stopped graying altogether. He and several former law enforcement officials were running a very successful, high-powered international investigation agency. Calame hunkered down next to Walker with an old pro's interest and respect as we listened to the inside version of a story we'd known only from the outside.

"By the time I got to Lewisburg," Melvin murmured, "I already had two major escapes on my record." By early 1970, Melvin had become part of a large-scale plan at Marion to bring in a whole crate of guns—fourteen .45-caliber automatics. The print shop's new plates were arriving in a series of shipments. Each crate weighed exactly 110 pounds 4 ounces. One of the guards would check the shipping number on the bill of lading with a matching number on file in the prison business office, then weigh each crate. Crates that passed these two examinations went into what they called a hot room, where a convict friend worked. A trustee in the business office phoned up some paperwork for one extra crate. A just-released inmate agreed to handle the outside work. Forged shipping papers and bills of lading were smuggled out of Marion by one of the convict's wives. "I had had a diagram drawn up of what the crates looked like, down to the type of wood he was to use and where the bill of lading was to be attached," Walker smiled faintly.

Then "someone snitched. Because all of a sudden, the guards started opening every crate that came in. Our forty-fives never reached the hot room. The guards opened 'em up right there on the dock. Everybody but me sort of gave up. No one had ever escaped from inside Marion before. They'd tried it with helicopters from the yard. But never from inside the prison itself."

The prison at Marion, Illinois, had opened in 1963 and replaced Alcatraz as the most secure facilty in the world. The penitentiary has eight bulletproof guard towers and a pair of fourteen-foot-high fences topped off with another four feet of curling, weaving razor wire. Every cell at Marion is a single, six and a half by eight feet, and is searched twice daily. Each cell has a solid steel door with a long narrow slit about eye level for food trays and head counts. Each cell has a window overlooking the prison grounds. The window has three two-part bars about an inch in diameter. The inner bar of solid steel is fixed at the top and bottom into the steel window casing. A hollow outer bar fits over the inner bar. Under a hacksaw blade, the outside bar just rolls. Melvin Dale Walker wasn't just the first inmate to escape from the inside; until now, he is still the only man to have pulled it off.

There were surely no two-bit crooks sent to Marion. Forty percent had escape records, and 60 percent had tried to kill someone. "One of the best escape men Marion had was telling me," Walker said, "how he tried to do it with a bar-spreader. I'd just been brought up from fifteen months in the hole [solitary confinement], accused of stabbing this guy from Texas." Not long after arriving at Marion in 1969, Walker was assigned to the morning kitchen detail. One morning a guard noticed splotches of fresh blood on the soles of Walker's shoes and on his white cook's apron. Suspicious, the guard checked the walk-in meat cooler. There he found another inmate lying, barely alive, in a pool of his own blood. Although Walker still denies stabbing the man, he spent the next fifteen months in isolation.

"That was in 1970, the spring of '70." Melvin Walker, I thought to myself, either possessed the best sense of hearing I'd ever come across or could tell fortunes because I hadn't actually got "How do you remember it was spring?" out of my mouth before he added, "The reason I remember it was spring, Mr. Rhodes, is because in isolation I had started reading the Bible." Then he told how he was watching *The Ten Commandments* one afternoon in the recreation room when he became violently ill and heard "a voice from God." Perhaps his life started to change, but not before he decided he wasn't going to accept this convict's word for it that bar-spreaders wouldn't work.

"So," Melvin said, looking at Calame, "I get me two bar-spreaders. The first one was an old turn-buckle contraption we take off of a bulldozer—threads on one end and a swivel on the other. The second one we get is an old vise someone steals for me out of the machine shop. By the time I get everything ready to go, it's two fifteen in the morning. The local weather station had said we would have cloudy skies that night and a seventy percent chance of rain. But from my cell, I could see a full moon, no rain, and no clouds. But lots of floodlights." He used both bar-spreaders simultaneously, his hands cramping so badly that tears ran down his cheeks. The bars separated just enough. ("In other attempts," Warden Charles Fenton later told the news media, "inmates were unable to even dent the cell bars.")

Walker shinnied down on a bedsheet rope and headed for a blind spot between the guard towers and the first fence, carrying a wool blanket to protect himself from the razor wire. He was visible to the officers in the message center on top of the administration building, but these officers, Walker knew, not only weren't allowed to shoot—they couldn't. They were sitting behind a four-inch bullet-proof window with no firing openings. Just as he made it over the first fence, his luck ran out. A guard in the closest tower fired a shotgun in the air and shouted, "Halt!" By then, Walker said, he was clearing the second fence.

"Miraculous," Fenton would tell the press, shaking his head in bewilderment, "how any man is able to zigzag his way through a hundred and twenty-six rounds of thirty-caliber machine-gun fire coming from the two east guard towers and live to tell about it."

"Only two hundred yards between me and freedom," Walker whispered. "I knew that those gunsights were useless in the dark without plenty of time to zero them in on me. The first tracer bullets from the east guard tower went high and blew windows out of the administration building. I'm just clearing the last fence when another tracer bullet comes within an inch of my nose and ricochets off one of the steel poles. When I hit the ground, I could feel dirt hitting both sides of my blue jeans and fresh mud fly in my eyes as I zigzagged full force up this grassy hill. All of a sudden I hit a ditch and both legs fly out from under me. The guards, I guess, think they killed me, so they quit shooting."

Crawling along the ditch under its cover of high weeds, he made it into a thickly wooded area about fifty yards up the hill, still close enough to see searchlights, hear the guard's voices, and hear the baying of the bloodhounds. "I ran most of the night with the bloodhounds yelping not far behind me. By morning I couldn't run another foot. The dogs found me hiding at the top of this big oak tree. I came down peacefully. When they led me down the hall into isolation, I heard someone whisper, 'Next time, Melvin, next time.' It was this big Mafioso boss named Frankie Carbo. Frankie Carbo didn't call many convicts by their first name."

Back in isolation, Melvin continued his Bible reading and began to think about making a commitment to God. "I wasn't sure how to go about it—or if I was even ready. One night a voice spoke to me audibly. It said, 'Your name is written in the book to enter the room.' I didn't know what it meant. The next morning, an officer opened my cell door, threw me a cardboard box, and told me to pack. Two marshals, he said, were there to take me to the penitentiary at Lewisburg, Pennsylvania."

Lewisburg, like Marion, is a maximum-security penitentiary, but it is older and grayer. Located one mile north of the small town of Lewisburg, 200 miles from Washington, D.C., 170 miles from Philadelphia, it sits on twenty-six acres of generally flat land. Around the perimeter runs a concrete wall thirty feet high, supporting six armed guard towers. There are two ways in and out. The main gate, off U.S. Route 15, is where visitors, lawyers, and other bearers of good tidings leave their cars just outside the wall, identify themselves at the main guard tower, and prepare for a thorough body search once they're inside the administration building. The second way in or out is the service entrance with its sally port.

Six cellblocks—A through F—lie systematically, like carefully placed dominoes, behind and on either side of the administration building. The prison dental lab, hospital, and segregation unit squats next to A block. The commissary is at the other end, next to E. A one-lane industrial road, used for maintenance and garbage trucks, begins at the main gate, curls around each block, passes the mess hall, and eventually comes to a halt at its armed sally port before the back gate. The sally port exists to bring everything to a complete stop. It looks like a covered bridge made of fortified chain link fencing with heavy metal gates on either end. When an authorized vehicle approaches, a guard electronically opens the gate. When the rear of the vehicle clears the gate, it immediately closes, confining the vehicle within the sally port. Once the vehicle has been thoroughly searched for convicts and other contraband, an officer in the adjoining control tower electronically opens the forward gate for it to proceed. The road then continues another quarter mile to a second gate. One other thing. The road leading to the sally port runs parallel to the inmate exercise yard, separated from it only by a six-foot chain link fence. And one more thing. Just inside the exercise yard, next to the fence and not forty yards from the sally port are two wooden park benches.

22 McCoy in Prison
1972–74

Richard's first twenty months in Lewisburg were dispiriting and monotonous. The prison regulations stifled his mind. He became despondent at times, grieved deeply over his children, and considered suicide, but "getting killed going over the wall," he wrote a friend in Salt Lake City, "would be much less painful to my conscience."

Richard could read and write better than most of the guards—he was almost a college graduate—so rather than being assigned to educational programs, he got the dental lab, exactly where he wanted to be. Karen and the kids headed back to Cove City, North Carolina. She and Myrtle drove up to Lewisburg and visited Richard as often as gas money and the warden would allow. For a while Richard received bags of what read like fan mail from people he hadn't heard from since high school. Some he didn't know at all.

Richard wrote regularly to Dave Winder, inquiring mostly about the status of his appeal to the Tenth Circuit Court in Denver on the Fourth Amendment issue raised by the faulty search warrant. On 7 May 1973, the conviction was affirmed. "It's disappointing, I know," Winder wrote Richard, "but we're not through yet." Next Winder filed a Writ of Certiorari with the United States Supreme Court asking the people's court of last resort to permit oral arguments over this same Fourth Amendment problem.

On 6 December 1973, the United States Supreme Court denied Winder's motion for oral arguments. Winder wrote Richard, "Don't give up yet. We still have Judge Ritter as our ace in the hole."

Rule 35 of the Federal Rules of Criminal Procedure allows the sentencing judge 120 days subsequent to any appeals to reduce or modify the original sentence. Ritter often did. Accordingly, Winder asked Ritter to reduce Richard's sentence to the minimum—twenty years. Myrtle added her pleas. Karen, she said, had been unable to find a position teaching school in the Cove City area because of the publicity, and Myrtle was doing her best "to furnish them a home with her limited means." She concluded hopefully, "I know that you have great love in your heart for your fellow man and I beg you do something to help my son." Richard wrote me on 23 January 1974, asking me to appear with Winder in any hearing he could get from Ritter. And he also wrote directly to Ritter, explaining his background. It was an illuminating, even moving recital:

During my formative years, it was still the in thing to serve one's country so at nineteen I followed in my father's footsteps and enlisted in the army. During my seven years of active duty, I strived to get into the best units and volunteered for the toughest and most challenging training. After completing parachute school and volunteering for the Green Berets, then came two more years of training in advanced demolition and guerrilla warfare. In 1964 I was sent to Vietnam as an advisor to the South Vietnamese forces where, during combat operations, I was shot and wounded. I've witnessed the death of many good friends. That experience was so distressing that I left active duty a few months after returning home. In trying to get my head together, I decided to return to college. That was in the spring of '65. There I met my wife Karen and married her the following summer. After that I went to work to support my family, but my personal life was not working out so I returned to the only life that offered a challenge. I reenlisted, and volunteered for helicopter training. After a year of intensive training, I returned to Vietnam in 1967. You are aware of a few of my experiences mentioned by my lawyer. As he said, I was awarded the Commendation Medal for Valor. I only mention that to illustrate that I have never shirked my duty in the face of danger and actually sought out difficult assignments. After Vietnam, I served two years in Germany, but in the spring of 1970, after seven years of active service, I deferred to the wishes of my wife and ended my military career. I was scheduled at that time to return to Vietnam for a third tour of duty, but my family, being aware of my habit of getting into things, was concerned that I was pushing my luck. Perhaps they were right, but there are worse things than dying honorably in the service of a man's country. Considering what's happened since, along with the disgrace and suffering my family has suffered, an honorable death would have been preferable.

After leaving the army, I moved to Provo and enrolled at Brigham Young University where I majored in law enforcement. Due to my age and limited finances, it was necessary to carry heavy academic loads, enroll in summer sessions, and take night classes. But I also found time to serve in the Utah National Guard, work part time as a salesman, and devote time to the church and the Boy Scouts.

I'll bet those Scouts loved him, I thought irrelevantly when I got to this point. But I wonder how all those good Mormon bishops and good Mormon parents are explaining to their teenagers that they should never under any circumstances think for even one minute that Richard McCoy was a fine, upstanding model for youth. Richard went on to explain his medical condition, the future of an invalid that awaited him, and the constraints of establishing a career to take care of Karen and the children. Then he continued:

Maybe you're wondering whether I was capable of harming anyone. If you don't mind, I will go back for a few moments to give you a better insight into my personality. Some of these incidents you may be aware of through the trial and presentence report.

During my first tour of duty in Vietnam, I was wounded. The only reason, Your Honor, was because I was unable to kill another man up close.

On January 8, 1972, three months prior to my arrest, I assisted in a life-saving mission involving an airplane crash. There were three of us directly involved. We were members of the Utah National Guard and were utilizing a guard helicopter. As the aircraft commander, I was directly responsible for the success or failure of the efforts involved. The downed aircraft crashed in trees and deep snow on the side of Mount Nebo, forty miles south of Provo. The three men on the ground were seriously injured and were suffering from exposure. The crash site was at the 8,200-feet level. We had to contend with strong winds, low clouds, and a precarious and almost inaccessible landing site. The snow was waist deep and it was impossible to land. It was necessary to hold the helicopter at a hover against the slope of the mountain while my co-pilot and crew chief waded through the snow to the injured men. Obviously it was not an impossible task but it did take a bit of finesse and some daring to accomplish the rescue. One small miscalculation and all six of us could have perished on the side of that mountain.

Richard then described the rescue operation in Vietnam in which he picked up the survivors from two downed and burning helicopters and for which he received the Distinguished Flying Cross. He believed the recognition for his bravery could stand on its own merits, but he wished to make a clarification:

While U.S. Forces often provided support for the Vietnamese, our pilots were not compelled to take hazardous missions for them. We saved those risks for our own people. When assistance was needed, some of our pilots would often have "mechanical" problems or get "disoriented" en route and fail to show up. This is why volunteers were utilized. I had very little personal contact with the Vietnamese Nationals on my second tour; but I had learned to respect and admire them in 1964 when, as a foot soldier, I lived and fought with them. What I did on many occasions, I did because they were comrades in arms. If the situation were reversed I knew one of them would render similar assistance.

Yes, I thought, there was no denying it, Richard could offer convincing circumstances in mitigation of further punishment.

Ritter was in no hurry. He let the motion for reduction drag on until the 120 days passed and then some. Four or five months later, Ritter suddenly got interested. He called me up in a big hurry. We'd talk about it at lunch that day, he said. "How about George Lamb's place?" I didn't like the idea. Lamb's Cafe fed more lawyers and people likely to need lawyers than any four places up or down Main Street. There Ritter was pampered like royalty, fed more than he ordered, belly-laughed his way through dessert, and promised every waitress under thirty a trip to his farm. No, Lamb's was not the place to talk business with Willis Ritter. What's more, I wanted to see his expression when we walked into the newly opened D. B. Cooper Restaurant and Bar.

His expression, as it turned out, didn't change, so Calame and Winder hadn't, as Ritter would have put it, "taken sanctuary in the breast of the court" by whispering any secrets about Cooper and McCoy. We spent a good part of our Beefeaters pushing the McCoy file delicately back and forth, from my side of the table to his, then back again. He wondered whether we should get an opinion from Calame who was, as far as I could remember, along with Charlie Shepherd the only two FBI agents Ritter ever took sides with. The rest of them he was suspicious of and felt around under their chairs after they left his chambers. I reminded him that Calame had retired back in 1972 and was originally from Iowa, without bothering to mention that he'd stayed in Salt Lake City. "Well, let's get the next one," Ritter said. "The one that took his place." The man's name, I told Ritter, is Maurice Slocum. But he isn't a working SAC like Calame, so I very rarely see him."

I wanted Ritter to make the decision on his own, as he always had, without consulting the FBI. Although I wasn't convinced that the forty-five–year sentence was too long, I did tell Ritter I liked Richard McCoy and was afraid he'd commit suicide if the sentence wasn't shortened.

"I liked him, too," Ritter said waggling his head cordially, "but war, we've found out, does funny things to men. Some," he said, thumbing through Richard's file, "turn to alcohol when they come home. Some turn to dope. Some men take it out on their wife and kids. But this bird," Ritter said, closing the file, "is different. This bird has tasted human flesh, as we say in the judging business. He's got a piece of it, it seems to me, still caught in his throat. And I'm convinced," Ritter was tapping his fingers on the table, "convinced he won't get it completely out of his system until he kills someone— or someone finally has to kill him."

23 FBI Dirty Linen

Maurice Slocum, Calame's dapper little replacement, I found, had quietly fallen off the face of the earth by the tail end of 1973. From the beginning he seemed to resent Calame, refused to accept his hypothesis about the McCoy-Cooper connection, and never reassigned the case after Jim Theisen was transferred. Slocum's lack of interest, I believe, broke the investigative chain. I hadn't talked to him much during 1973, so when I asked for the SAC in late June 1974, I was not especially surprised to hear a new voice on the line.

He had, he explained, recently replaced Slocum, who had been transferred back to the Detroit office. "Bigger office," he said, as if he'd helped make the decision. "More responsibilities!"

"A promotion?" I asked him.

"We-ell," he answered, sounding even heartier as he got vaguer, "you couldn't actually say it was a promotion." The irony of most cover-ups, we'd just learned from Watergate was that loud denials and an inescapable pattern seemed evident from the very beginning. "He . . . I heard," he said, "was supposed to have done something or another . . . " (he was still ferociously cordial but stammered slightly over the words) "with so and so . . . that must have necessitated Mr. Slocum's transfer."

A transfer to the Detroit office, I'd always heard, or the one in Butte, Montana, was equal to life without parole. Sanitariums to hide burned-out agents whose hands shake when they pour their first drink in the morning or the young, handsome agent whose libido has gone on a rampage. I didn't need to ask any more questions.

On 19 July 1974, Willis W. Ritter signed his name to a brief document, the key sentence of which read: "The defendant Richard McCoy's motion for reduction of sentence is hereby denied." In Lewisburg, Pennsylvania, Richard Floyd McCoy and Melvin Dale Walker had been planning a break-out for two months.

A week or so later, I was invited to an Eighth and Tenth Circuit Judicial Conference back in Springfield, Missouri. Clarence Kelley, who had replaced Hoover after the Patrick Gray interregnum, would be the guest speaker with a couple of United States Supreme Court justices as special guests. That allowed even more pomp and ostentation. Whenever the federal judiciary throws a party, it far exceeds the rubber chicken and English peas that garish politicians make impossible promises over.

The conference opened with a formal dinner party. I didn't notice anybody expressing disapproval of either the food or drink, and we were a pretty mellow gathering by the time Clarence Kelley, a huge, ruddy-complected man, arose. He hovered over the podium with the grace of an overweight prizefighter. He at first seemed out of place. He suffered, I imagined, from high blood pressure and sweat profusely—sheets of it streaming off his broad crimson forehead and disappearing somewhere down in his notes. The longer he talked, the redder he got. But when Director Kelley finally finished up, J. Edgar Hoover, I remember thinking, never received a more enthusiastic ovation. With the applause still in the air, a line formed between the tables leading up to the speakers' table. I was about fiftieth.

The line started out at a snail's pace, then came to a complete stop when the old judge from Kansas wearing the hearing aid reached Mr. Kelley. I shifted from foot to foot for a while, then gave up my place in line to join an even bigger gathering outside the men's room. Suddenly I remembered a small men's room with a single urinal up one flight of stairs on the mezzanine that I'd discovered earlier during registration. I'd just taken over its only urinal when the door flew open and this big red-faced guy in obvious pain burst in, followed by two bodyguards, and danced around behind me.

Out of respect for human suffering, I stood there no longer than absolutely necessary. From the mirror over the washbasin, I could see Kelley behind me, wheezing nervously, then catching his breath long enough to light a filter tip and stick it in the corner of his mouth. I decided against interrupting Mr. Kelley, but told him when he joined me at the sink that my name was Rhodes and that while I worked out of the Salt Lake office, I was born and raised in Hannibal. "I wasn't aware you were also from Missouri," I said, "until your speech tonight."

"Kansas City, Judge," Kelley said, almost deferentially. "Still have a home there. May one day retire there, Judge." Not even the director of the Federal Bureau of Investigation wanted to appear disrespectful to someone who may later show up in a black robe—so everyone at a judicial conference is Judge, Your Honor, or Mr. Justice until told otherwise. With most people, I generally never felt a correction was necessary. But with Kelley I did.

"No, no," I remember enunciating, "chief probation officer, District of Utah." I told him I'd met his SAC, Maurice Slocum, but hadn't really got to know him before he was suddenly transferred to Detroit.

Kelley knew I was fishing, but I don't think he minded too much. "I fired him," Kelley said, "had him dead to rights, too, Judge. Two inspectors flew out to Salt Lake City, followed him around, and caught him redhanded in something he shouldn't have been into! He appealed my ruling to the Civil Service Commission and eventually they went over my head and reinstated him. Finally," Kelley said, drenching his thick gray hair in the washbasin and combing it straight back, "we had to transfer him. But if you're interested in knowing exactly what happened," he tucked the comb back in his pocket, "get in touch with Russ Calame, Judge."

I didn't exactly call Russ Calame from the airport when I got back to Salt Lake City, but my curiosity about Slocum was whetted, so when a couple of agents dropped by on an unlawful flight investigation, I asked about Slocum.

It was hunting season, they both agreed. "November or early December," Jim Stewart said, "probably between deer and geese seasons. Shepherd and Morton were buying shotgun shells." Shep and Morton accidentally spotted the boss's bureau car at Fashion Place Mall. "At first they thought he was checking on them," Stewart said, "them buying shotgun shells during working hours." But they wondered why he'd spread the morning paper across the steering wheel to hide his police radio. So they backed off a ways and waited. They had no trouble seeing Slocum hurry toward his bureau car, coat collar turned up, hands buried deep in both pockets. They didn't have any trouble seeing the tall ash blonde clinging to his left arm, either.

"Well, hot damn," Morton drawled at Shepherd in his deep Bear Bryant accent. "No more'n buy a box of shotgun shells, and we get us up a bird."

For the first time with Slocum, agents had options. Shep was prepared to go either way. He'd just made supervisor. They could back off and leave it alone, or they could go ahead. But above all, don't rush it. Wanting to keep their options open, they tailed Slocum and the blonde to an exclusive condominium complex known as Three Fountains East, at about Ninth East and 4900 South in Salt Lake City.

A white brick trellis, nearly covered with clinging ivy, supported a heavy black metal security gate where the boss drove in. This main entrance, they discovered, was also the only exit. Suppose the boss was only dropping the lady off, and they were pulling in while he was driving out? In that case, Jim Stewart pointed out, they may as well climb out with guns blazing and blow the patent-leather bastard full of holes right there in the driveway. It would be a lot easier to convince a jury that it was a regrettable but simple case of mistaken identity than to explain to Slocum why they were following him. "So they both agreed it was too risky," said Loveless. "At least for the time being."

But they didn't forget. They didn't like Slocum. Self-righteousness and hypocrisy. That's what did him in.

He'd hold meetings with the female clerks. Chide them about their dress and quote statistics on secretarial infidelity—by which he meant both changing jobs and messing around—within the FBI. "Since Mr. Hoover's death," he'd tell them, "the public is watching us even closer," he'd waggle his finger, "so it's not only necessary to do a good job, but important as well that we all look good while we're doing it."

Suddenly, Slocum became the target of an around-the-clock FBI investigation. Within forty-eight hours, agents had discovered a pattern. At 8:30 every morning he would leave everyone else digging into police work and drive south on State Street to a small, well-hidden public parking lot. A tall, well-shaped ash blonde about forty was never far behind. These front-seat meetings continued every day for a week. Agent Dave Loveless's young daughter was seriously ill; he had petitioned Slocum several times for a transfer to Provo to be closer to her treatment. The answer, each time, was unequivocally "no." So when Agent Bill Olmstead asked Loveless if he would do a stake-out with him in Bill's old Chevy van at the parking lot and photograph Slocum the next morning, Loveless's answer was an unequivocal "yes."

"It was a lot easier than we expected," the agents declared with professional satisfaction. "The boss pulled right in behind us." The rear windows of the van were covered with cardboard, except for the camera peephole. From the van's higher angle, their high-speed 24 by 75 film captured at close range how quickly middle-aged passion turns to perspiration in the front seat. The lady, they found out later, was the wife of a very successful Salt Lake City business executive.

Once the agents had the "goods" on Slocum, it was merely a matter of how best to advise superiors in Washington. Once FBI headquarters was given the ball, they could run with it and run they did. Within the week, two inspectors from Washington flew to Salt Lake City and got what they came for. Director Kelley put Slocum under a sort of office arrest which required that he report to the office every morning with a sack lunch and stay within the confines of the SAC's office space so that he was available to the inspectors for interview but for the most part isolated from other employees.

It was at this time according to Harry Jones and Jim Downey, two of the most capable agents in the office, that Slocum decided to get even by spying on them as they signed in for work the first thing every morning.

The FBI, from its inception, had had a daily log where every agent, every morning, entered the exact time he arrived and signed his name attesting to its correctness. (Agents, still today, need to average 110 minutes of overtime each day to remain eligible for extra benefits.) A new sign-in sheet was started each morning by the first agent to arrive. This was how it worked. The first agent arriving at 7:00 A.M. would write his arrival time as 6:30 A.M. This not only allowed him thirty minutes of extra overtime but also allowed everyone else a thirty-minute cushion. It was dishonest, so not everyone did it. But some did out of peer pressure.

Slocum and one of his clerks started arriving in the office before anyone else. They hid in the vault with the lights off and the door cracked just enough to watch agents arrive and sign in. The clerk sat in the back of the vault with a flashlight and wrote down what Slocum told him to. "Jim Stewart—my time is seven–forty-four," Slocum would tell the clerk. "We'll check my time," he'd say, "against what Stewart listed as his arrival time." Then they'd do the same on Downey and Twede and Olmstead and Empey. After everyone had arrived and signed in, Slocum would slip out of the vault, run to his office, and compare his times against those of the agents.

Sure enough, Slocum caught some of them fudging on their arrival time. Later, the agents pretty much agreed that the seriousness of Slocum's extramarital activity was aggravated by his revengeful effort against agent personnel and that the combination resulted in Kelley's recommendation to fire Slocum. Kelley's recommendation was overruled by the Civil Service Commission and Slocum was busted several grades, demoted, and transferred to Detroit as an agent on the bricks. Slocum was there but a matter of months when he retired and moved back to Omaha, Nebraska. Not long after that, Slocum died—heart failure, someone said, was the cause.

Looking back now, years later, one can only speculate on the importance of Slocum's lack of interest in the Cooper-McCoy connection. I believe completely, however, that when Maurice Slocum, for whatever reason, chose to chase women instead of Calame's hypothesis, he was playing, like the Reno agents, into D. B. Cooper's hands.

24 Escape from Lewisburg
10 August 1974

The goal that I strive for is freedom
The lives I may take are unknown,
Yet I'll plot and I'll pray—
Lay and wait for the day
'Til my spirit and flesh are both free.
Only God can say where he'll lead me.
My fate, it lies in his hands.
So accept this warning as wisdom:
[In] this hell I can no longer stay.

Melvin Walker, 1974
Lewisburg Federal Prison

Melvin Walker, going over the past at my cramped dining-room table that February 1987, was vague about how he and Richard met. Some chemistry may have brought them together, like geese getting restless at the same time until the whole flock springs into the air together to migrate. "Once Richard was assigned to the dental lab," Walker recalled, "he started experimenting with different kinds of dental plaster."

Richard confided feelings of personal inadequacy about his appearance to a sympathetic doctor, who had him transferred to the Medical Center for Federal Prisoners at Springfield, Missouri, in November 1973, where, according to Walker, he had "cosmetic surgery" that narrowed both ears and laid them flatter to his skull. Richard tried to escape from the Springfield facility, failed, and was returned to Lewisburg but with no particular prejudice. "The FBI'll have to look twice now," Richard told Melvin when he returned to Lewisburg.

Around the first part of August 1974, I received a report from Lewisburg on Richard's "institutional adjustment." Among the computer-generated information at the top of the report was Richard's date for parole eligibility: 8 April 1987. Aside from getting a "disciplinary report" for using a public phone without permission and trying to escape while he was in Springfield, Richard had been a model prisoner. The report read:

> McCoy works in the Central Dental Laboratory as a clerk and receives very good work reports. He is considered a very conscientious worker and one who could be depended upon to carry out the duties assigned to him. He maintains a good attitude and does his work as required at all times. He is housed in a cell and has good response to housing routines and regulations. He does not cause any difficulties and seems to have respect for authoritative figures.

"Richard," Melvin said, "had heard about my talents for making things with these hands and sent word through Larry Bagley, the cell block orderly, that he wanted me to make him a toy forty-five–caliber pistol. I agreed. The next thing I get through Bagley is magazine pictures of an army forty-five and a block of wax from the dental lab. Took me the biggest part of a day," Melvin said, and I thought, maximum security may be able to suffocate a man's I.Q., but it doesn't dilute his ego much, "even down to the smallest screw and the grooves in the handle. Richard sent word back through Bagley that Michelangelo couldn't have done it in less than a week." Richard made the mold himself in the dental lab while the dentist was on leave and cast the finished product out of a hard plaster of Paris they use in making false teeth. "Richard and me," Melvin continued, "experiment with different colors of paint until we come up with this blue-steel look that you can't tell from a real gun."

From the second floor of Dog Block, inmates along the north wall watched favored convicts planting corn along the six-acre strip between the first and second gate. It was well into May before the weather was warm enough that they could take off their shirts and soak their sun-starved bodies. Then they watched it grow. They could only guess how long it would take for field corn to grow tall enough to hide four grown men. And what went on beyond the second gate where the two-lane blacktop ran?

Then, as if it finally dawned on Walker who all three of us were and what we were doing, he surprised us both. "Why don't we skip all this little stuff," he said to Calame, "and get on to the night you guys kill Richard." I looked at Calame, and he raised his eyebrows like, Hey, Rhodes, you're the guy that has to sleep in the same room with him tonight—and then just that quick, it all blew over. "Calame and I," I said, trying to ease the tension, "of course we want to hear about the shootout, too. But first we want to know how you slipped through the sally port. And about that second gate. And how much help you got out of Karen."

"Actually," Melvin said, "I didn't want to go with McCoy. All I knew about Richard McCoy was that he jumped out of an airplane with half a million dollars. I didn't know about him and the Green Berets in Vietnam. Larry Bagley and I had a good plan of our own," Melvin said, "where we'd leave through the education department in foggy weather. But I needed a gun and a bar-spreader. Finding someone at Lewisburg you could trust to make you anything wasn't that easy either. So . . . " Melvin summarized, "Larry and me were having our own problems. Richard sends word he wanted to meet with me. 'Hear me out,' he said, 'then decide.' I have to admit, it was a good escape plan. But I wanted a real pistol to take along. One other thing I didn't like about it. Richard was too trusting. That and I didn't think if it came right down to it he'd kill anybody." But Melvin sent back a final message: if he couldn't find a gun before the field corn between the two fences was tall enough to hide a man, then he'd come with Richard.

"I'm lost," Calame said. "When is this we're talking about? What month?"

"The denial," I said, "on that motion to reduce his sentence came in mid-July 1974."

"And we left Lewisburg in August," Melvin Walker said. "August 10."

4 CRASH OUT OF LEWISBURG

Lewisburg, PA. (UPI) 8-11-74—Four armed convicts, including a former Mormon Sunday School teacher involved in a bizarre 1972 hijacking, crashed a commandeered garbage truck through a gate at a federal penitentiary Saturday and disappeared into the central Pennsylvania mountains.

State police, FBI agents and local authorities searched a heavily wooded area 15 miles west of here for Richard F. McCoy, 31, and three other convicts. McCoy was convicted of hijacking a United Airlines jetliner April 7, 1972, obtaining a $500,000 ransom and then parachuting at night near Provo, Utah.

The three others, all convicted of armed robbery, were identified by police as Joseph Havel, 60, Philadelphia, serving 10 years; Larry L. Bagley, 36, of Iowa, serving 20 years, and Melvin D. Walker, 35, serving a total of 55 years for four bank holdups and one escape.

State police said the convicts had at least one gun and some knives.

"They don't have much to lose," a state police spokesman said. An FBI spokesman said the terrain was some of the most rugged in the state.

Authorities used two police helicopters, about 30 state troopers, FBI agents, and other law officers in the search.

The FBI said the convicts showed a gun to a prison guard at the first of two back gates to the maximum security prison. The guard opened the gate, the FBI said, and the inmates then crashed the truck through a second gate to freedom.

About 15 miles west, in the small community of Forest Hills, the convicts accosted a man and two women and stole the man's car, the FBI said. The man and two women, who were not identified, were left bound but unharmed.

Richard's escape plan had been put together long before 10 August. "Either the second or third Saturday in May," murmured Walker, "the three of us, Richard, Larry, and I, started dropping by the exercise yard right after we came from the commissary. One of the three of us made it a point to keep enough money on the commissary books to buy ice-cream bars every Saturday. We'd ask for a large paper bag and sit an hour or two on these wooden benches along the fence that leads to the sally port. We were there faithfully every Saturday morning until the guards got used to seeing us. Richard was the fastest of the three. I was next. Every idiot there, I think, except the guards, knew why we were foot-racing and running wind sprints.

"At nine o'clock every Saturday morning, this big white snub-nosed garbage truck driven by one of the prison trustees pulls just inside the first gate. The routine, we noticed, was always the same. When the trustee drove the truck inside the sally port gate, one of the guards would jump up in the cab and ride along with him while he made his rounds. After all the garbage was collected, the convict driver would pull up to the back gate and turn his engine off. The guard would then climb out and hurry around to the back to make sure there wasn't a convict hiding under it. When the guard was satisfied everything looked all right, he would wave to another guard up in the sally port gun tower who then walks to the back of the tower and pushes a button that opens the gate. The inmate then pulls the truck inside the sally port and stops. Always the same, at exactly nine thirty. The guard on the ground then walks around behind the truck, and lights up a cigarette while the gate closes, okay?''

"Did the guard on the ground have a gun?" Calame asked. "The one who rode in the garbage truck?"

"No."

"What about the one in the tower?"

"The day shift was older guys with more seniority," Walker said, his lips barely moving, "and from what some of the inside officers let slip weren't very good shots. But to answer your question, yes, they had plenty of firepower. Keep in mind there were two other guard towers on either end of the wall."

Guards, I remember thinking as I listened to Melvin, tell a hell of a lot better jailbreak stories than convicts do. I'd visited most of the federal prisons and attended conferences with wardens and correctional officers who after a few beers couldn't wait to tell about their days at Alcatraz or Marion. Mainly it was the riots and escapes they liked most to reminisce about. Generally, though, I think they would prefer it take place in another part of the prison or at least not on their particular shift.

Walker was continuing, "We had eleven seconds we figured to jump this six-foot fence in front of the benches and run fifty yards into the sally port before the gate closes. Either me or Richard would do it. Because we couldn't see what the second gate looked like, we couldn't be sure if the truck would make it through all the way. Richard and I were pretty sure we'd make a hole with that garbage truck big enough to crawl through on foot, but until the corn got high enough, there was nothing but open spaces. We'd be an easy target."

Calame was taking notes. "Was Karen any help? Or Richard's mother?" he asked.

Walker sounded faintly surprised, "We couldn't have done it without Karen.

"Karen visited regularly, bringing twenty or thirty dollars each time. That bought us enough candy bars, cheese sticks, beef sticks, and Cokes to provide quick energy during our getaway. Karen took photographs, too, of the second gate, the cornfield, and other landmarks for ten miles along the blacktop road to a small bridge, then up a logging road. Richard had hidden the plaster of Paris forty-five in a false ceiling in the dental lab along with army fatigues for each man. Walker enrolled in an arts and crafts course and made backpacks. Bagley put together a first-aid kit from a friend at the hospital."

"What about Havel?" Calame asked. "Where does he figure into this?"

Joseph Havel was the friend of a friend of Richard's who went home on parole and persuaded Richard to include Joe in the breakout in exchange for hiding a car, money, clothes, food, and guns near the blacktop road. Walker said he reluctantly agreed. He would not have told Havel details of the plan, but Richard's trusting nature won out on that issue. Havel was about sixty, five eight or eight and a half, 155 pounds, "but tough," insisted Walker. "He's an armored car robber. Brinks, I think. We warned him he was going to be exposed most to the guard towers on the right side of the truck and ran a risk of getting shot up. He said, 'So what. We're going out together ain't we?'"

Richard's friend was supposed to send Richard a postcard letting him know everything was taken care of. It never came.

On the night of Friday, 9 August, inmate friends helped smuggle the supplies out of the dental lab and into the four men's cells. On Saturday morning, all four wore fatigues under their prison khakis, stuffed their supplies into a big brown paper sack, and layered ice-cream bars on top. Their appearance was absolutely routine to the guards by then. "But we were so jumpy that morning," Walker said, "that when a blue station wagon with four men in it drove into the sally port, we thought about calling it off." Walker was adamant about going ahead. They couldn't possibly get the supplies, he said, back into the cells and keep them hidden over the weekend.

"The plan," breathed Walker, "was for me to throw the backpack over the fence and Richard, being the fastest, was to jump the fence and take it from there. All three, Joe Havel, Larry Bagley, and Richard sat there like they was froze. And all of a sudden, instead of throwing the backpack over the fence, I make one big lunge at that fence and take everything with me. We had black knit stocking caps with holes cut where the eyes go. Even faster than I'd expected and way before any of the alarms sounded—just as the sally port guard turned to watch the gate close, I'm standing there in front of him with that black stocking cap pulled over my face and this big blue forty-five leveled right between his eyes. He went into a state of shock, fell at my feet, and crawled up next to the guard tower. I stepped over behind the truck and pointed the forty-five at the guard up in the sally port guard tower and yelled at him to push the button to open the next gate. When he got a glimpse of the gun he backed up real slow, then fell to the floor. As he ducked down, I climbed up between the bed and the cab where the hydraulics are. As I grabbed at the truck cab with both hands that plaster-of-Paris forty-five shatters like a dime-store looking glass. I can see Richard and Larry Bagley through the back window trying to drag the trustee out of the truck on the driver's side to keep him from being exposed to the gun tower on the right. He sees their knives and won't budge—thinks they're out to kill him. I could see Joe Havel trying to climb up the passenger side of the truck, which exposed him to the tower—and I could tell he wasn't going to make it. Shots, first one, then a dozen, start coming faster from both guard towers. Richard throws the trustee out his side of the truck just as Larry releases the emergency brake and throws the truck in low gear. Just as we lunge foward, I see Joe dart from the right side around in front, and as he gets to my side I grab him by one arm, and hold him while we crash the first gate. These two big pulleys that hold the gate up on both sides come flying off. Gate and all's hanging across the hood and tears the windshield out. The second gate we come to down through the cornfield is the one we'd all worried so much about. Larry is going maybe fifty when we hit that chain link double gate, and as we crash it, it tangles up with the gate over our hood and, lucky for us, they both jerk clear. When we hit the blacktop, thanks to Karen McCoy, we know exactly where we are. She'd also timed it perfect from where we were to turn, just before the police, coming from the next little town, could get to that point."

Most people, I suspect, don't often get to see an ordinary old snub-nosed garbage truck barreling down the middle of a narrow two-lane blacktop at seventy miles an hour with escaped convicts hanging out of every door. A kid on a bicycle coming toward them jerked the handlebars just in time and landed head first in a dry creek bed.

Calame said, "Judas Priest!"

On the old logging road, they passed a two-story farmhouse with an old man and two old women just walking out to get in the car. They pulled off the road and ran back to take the car. "It was a comedy scene," recalled Walker, smiling a little. "I said, 'Everybody out. We need the car!' One of the ladies said, 'What do you thugs want our car for?' I said, 'Lady, we just escaped from a federal penitentiary and we're desperate. Somebody is going to kill us if we don't hurry.' And she said kind of sarcastic, 'Oh, you're desperate, are you?' We all had to laugh. We took them back inside and tied them to chairs. Richard asked if anyone took medicine. The old man said he took heart pills. Bagley and Havel made a quick search of the house for weapons but didn't find any. So we give each of them a drink of water, give the old man his heart pill, and run for this light-colored four-door Chevy. Just as we pull back on the blacktop we see this police car come flying by towards the prison with his red lights flashing. Didn't pay a bit of attention to the four of us."

They drove north about forty miles, pulled into an abandoned logging road, and prepared to wait it out until dark. They could hear helicopters and National Guard convoys moving back toward Lewisburg. Melvin and Richard shaved each other's heads. Then they drove into a small but swanky tourist mountain town, lifted some Ohio license plates for the car, and spent half of their four hundred dollars on less conspicuous clothes than army fatigues.

They began driving toward North Carolina, deciding en route to rob a bank. "Richard remembers a cousin he says we might get a gun from," Walker continued, with a story that sounded odder and odder. "Turns out he's a police officer, so I jump out of the car, Havel and me. I'm against it. Richard comes back an hour later with this little twenty-two he says can't be traced."

GRAB 2 LEWISBURG ESCAPEES
HUNT 2 OTHERS IN N.C. BANK ROBBERY

NEW BERN, N.C. (AP)—Authorities say four men who robbed a Pollocksville, N.C., bank were convicts who escaped from the federal prison at Lewisburg, Pa., last Saturday.

Officers said three men walked into the bank and took an estimated $10,000 at gunpoint, then fled in a car driven by a fourth man.

They said the bandits then switched to another car with Ohio tags. It was subsequently spotted by a police helicopter on an unpaved logging road in the Great Dover Swamp, about 15 miles west of New Bern.

Officers aboard the helicopter exchanged fire with the fugitives as they abandoned the vehicle, police said. Officers said no one was hit in the burst of shots.

Arrested later as some 50 officers swarmed into the area were Joseph W. Havel, 60, Philadelphia and Larry LeRoy Bagley, 36, Des Moines, Iowa.

Still being sought were Richard F. McCoy Jr., 32, of nearby Cove City; and Melvin Dale Walker, 35.

25 The Manhunt

Pollocksville was about twelve miles south by southeast from Cove City, and North Carolina's Great Dover Swamp weaves its way almost unnoticed between the two small country towns. Richard's distant cousin, Charles McCoy, was mayor of Cove City and chatted happily to the news media as FBI agents searched acres of snake-infested swamp. "Most of the FBI think he's already out of the area, and I'd bet my pants on it," the mayor said. "Might lose 'em, but I'm bettin' I wouldn't. It's like throwin' a rabbit into a briar patch," Charlie related gleefully, with a proper Southern joy in seeing a family member put one over on the feds. "Richard used to wade into those swamps with his brother Russell just to see who could catch the most snakes barehanded and pop their heads off."

Edward J. Krupinsky, North Carolina SAC, surrounded the swamp and then brought in an expert tracker. "We have to go in," he told a TV camera crew. "He's got so many relatives and friends down here who would assist him if we pull back."

Local people around Cove City and New Bern readily admitted they'd give Richard McCoy the shirts off their backs "if he showed up at my doorstep asking for it." Richard, as a boy, had helped most of them cut and stack the fat brown tobacco leaves. So they didn't exactly feel threatened and outraged by the possibility of escaped convicts in their midst. Most didn't even stop to look up when a helicopter went whacking over.

But it was helicopters that first spotted the four escapees in a cornfield carved out of the Great Dover Swamp. Melvin and Richard ran in one direction, Larry and Joe in the other. When one National Guard copter began hovering lower over the cornfields where Richard and Melvin were hiding, Richard jumped up and began firing that puny little .22. The pilot, seeing the firing flashes, started shooting back.

Melvin told Richard to keep firing as the two of them jumped feet first into waist-deep swamp water and half a dozen curious white-faced milk cows lined up on the other side of the bank to watch. Wet but not lost, the two set off on foot through Dover Swamp, just as night rolled over its thick, clinging foliage. Richard was at home in jungle country and getting closer to Karen and the kids every minute, while Melvin, for most of the next five hours, felt lost and scared. "Not much farther," Richard told an exhausted Melvin Walker as they both swatted horseflies and giant mosquitos. "We'll eat when we get there."

It was after ten when they reached the house of Richard's aunt, Myrtle's sister, the happiest face they'd seen in two days. "The first thing she did," said Melvin, "was turn the lights down and help us out of our wet clothes. 'Oh my God,' she told Richard, 'your mama's been worried half to death, boy.'" They ate what she'd eaten that night—tomato and mayonnaise sandwiches. Best they'd ever had. While Richard and Melvin sat counting out twenty-dollar bills from the Pollocksville bank robbery, Richard's aunt drove to Cove City to tell Karen where to meet them. She found a nice stack of new twenties waiting on the kitchen table when she got back. "Like Jesse James and Frank James was credited with doing," Melvin said.

According to Melvin Walker, Barnum and Bailey must have been running the dragnet that night, because it had holes in it big enough to parade an elephant through. "Richard," Melvin said, "was always cool and under control. But when he first sees Karen parked off this little dark country road waiting for us, he about cracks up." With her was another aunt of Richard's—Jane Kornegay, about his own age. She'd done the improbable feat, for a McCoy, of forming a close relationship with Karen and obviously didn't mind the excitement, even if it came with some risk. It was Jane's car, a late-model maroon Chevrolet, that she and Karen had brought. Karen and Aunt Jane quickly told about the capture of Joe and Larry. From where the four were sitting, they could see the lights of a stopped passenger train, with FBI and more uniformed police officers than you could count crawling all over it.

Karen told Richard, giggling, "The highway patrol just stopped and warned us about driving the back roads. Said, 'There's a couple of dangerous criminals loose in this area, so don't you two ladies stop and pick nobody up, okay?' " All four of them laughed.

26 The Killing
9 November 1974, Virginia Beach, Virginia

As Walker told it, the reunion between Karen and Richard was tender. As she described working her way through the roadblocks, Richard said, "You did all that for me?" his voice full of love and admiration. Then he gave her a lot of money from the Pollocksville bank robbery and told her there would be more to come. Melvin Walker said, "At that point I had not seen the bad side of Karen McCoy."

Karen and Richard reminisced softly that night in the front seat about the children, their little red house in Provo and a lot about the Mormon church. Melvin told Calame and me that Richard was still agitated about being excommunicated. "I heard something, good or bad, about the Mormon church and Joseph Smith, its founder, almost every day," Melvin said, shaking his head, "so I ought to know." Religion had been a big part of their daily conversation.

The picture of Karen McCoy that emerged from Melvin Walker's quiet murmur was full of surprises. Not just that she'd helped in the escape and, with Richard's Aunt Jane, slipped them through Cove City roadblocks and driven them to Virginia Beach just before breakfast. That's what we expected. But Melvin also told us he knew for a fact that Karen was dating an FBI agent from the Cove City area while he and Richard were hiding out, and finally cut a deal with the FBI to finger him and Richard, but only with the understanding no one got killed. I remember thinking, I wish Jim Theisen were here. He had Karen pegged from the very beginning. We'd kept in touch during those past fifteen years while he was back at FBI headquarters.

His certainty about the McCoy-Cooper connection had remained unshakable all those years. "We were relying on you to break McCoy, Rhodes," Theisen would complain long-distance. "Why did you think Calame and I went to all that trouble briefing you?" Then for the hundredth time I'd explain, and we'd both laugh, how Willis Ritter had thrown a wet blanket over what little I'd done. Then Theisen, who was where he could see things happen, would lament how he, over the years, had watched the McCoy-Cooper theory slowly disappear through bureau cracks.

Then the hiding began. Richard and Melvin took a motel room, while Karen and Jane drove straight back to Cove City. Jane's husband got worried when she didn't come home all night and called the FBI. Jane got called before a federal grand jury, but never told them one single thing about Richard and Melvin so they couldn't indict her.

The first four days in Virginia Beach, Melvin and Richard came out of the motel only at night. But Richard was not his normal easygoing self. He missed the children. "He got jumpy," Melvin added, "when he saw my picture on the FBI's top ten wanted poster." He became suspicious of running into an ambush. His guilt over the excommunication, for some reason, seemed to accelerate. The motel stank, and the Pollocksville bank money was about gone.

"Richard and I," as Melvin put it, "decided to get out of that rat trap and indulge ourselves on everything we'd ever been without. First we needed some decent identification. So we went looking for a man about thirty-five to forty, five feet ten inches tall, a hundred eighty pounds with blue eyes. Someone I could pass for. We found him late that next Saturday night, the twenty-fourth of August, coming out of a bar. Just as he unlocks his side of the car, Richard spins him around and we slam him in the front seat between us. He about beat himself to death trying to empty his pockets. We never hurt the man and when we let him out, he thanked us for the ride. That's when I assumed the identity of Herbert J. Moon.

"You and Richard wore masks when you robbed that Maryville bank, didn't you?" Calame cut in. "The one in Tennessee."

Walker looked at him calmly. "We've never been charged with it."

"I know," said Calame, "but I'm curious. I hear they've never cleared that robbery either."

Then followed a long discussion between Melvin and Russ Calame over statutes of limitation and witnesses' memories after thirteen years. Eventually Calame and I agreed, without making any promises, to do what we could to help if Melvin were ever charged with the Maryville robbery. Nonetheless, I got the feeling that Walker felt Calame—and me, too—still had the hammer in our hands and were saying things that, if tested, we might not back up.

So Walker told us how he and Richard had stolen a car in Virginia Beach, driven to Knoxville, Tennessee, stolen another, and gone on with both cars to Maryville. "Next we located a nice little bank with a lot of highways leading in and out of town. And we took it on a Friday morning. Banks have more money on Friday to cash payroll checks. We put on some white coveralls, Richard and me, and wore yellow hardhats like construction workers. We walked in the front door with our guns drawn and ordered everybody on the floor. The next thing we did was have the tellers empty their trays in the big laundry bag. We were in and out in less than two minutes.

"Then we drove down to Gatlinburg, Tennessee, and spent the night at a Howard Johnson. We had the money out on the bed counting it when Richard turned on the TV. The movie was *Butch Cassidy and the Sundance Kid*. It was like watching ourselves. We counted out $76,000—enough, as Richard liked to say, to indulge ourselves for a while longer."

Walker, still using the name of Herbert J. Moon, registered the title of a dark blue 1971 Ford Limited and also leased a brick, three-bedroom rambler at 733 North Great Neck Road in a very good Virginia Beach neighborhood on 7 September 1974. They had no long-term plans except for that simple goal of self-indulgence. Melvin, shaking his head, told how Richard had been planning another airplane hijack, but Melvin was against it. "I couldn't have jumped out of the back of one of those big things if the whole front end was on fire."

The house was a fantasy of luxury—oriental rugs, thick soft cushions, paintings of a Bengal tiger and tropical birds on black velvet, an antique black marble nightstand that cost five hundred dollars, and a dark green porcelain vase. "All in all, I think we spent over five thousand dollars on new furniture," Walker recalled.

"Never spoke to either one of them," was what David Mecartea, a next-door neighbor, later told FBI agent Nick O'Hara, "but they both seemed very pleasant. Couple of things did seem a little strange. Neither one of them appeared to have a job, and then they'd leave town for three or four days every now and then."

Between 7 September and 9 November 1974, Richard and Melvin made four night trips to Cove City to see Karen and Jane. On their last trip in mid-October, Melvin said, they put a trailer hitch on the Ford and took Chanti a registered Arabian horse for a birthday present. Karen and Jane arrived at the house on Great Neck Tuesday night, 5 November, for a sort of farewell party. "I had bad feelings about Karen and Jane coming that night," Melvin said. "I told Richard I was afraid they might be followed. But . . . " Melvin took a deep breath and closed both eyes as if it were still painful to recall, "we were moving to Alabama that weekend, so I told Richard it was all right. It was later that I learned about Karen cutting a deal with the FBI to sell us out."

On 6 November 1974, in Virginia Beach, eighty-eight days after their escape from Lewisburg, Richard said good-bye to Karen for the last time. Just after Karen and Jane left for Cove City, Richard and Melvin started early that Wednesday morning for Tuskegee, driving the horses to the 185-acre farm they had rented a month earlier. The plan was for them to come back Saturday to pack, put most of the furniture in storage, and leave Virginia Beach for good on Monday, 11 November, Veterans' Day.

It was nearly sundown when Melvin and Richard arrived in Tuskegee that damp November day. Cold lay on the ground, and there was no electricity yet in the old two-story house or beds to sleep on. "Richard," Melvin said, "acted kind of strange when he got out of the car. He left me to unhitch the horse trailer and lead the horses up to the barn while he absentmindedly saunters off down behind the house. Although I started to stop him and ask what his problem was, I never did."

Melvin took a deep breath, then hesitated. "Could I ask a personal question?" he said, looking at both of us.

"Yes," Calame responded.

"Well," said Melvin uncomfortably, "does all this really have to come out in your book, Mr. Rhodes?"

"Only if it's important," I told him, "and isn't going to get someone killed. Other than that," I said, "it just depends on whether or not I like it."

"I liked Richard," Melvin said, "but if it hadn't been for all that money, I don't think Karen would have had anything to do with him." While Melvin was unloading the car, he discovered something. At the Great Neck house, they'd always kept the Maryville bank money in a brown attache case in the trunk of the Ford along with several guns. And they always parked the car in the attached garage. But there was access to the garage from the kitchen. Tuesday, just the night before, there had been $36,000 in the trunk. "Now," said Melvin, "when I check the money Wednesday, down at the farm, there's only $16,000 left. Karen took $20,000 Tuesday night, and Richard McCoy knew it! So, I'm walking down this narrow lane behind the house, my shirt unbuttoned and a pistol sticking half out of my waistband and here's Richard walking toward me with his head down. When he suddenly looks up, his eyes start at my waistband where the pistol is, then come up and meet mine. That's the first time I'd seen Richard McCoy's eyes show fear. I really believe Richard was asking himself whether I was going to allow $20,000 to go to Karen without killing somebody. It seemed like a minute or more went by, still no one said anything."

Richard then turned toward the house as if he didn't care if Walker shot him in the back. Instead, Walker fell in line walking behind Richard. Neither man realized as they walked single file toward the house that night that the $20,000 would never have done either of them any good anyway. Only Karen knew that—Karen and one of the agents assigned to the Charlotte, North Carolina, office of the FBI.

In the Norfolk FBI office, Special Agent Nicholas V. O'Hara was case agent in charge of the stakeout those three long, exhausting days, Thursday, 7 November, to Saturday, 9 November 1974, at 733 North Great Neck Road. Jerry Coakley of Norfolk was SAC and actually running the show, O'Hara later told Russ Calame and me, "but he supported his men all the way and let us do what we had to." Nick O'Hara would have been in his early thirties back in 1974, athletic, just under six feet tall, and a little under 180 pounds. A native of Madison, South Dakota, Nick went with the FBI in the early sixties, right out of law school.

Thursday evening O'Hara, accompanied by Kevin McPartland, Martin F. Houlihan, Joseph Smith, Joe O'Brien, and Gerald

Coughlin, notified the Virginia Beach Police Department at 6:00 P.M. that they were in town and then took up surveillance at 733 North Great Neck Road, code-named Touchdown. The Golf Ranch Motel on nearby Laskin Road, code-named Clubhouse, housed other agents. One block south, at 705 Earl of Chesterfield, a tall two-story home code-named the Tower, four agents, Arnold, Roball, Jester, and Weschler, and their binoculars, could see the house on Great Neck clearly from the upstairs.

Roadblocks to reroute traffic would be set up at the corners of Plantation and North Great Neck, at Plantation and Simpkins Lane, at Simpkins and Dodd Drive, at Wolfsnare Drive and Great Neck, and at Plantation and Earl of Chesterfield. O'Hara later told Calame and me in his strong, clear voice that never wavered for a second, "Roadblocks especially would be implemented only upon Walker and McCoy returning to the area. Once they're at the house" (O'Hara was recalling the Virginia Beach incident as if it were yesterday), "we close the entire neighborhood off."

After the roadblocks were made ready, occupants along the rear and on either side of 733 North Great Neck Road would either be moved or put on alert. Agents in the back along Simpkins Lane were given M79 grenade launchers with at least a dozen CS tear gas shells. Six unmarked FBI cars would, it was hoped, go unnoticed along North Great Neck Road and Simpkins Lane. Cars one and two were told to drive directly across the front lawn of the suspect house and take up positions in the rear. Agents occupying cars three through six, covering the front, would also have M16 rifles, twelve-gauge shotguns, a grenade launcher, and police bullhorns.

Neither Calame nor I actually expected O'Hara to confirm Melvin Walker's claim that Karen McCoy had fingered her husband to the FBI. What O'Hara first said to Calame, after a proper FBI handshake, was, "Russ, you know that out of respect for my source of information, I can't discuss it, but you already know how we got them."

"Not really, Nick," Calame said. "We only think we know. All we have now is what Walker told us, and his version puts the monkey on Karen." Calame added, "We had earlier theories that it could have been one of McCoy's relatives, or you found the house with a wiretap on a telephone that Karen or Myrtle were using to call Richard."

"No," said Nick. "There was no wiretap."

"Then who was your informant, Nick?" asked Calame, as casually as if he were asking for the halftime score in a football game.

"Mr. Calame," repeated Nick softly, "I can't tell you my source. You know that. But if you were to use your hypothesis that Karen McCoy was my source, that *hypothesis*"—he leaned, ever so slightly on the word—"would be a very interesting hypothesis."

On Saturday, 9 November 1974, the day of the killing, Richard and Melvin pulled out of Tuskegee, Alabama, just before noon and headed back to Virginia Beach to pack up and store the furniture. They took turns driving, and neither one mentioned the missing twenty thousand dollars. "Hindsight," Melvin Walker explained to Calame and me, "now tells me we should have been thinking ambush. When Karen McCoy took the money, she must have been pretty sure she wouldn't see either one of us again and couldn't stand to see all that money turned over to the authorities."

According to Walker, he and Richard became part of a conspiracy that had begun a week earlier between Karen and the FBI, a conspiracy in which Karen agreed to tell everything she knew about the house at 733 North Great Neck Road, about the dark blue 1971 Ford with the trailer hitch.

Richard, when it was his turn to take the wheel, talked constantly, said Melvin, about the Mormon church and about his admiration for its founder, the prophet Joseph Smith, until Melvin dozed off in the back seat. Richard would wake Melvin to point out how calm the Atlantic Ocean was for November and how much warmer Virginia Beach winters were than those in Provo, Utah.

"Tell me again," Richard asked, "what's the name of those evergreens there along the front of the house?"

Melvin told him for the tenth time they were arbor vitae and finally asked him why.

Richard turned and looked at Melvin sprawled out in the back seat as if he were about to reveal something very important about the bushes. But he didn't. He instead turned back to the road, whispering "arbor vitae" over and over to himself. Melvin wasn't able to tell Richard that the translation of the Latin name was "tree of life."

It was exactly 10:50 P.M. that Saturday night, 9 November, and Richard was still behind the wheel, when his headlights began to pick up road signs letting them know Virginia Beach was right up ahead. Melvin said he thought at first it might have been a roadblock when Richard suddenly swung the car over on the shoulder and came to a quick stop. "They say most people have a premonition about death," Melvin told Calame and me, "and I know for a fact that Richard McCoy felt something strange that night."

"Because," Melvin said slowly, feeling his way through something he had seen but still didn't understand, "coming from the east, there's this huge ball of light traveling at a tremendous rate of speed." Melvin said the first thing he reached for was his .38. The next thing was a pair of binoculars. What Richard told Melvin as they both sat there stiff as starch was, "No plane ever made can travel that fast." "Whoosh!" Melvin said, squirming around a little in his chair, "like a giant beacon or flying saucer, it was over the car and then gone in no time. Nothing like either one of us had ever seen before."

Richard seemed calm but puzzled. He put the Ford in gear again and told Melvin, "On Monday, we can finally start to relax."

Richard and Melvin had ensured against both of them being ambushed at once by a procedure they followed each time they drove back to the house on Great Neck Road. Four blocks from the house, taking turns, he or Richard would slip into sweats and jog home. The driver would give the jogger time to get home, then pass the house and circle the block. If the garage door was up and the light on when he drove by the house, he'd know the house had been checked.

As Richard pulled the dark blue Ford over to the curb that night, he asked Melvin if he'd check the house. "It's your turn," Melvin protested, "and I'm half asleep. I'll drive the car and you check it out." Richard had never asked Melvin to take his turn before, had never tried to avoid any shared risk. But he again asked Melvin to do it "just this once." Even said, "Please." But Melvin stood firm.

At 11:10 P.M. Richard tucked a .38 Smith & Wesson in the waistband of his light-brown jogging suit, mumbled something, Melvin said, about things not looking just right, and quietly shut the car door behind him.

If Richard was looking for warning signs that night as he half-loped across the intersection of Plantation and North Great Neck, there were none. Only an unexpected drop in the temperature and a cold, damp wind coming in off the Atlantic Ocean. The streets seemed a little quiet for Saturday night. A hunter's moon rode lopsidedly against the clouds and midnight blue of the sky. A dog barked over on Plantation, another on Wolfsnare. By the time

Richard's long legs cleared the arbor vitae bushes in front of the house, he was on the top stair and could see his own breath. At that very moment, when he turned the key and the front door slowly opened, the final chapter of the D. B. Cooper–Richard McCoy story was about to be written.

Once inside, Richard suddenly realized he wasn't alone. What went through his mind, as he stood there with no place to run, is anybody's guess. He and Melvin had discussed for months what exactly they would do when that day finally came. Melvin had told Richard it all depended. "If you shoot it out, I'll shoot it out with you. But only if I can see we can make it. When I decide we can't, my hands go straight over my head." Richard, his own intentions fixed, it seemed, in concrete, told Melvin, "Not me! I'd rather die a thousand deaths than spend one more day in Lewisburg Prison."

Before Richard could hit the light switch or get his eyes adjusted to the dark, a hand-held walkie-talkie accidentally crackled in the next room where Nick O'Hara and two other FBI agents had been relying entirely on the element of surprise. "It's dark in there," O'Hara later told Calame and me, "but we could tell it was McCoy." Streetlights reflecting through two large front-room windows provided plenty of light for a clear and certain identification. As McCoy's hand fidgeted for the light switch, Houlihan's radio blared something out and all hell suddenly broke loose.

McCoy reached for his gun. "The three of us," O'Hara said, "are standing just inside the dining room, not more than twelve to fifteen feet from McCoy. Kevin McPartland, he's on the south side of the doorway with a twelve-gauge pump and I'm on the north. Marty Houlihan has, I believe, a three-fifty-seven handgun, and he's standing just behind Kevin and me, but more in line with the open door. Both inside and out, there were about twenty of us. Agents Gerald Coughlin, Joe O'Brien, and an agent named Smith were on the outside, hidden in some evergreen bushes. As McCoy brings this snub-nosed thirty-eight about chest high and turns toward me and Houlihan," O'Hara said, "I holler 'FBI!' and start to tell him to move quietly and shut the door behind him because we don't want to spook Melvin Walker. But," O'Hara said, "McCoy gets one off, just over Marty Houlihan's head."

Richard McCoy must have stood there in the dark that Saturday night as he had lived most of his life, alone and frightened, inside himself, watching two long, black, thirty-inch shotgun barrels, as if in slow motion, swing in his direction and explode in deafening unison. Neighbors said they heard only one great big WHAM!! when it happened. The smell of gunpowder was strong in the small front room and fire-flickers from the two shotgun blasts danced against the east wall.

"We all three fired at once," O'Hara said. "Houlihan and McPartland both miss. I catch McCoy with one round of double-aught buckshot just above his left nipple. His head jerks back, and it sounded to me like he said, 'I'm killed!' McCoy clutches himself with both hands," said O'Hara, "and stumbles backwards off this concrete front porch." Blood started to flow immediately through his light-brown jogging top and ran down into the seat of his pants.

Medical Examiner Charles Springate, M.D., would later undress, identify, and describe the body as "a well-developed, well-nourished white male." According to Springate's autopsy report the body had suffered a massive hemorrhage as nine double-aught pellets entered the upper left chest, breaking ribs, puncturing a lung, and tearing out soft tissue. There was a large amount of blood on the clothing. Springate's autopsy report continued: "Rigor mortis is well-developed in the jaw, neck and extremities. The body temperature is cold from refrigeration. The body is slender and clothed in a long sleeve dress shirt, tan trousers with belt and undershorts. The right rear trouser pocket contains $1.15 in change. . . . Attached to the left big toe with a piece of wire is a red evidence tag with various notations. *Cause of death*: shotgun wound to upper left chest from 10 to 12 foot range." As medical examiner, Dr. Springate could tell almost everything about Richard McCoy except what was on his mind at the moment of death.

"When I reached the front door," O'Hara continued, "I could see one of my agents kneeling in some arbor vitae bushes, cradling McCoy in both arms and hollering, 'Somebody run! Get some bath towels quick! Before this man bleeds to death.'" O'Hara walked out on the front porch, jacked another shell in the chamber, and said, "Fuck him! The son of a bitch just tried to kill me in there!"

"This agent . . . " I began.

"We'd staked out about twenty of them around the house," explained O'Hara. "Three of them were in the bushes right near the front. Smith just got to McCoy first."

"Smith?"

"Agent Joseph Smith," O'Hara said, seemingly not aware that a Joseph Smith had been the founder of the Mormon church.

Russ Calame and I glanced at each other. Truth really is stranger than fiction. A mere coincidence, some people will say, and maybe it was. But with approximately sixty-five hundred agents in the FBI at the time, the one named Joseph Smith was kneeling in the arbor vitae bushes near midnight, holding Richard in his arms, trying to save a life rather than take one. And in his arms, Richard McCoy, the excommunicated Mormon convert, died.

O'Hara said he ran out in the yard when he saw a blue '71 Ford Limited cruise by, then suddenly pick up speed. "When I saw that trailer hitch," O'Hara said, "I knew it was Walker." How did he know? He wouldn't say how that trailer hitch figured in. Most likely someone, I thought, filling in my own gaps, who saw the horse trailer that night Richard and Melvin delivered Chanti's birthday gift to Cove City. Probably that person was the FBI's source of information.

Melvin Walker ran bumper to bumper with two unmarked FBI cars at high speeds around Simpkins Lane, Wolfsnare, and up and down Plantation Drive. When agents got close enough to stick a twelve-gauge shotgun in his ear, he did exactly what he told Richard he'd do. Both hands flew over his head. Not a shot was fired.

"Not bad for one night," Nicholas V. O'Hara told his men. "Melvin Walker, an FBI top tenner, caught, and a major fugitive killed."

Melvin Walker went back to the prison at Marion, found God, became a born-again Christian, and was released on parole in 1981. He now lives a quiet life with his wife and two children in a large southwestern city where he works as a truck driver.

Richard McCoy's body was released to his family the Monday after the killing. Funeral services were held Wednesday, 13 November 1974, in the New Bern Ward chapel. Richard was later driven to the McCoy family farm in Cove City, North Carolina, where he was put to rest in the family cemetery. Melvin Walker brought photographs of the funeral when he visited me in Salt Lake City in February 1987. One was a close-up of Richard in his casket. Another was of the family.

The day of the funeral, Karen, according to John J. Coneys, assistant special agent in charge of the Norfolk office, accused the FBI of shooting her husband deliberately. Irate over the publicity, she demanded that everything recovered by the FBI be released to her on threat of a lawsuit. That included the horses, saddles, furniture, and the 1971 Ford, which contained an assortment of weapons and $16,000 in cash. The bank at Pollocksville, North Carolina, and the one Richard and Melvin robbed at Maryville, Tennessee, both filed claims to recover the $92,000 that they had lost. A settlement, according to Coneys, was made between Karen and the two banks.

Epilogue

This close to the end of the story, the mystery of D. B. Cooper seems smaller and less important than when I first started working on it five years ago. If it is true, as evidence seems to indicate beyond a reasonable doubt, that Richard McCoy and D. B. Cooper are one and the same, then Richard McCoy's secret lies buried with him, deep in the McCoy family cemetery.

Ironically, the deeper Russ Calame and I dug into the life of Richard McCoy, the more our mystery-thriller turned instead into a story of human weaknesses. A tale of broken vows, of greed, and possibly even betrayal. Yet as much as anything else, it's the story of a Vietnam hero and what so often happens once the killing subsides and everyone goes home.

And no, it wasn't John Steinbeck, I've since learned, nor Ernest Hemingway whom the tall Lee Remick-looking reporter with the green eyes and red shoes made such a fuss about that day in the courthouse hall. Found among the many notes of F. Scott Fitzgerald, long after his death, was a scribbled invitation to a friend: "You show me a hero," Fitzgerald had written, "and I'll write you a tragedy."

Index